How the Suddu. Pot Began

By
Bettye Gyle (Sudduth) Guillory
The Family Matriarch

William and Lucy (Mikens) Sudduth Sr.

First Amended Edition

Preface

This book was beautifully done with much love and care. The author has included highlights as well as some low points in a family's long history. Bettye has featured many photographs and myriads of irresistible looks into the lives of loved ones, those who have gone the way of the earth and those who are still living today. This book will not only capture the hearts of the family members that are associated with this particular lineage, but is bound to give insight, inspiration and encouragement to others to embark upon a new journey, to discover their family history.

Table of Contents

Table of Contents.. - 5 -

Table of Figures.. - 9 -

A Prayer for all who may read this Book.......................... - 12 -

Introduction.. - 13 -

Acknowledgements.. - 19 -

Forward.. - 24 -

Chapter- 1 - How the Sudduth Melting Pot Began.................. - 25 -

  1.1 Paternal Grandparents - William and Lucy (Mikens) Sudduth the Senior.. - 25 -

  1.2 Maternal Grandparents -Benjamin and Molly Culpepper....... - 26 -

  1.3 My Dad's Parents and Family.................................. - 28 -

    1.3.1 "Will "Sudduth Jr. .... - 28 -

    1.3.2 James "Jim" Sudduth.. - 29 -

    1.3.3 Olivia Sudduth.. - 29 -

    1.3.4 Lucinda Sudduth.. - 29 -

    1.3.5 Mathilda Sudduth,.. - 30 -

    1.3.6 Lucy Sudduth... - 30 -

    1.3.7 Leonard "Lynn" Sudduth .... - 31 -

    1.3.8 George Sudduth... - 31 -

    1.3.9 Chares J. Sudduth... - 31 -

    1.3.10 Elsberry "Ebb" Sudduth.................................... - 31 -

    1.3.11 Joseph "Joe" Sudduth..................................... - 31 -

    1.3.12 John Sudduth... - 31 -

Chapter 2 -William Sudduth II -"The SUDDUTH Legacy Moves West".. - 32 -

  2.1 William Sudduth III "Doc" Sudduth.......................... - 33 -

  2.2 Mary Lucy Sudduth and Sumpter Spann's Family.............. - 36 -

    2.2.1 Ella Mae Spann Eggleton.................................... - 37 -

    2.2.2 Theodore "Teddy" Spann..................................... - 38 -

    2.2.3 Dewey Larry Spann, Sr. .... - 38 -

    2.2.4 William Spann, Sr. .... - 40 -

    2.2.5 Mathilda Ruth Spann Logan.................................. - 41 -

    2.2.6 Dorothy Spann Roberson..................................... - 43 -

    2.2.7 Marcella Spann West.. - 44 -

    2.2.8 Enoch Spann.. - 45 -

      2.2.8.1 Calvin Spann: Mary Lucy (Sudduth) and Sumpter Spann's Baby Boy.. - 46 -

        2.2.8.1.1 About Calvin David Spann Sr. 8 Children: .... - 48 -

      2.2.8.2 "The Saga of the Sudduth Clan"..................... - 49 -

        2.2.8.2.1 Preface: .... - 49 -

        2.2.8.2.2 The Sudduth Clan: .... - 50 -

  2.3 Larry Bryan Sudduth.. - 55 -

  2.4 Georgia Sudduth Taylor..................................... - 59 -

Chapter 3 -"James Journey to the Oklahoma Bible Belt".......... - 63 -

  3.1.1 PREFACE.. - 63 -

  3.1.2 INTRODUCTION .... - 65 -

  3.1.3 The Eight Children of James and Mattie Named above ... - 66 -

    3.1.3.1 Cramer Sudduth Sr.. - 67 -

    3.1.3.2 Charles Sudduth.. - 69 -

3.1.3.3 Arrie Flynn Turner (Sudduth)...................... - 72 -
3.1.3.4 Ila Parker Sudduth........................ - 72 -
3.1.3.5 Mazie Holland (Sudduth)........................ - 74 -
3.1.3.6 James/Jimmy........................ - 74 -
3.1.3.7 Ruth........................ - 74 -
3.1.3.8 Adolphus........................ - 75 -
3.1.4 The Grand Children .... - 75 -
3.1.4.1 CHARLIE'S FAMILY........................ - 75 -
  3.1.4.1.1 Juanita's life .... - 75 -
  3.1.4.1.2 Vernell .... - 76 -
  3.1.4.1.3 Charles Jr. .... - 76 -
  3.1.4.1.4 John D. .... - 76 -
  3.1.4.1.5 Joseph (Joe) .... - 77 -
  3.1.4.1.6 Betty L & Robert (twins) .... - 77 -
3.1.4.2 ILA AND FRANK PARKERS 13 CHILDREN........................ - 77 -
  3.1.4.2.1 Herman .... - 77 -
  3.1.4.2.2 Emma .... - 78 -
  3.1.4.2.3 Ruthy Mae .... - 78 -
  3.1.4.2.4 Fred .... - 78 -
  3.1.4.2.5 Maxine .... - 79 -
  3.1.4.2.6 Leroy .... - 79 -
  3.1.4.2.7 Carl .... - 80 -
  3.1.4.2.8 Curtis .... - 81 -
  3.1.4.2.9 Frank .... - 81 -
  3.1.4.2.10 Eugene (Ed) .... - 82 -
  3.1.4.2.11 James (Uncle Bat or JC) .... - 82 -
  3.1.4.2.12 Elizabeth (Aunt Doolie) .... - 82 -
  3.1.4.2.13 Billy .... - 83 -
3.1.4.3 MAZIE'S FAMILY........................ - 84 -
3.1.4.4 JIMS FAMILY - Leanna's Story........................ - 84 -
3.1.5 The 58 GRANDCHILDREN OF ILA SUDDUTH-PARKER .... - 85 -
3.1.5.1 Ila's Granddaughter - Yvoughn's Story............. - 85 -
Chapter 4 - Memoirs of Siblings of whom Very Little is Known: Olivia, Lucinda, Mathilda, Leonard"Lynn,"& Elsberry Sudduth........................ - 86 -
4.1 Olivia Sudduth........................ - 86 -
4.2 Lucinda Sudduth........................ - 86 -
4.2.1 Ida Sudduth Burns........................ - 86 -
4.2.2 Jessie Sudduth........................ - 88 -
4.3 Mathilda Sudduth........................ - 88 -
4.4 Leonard Sudduth........................ - 88 -
4.5 Elsberry "Ebb" Sudduth........................ - 89 -
Chapter 5 - "Lucy Sudduth Marcus, "Mudda", the Tie that Binds".. - 90 -
5.1 Bettye's Memories of Lucy Sudduth Marcus .... - 90 -
5.2 Lucy's Grand-daughters remember their Grandmother - Mudda the ties that Bind........................ - 94 -
Chapter 6 - George Sudduth, "A Journey of Faith"........................ - 99 -
Chapter 7 - Legacy of "My Papa" Charles J. Sudduth & His Multi talented Family........................ - 102 -
7.1 Mama and Papa: Their Early Years .... - 102 -
7.1.1 Their Courtship .... - 102 -
7.1.2 Making a Living .... - 104 -
7.1.3 The family home .... - 105 -
7.2 Mama and Papa: Their Children .... - 105 -

7.2.1 Bonnie "Trudy" Leonard Sudduth Robinson .... - 106 -
7.2.2 Nathaniel "Buck" Sudduth .... - 107 -
7.2.3 Ella Mae Sudduth Lucas .... - 109 -
7.2.4 Calvin Elsberry "Ebb" Sudduth .... - 110 -
  7.2.4.1 Memories of Ebb - Twin Oaks, A Quiet Strength..... - 110 -
    7.2.4.1.1 Calvin Elsberry Sudduth .... - 124 -
  7.2.4.2 Calvin Elsberry Sudduth - A Genealogy............. - 124 -
7.2.5 Emma Lou Sudduth Larkins .... - 134 -
7.2.6 Napoleon Bonaparte Sudduth .... - 135 -
  7.2.6.1 Donna Jean Sudduth Kid - Legacy & children's bios. - 136 -
7.2.7 Maude Esther Sudduth Lawton .... - 138 -
  7.2.7.1 Children's memory of Maude........................ - 139 -
    7.2.7.1.1.1 Testimony of Gloria Williams - Maude's Daughter. - 140 -
    7.2.7.1.1.2 Marvin Lawton - Lawton Family Tree.............. - 142 -
    7.2.7.1.1.3 Victoria Jean Lawton Benson.................... - 144 -
    7.2.7.1.1.4 Crystal Nevada Thornton....................... - 145 -
    7.2.7.1.1.5 Phyllis Haber Lawton Williams.................. - 147 -
7.2.8 Charles Sheldon Sudduth .... - 148 -
  7.2.8.1 Children's memory of Sheldon...................... - 149 -
7.2.9 Bettye Gyle Sudduth Guillory .... - 151 -
  7.2.9.1 Marriage and Children............................. - 152 -
    7.2.9.1.1 Nesbia Greta Guillory Lopes .... - 154 -
    7.2.9.1.2 John Basil Guillory .... - 156 -
    7.2.9.1.3 Paquita Ylonne Guillory Goss Wheeler .... - 158 -
    7.2.9.1.4 Naomi Ruth McFadden-Edwards .... - 162 -
  7.2.9.2 My career in Cosmetology.......................... - 163 -
  7.2.9.3 Becoming a Book Author............................ - 164 -
7.3 Mama and Papa: Their later Years .... - 166 -
Chapter 8 -Joseph Sudduth, "Remnants of Grace"............. - 171 -
Chapter 9 - "John Sudduth's Genealogy"..................... - 176 -
Chapter 10 - Dora (Culpepper) Sudduth, "Experiences with the Father
and Miracles of Today"..................................... - 181 -
10.1 Introduction .... - 181 -
10.2 Truths Revealed in Visions .... - 181 -
  10.2.1 Truths Revealed in Visions, My Work .... - 183 -
  10.2.2 God's Children Are One .... - 184 -
  10.2.3 "Ask In My Name" .... - 184 -
  10.2.4 The Temple Of God Is Holy .... - 185 -
10.3 When Jesus Healed My Life Extended.................... - 186 -
  10.3.1 A Ruptured Appendix Healed .... - 187 -
  10.3.2 Healed of Hemorrhages .... - 188 -
  10.3.3 A Deadly Poison .... - 188 -
  10.3.4 Dye Poisoning .... - 189 -
10.4 Miracles of Today .... - 190 -
  10.4.1 The return of The Spirit .... - 190 -
  10.4.2 Operation of the Heavenly Physician .... - 192 -
  10.4.3 When the Doctors Were Cheated .... - 194 -
  10.4.4 A Broken Back .... - 194 -
  10.4.5 Hemorrhage of the Brain .... - 194 -
  10.4.6 Tuberculosis .... - 194 -
  10.4.7 Other Healings .... - 195 -
  10.4.8 Personal Guidance through Revelation .... - 196 -

10.4.9 Death .... - 196 -
10.4.10 The Reward of Faith .... - 196 -
10.4.11 "Whosoever Cometh Unto Me, I Will in No Wise Cast Out"- 198 -

10.5 Miracles of Today .... - 199 -
10.5.1 The Plot of a Deceiver .... - 199 -
10.5.2 The Prince of Peace .... - 200 -
10.6 Miracles and Visions .... - 200 -
10.6.1 The Power of Darkness .... - 200 -
10.6.2 Kidney Stones Pass .... - 201 -
10.6.3 Caterpillars .... - 202 -
10.6.4 Tumor .... - 202 -
10.6.5 Snake Experience .... - 203 -
10.6.6 Tuberculosis .... - 203 -
10.6.7 Gall Stones .... - 204 -
10.6.8 Baby's Life Extended .... - 204 -
10.6.9 Pneumonia .... - 204 -
10.6.10 Healed of Infantile Paralysis .... - 205 -
10.6.11 Tumor .... - 205 -
Chapter 11 - A Glimpse of the Culpeppers................. - 207 -
Chapter 12 - My Spiritual Quest.......................... - 210 -
Chapter 13 - " The Summary".............................. - 216 -
Addendum and Acknowledgements. . . . . - 219 -

Table of Figures

Figure 1 - Paquita Ylonne (Guillory) Goss, Wheeler.............. - 12 -

Figure 2 - Anthony Patrick Goss and his Lovely Fiancé' Patricia
Musumeci .... - 13 -

Figure 3 - Christina Portillo and Bettye Guillory............... - 20 -

Figure 4 - Bettye with Spiritual Grand-daughter Donna Olsen..... - 21 -

Figure 5 - Pastor Mary and Sr. Pastor Steve Schell, NW Foursquare
Church .... - 22 -

Figure 6 - Carol Reed and Bettye Guillory....................... - 23 -

Figure 7 - William Sudduth Sr. and Lucy (Mikens) Sudduth . . . .- 24 -

Figure 8 - William Sudduth II and Ella (Culpepper) Sudduth. . . - 31 -

Figure 9 - William (Doc) Sudduth III. . . . . - 32 -

Figure 10 - Juarez Sudduth............................... - 34 -

Figure 11 - Left - Juaretta's Daughters, Son-in-Law and Grandchild.
Right - Juarzetta and Hal Bass .... - 35 -

Figure 12 - Children and grandchildren of William Spann on left and
children of Calvin Spann on the right .... - 37 -

Figure 13 - Left- Ella Mae Spann Eggleton Velva Stewart Moore, Calvin
Spann Right - Ella Mae .... - 37 -

Figure 14 - Dewey Spann Sr. and family. . . . . - 37 -

Figure 15 - Dewey Spann. . . . .- 38 -

Figure 16 -Logan Family, the Mother of all in this picture "Mathilda"
is in the center with the plaid skirt and white blouse ...... - 41 -

Figure 17 - Enoch Spann and daughter Enid...................... - 45 -

Figure 18 - Calvin D. Spann(Calvin authored "The Saga of the Sudduth
Clan") .... - 47 -

Figure 19 - Left - Janice and her 3 children seated, Nadel standing.
Georgia with baby in lap Right- Nillus NaDell Justice .... - 55 -

Figure 20 - Velva (Stewart) Moore (daughter of Elizabeth) with her
Aunt Georgia Sudduth Taylor .... - 60 -

Figure 21 -Yvonne White...................................... - 61 -

Figure 22 L-R Billie Ruth Parker; seated left her dad a grand daughter
and seated on the right her mother, sisters and brother standing,
Billie Ruth on the right at the end. .... - 63 -

Figure 23 - "Jim" Sudduth's Daughters - Arrie, a neighbor, Mattie
Jim's wife, Bettye, Juanita (grand-daughter of Uncle Jim), and Ila
another daughter of James "Jim" .... - 65 -

Figure 24 - Mattie Victoria Lindsey-Price Sudduth, dob 8/25/1869 (Ga.)
dod 8/6/1956 - (Coweta, Ok)This is James "Jim"'s wife .... - 66 -

Figure 25 - Left:Cramer Sudduth Sr. and second wife Mae, Right: Cramer
"Son" Sudduth Jr. .... - 67 -

Figure 26 - Left: Margaret Sudduth Peavy Right: Peavy Family: Kent,
Cheryl, Kenny. Anna, Amanda, Phil and Kendra .... - 69 -

Figure 27 - The Charles Sudduth Sr.'s Family; standing L-R Joe,
Venell, Charles Jr.,Betty, John, Drocky Sitting L-R Juanita,
Malinda, Charles Sr. and a friend John Coop .... - 70 -

Figure 28 - Arrie Flynn Turner (Sudduth)...................... - 72 -

Figure 29 - Ruth Sudduth.. - 75 -
Figure 30 - Ida Sudduth Burns.. - 87 -
Figure 31 - Jessie Burns... - 88 -
Figure 32 - Leroy Sudduth son of Leonard Sudduth................ - 89 -
Figure 33 - Elsberry (1877 - 1911) and his wife................. - 89 -
Figure 34 - Left - Lucy Sudduth Edison Marcus Right - Laura Edison
    Thurston Lucy's daughter .... - 90 -
Figure 35 - George and Laura Edison Thurston.................... - 91 -
Figure 36 - Top - Manch Marcus, son Edwin Marcus Bottom - Edwin Marcus
    Sr., Grunetta Marcus, Edwin's wife and their first child Edwin Jr. -
    92 -
Figure 37 - Calvin Elsberry Jr, Trudy in front, Bettye Sudduth
    Guillory, Ruth Rogers, Kathyn Wainsbourgh, Sam Rogers, Laura
    Thurston, Beatrice Sudduth, Elsberry Sudduth Sr, seated BeBe
    Chapman daughter of Bea and Ebb .... - 95 -
Figure 38 - Patricia Rogers Buckner-Michael daughter of Ruth and Sam
    Rogers .... - 97 -
Figure 39 - Anita Marcus Culp....................................... - 97 -
Figure 40 - L-R Charles J Sudduth, Lucy Sudduth Marcus, and George
    Sudduth .... - 99 -
Figure 41 - George Sudduth's Family; his wife Aunt Lizzie seated on
    right, 5 sons & 2 daughters with grand children .... - 100 -
Figure 42 -Papa Charles J. and Mama Dora (Culpepper) Sudduth... - 102 -
Figure 43 - Top Row Left Trudy, Buck, Ebb, Emma, Ella 2nd Row Maude,
    Dora (Bettye 3 on Mama's lap), Polly, Charles J with Trudy's baby
    Freddie, Sheldon with rabbit .... - 105 -
Figure 44 - Charles J. and Dora (Culpepper) Sudduth's 9 Children L-R
    stand Ella-Mae, Bettye Gyle, Bonnie Leonard "Trudy", Maude Esther,
    Emma Lou, L-R Squatting: Napoleon "Poly", Elsberry "Ebb", Nathaniel
    "Buck" , Charles Sheldon Sudduth Sr. .... - 106 -
Figure 45A - Calvin Elsberry Sudduth and his wife Beatrice..... - 124 -
Figure 45B - Calvin Sudduth Family (Puggy, Calvin Sr., Beatrice,
Calvin Jr., Katherine, Beth, Dora Della)

Figure 46 - Donna Jean Kidd (1977), Daughter of Napoleon....... - 136 -
Figure 47 - Top Row - Lanette Kidd, Judy Dyer, Rudy Dyer, Donna Jean
    Kidd, Carla Jackson Lower Row - Michael Dyer, Linton Kidd, Chalmus
    Kidd .... - 138 -
Figure 48 - Maude (Sudduth) Lawton.................................. - 139 -
Figure 49 - Gloria Williams... - 140 -
Figure 50 - Muade Sudduth Lawton and Marvin Lawton............. - 142 -
Figure 51 - Victoria Lawton Benson................................. - 144 -
Figure 52 - Crystal Nevada Thorton................................. - 145 -
Figure 53 - Crystal, Rock, and Ron Thornton..................... - 147 -
Figure 54 - Left - Sheldon and Mildred Jones Sudduth (1st wife) with
    Nadine and Charles. Right (2nd wife) Ruth and Sheldon Sudduth- 149 -
Figure 55 -Paquita Y Guillory Wheeler, Bettye Guillory, Johnny
    Guillory, and Nesbia Guillory Lopes .... - 153 -
Figure 56 Bettye's 3 children and 9 of her 11 grand children... - 154 -
Figure 57 - Tony, Gina, Nesbia, and Rhonda Lopes.............. - 155 -
Figure 58 Suzette Lynn Georgia (oldest daughter of Johnny Guillory),
    Bettye Guillory (Johnny's Mother), and Senta Georgia (Suzette's

first daughter 2 more were born after senta; Betty's great granddaughter) .... - 157 -

Figure 59 - Johnny Guillory and daughter Leslie Lattanzio...... - 158 -

Figure 60 - Angela Goss.. - 159 -

Figure 61 L-R Deryck and Estrelletta Goss, Daughter Angelina Niclole
Goss .... - 160 -

Figure 62 - The Halleluiah Christian Theater Group of Seattle. Paquita
is seated in bottom row center with the lavender blouse and boots
on. .... - 161 -

Figure 63 - Naomi Ruth McFadden............................... - 162 -

Figure 64 - Mama and Papa Charles (2 years before his passing in 1945)
.... - 166 -

Figure 65 - Left - Joseph Sudduth 1870-1917 Right - Daughters of
Joseph Sudduth: Naomi, Rose, and Ruby Sudduth .... - 171 -

Figure 66 - Leonard Joseph Parker and Rose Sudduth Parker...... - 171 -

Figure 67 - Ophelia (daughter), Gywn (granddaughter), and Rose Sudduth
Parker .... - 172 -

Figure 68 - Joseph and Ramel McCleland Eubanks................. - 174 -

Figure 69 - L-R John A.Sudduth, wife Holly Mae (Mattox) Sudduth - 176 -

Figure 70 - John A. Sudduth's children........................ - 178 -

Figure 71 - Robert Blakesley................................... - 179 -

Figure 72 - Indigo Davis the little daughter of Charles Davis the 3rd
and his wife Lena .... - 209 -

Figure 73 - Elizabeth Petersen holding her baby Makayla; Bruce
Petersen the proud grand father, and father of Elizabeth ... - 216 -

Figures 74 - 88 Can be found in the Addendum at the end of the book

A Prayer for all who may read this Book

By: Paquita Y. (Guillory) Wheeler

Please, Holy Spirit, translate my meager words into a deluge of cleansing and renewal. I pray that those who have been marred will allow reconstruction by the hand of the Potter to mend places in their lives, amidst affairs and struggles, needs and incidents. May the peace and calmness of knowing the Eternal God of Heaven, cause the birth of fresh dreams; but most of all, may it lay to rest old fears.

In Jesus Name

Amen

Figure 1 - Paquita Ylonne (Guillory) Goss, Wheeler

My youngest daughter Paquita who wrote the opening prayer; has written the Forward in this book also; every time I read the Forward it brings tears of elation to my eyes; when you read it I am sure you will be touched deeply also, your heart will be warmed and your spirit will be moved by the anointing of the Holy Spirit upon her.

Introduction

Section 1.01 Several years ago the Lord put the desire in my heart to write this book about our family tree. I began to pray *"Lord, please give me Wisdom, knowledge, and direction." May I also give information concerning our ancestors, especially to our descendents?" It was then revealed to me in my Spirit to use as my theme: "Plant seeds of Wisdom, Love and faith".*

Section 1.02 I, Bettye Gyle (Sudduth) Guillory, and Lucille (Sudduth) Johnson are the only two left on this planet earth of 58 grand children of our Paternal Grandparents, I feel that the Lord has chosen this time for me; a perfect time to put in book form all that I know and other members of the Sudduth family know about our ancestors, their lives, specially memoirs of the older members of our family tree. My prayer and hope is that others, all who read this book may feel love, receive wisdom also, and their faith in God be increased.

Section 1.03

Figure 2 - Anthony Patrick Goss and his Lovely Fiancé' Patricia Musumeci

The picture above is Anthony Patrick "Tony Goss" (my first born grandson) with Patricia his beautiful bride to be. They will be married in Jamaica this coming July the 12, 2008. By the time you read this book they will be Mr. and Mrs. Anthony P. Goss. I received this special card from them. You are about to have the pleasure of reading the words below; this card touched me deeply. The verses made me feel like "My life has not been lived in vain". "Tony G." is the grand son who never misses sending this grandma (Nana) meaningful cards with special words that come straight from his heart. He and Patricia always touch my heart with not only cards but monetary gifts for every occasion.

One birthday, Tony sent me a very special card I cherish and have kept. It says "I have planted seeds of faith and love in his heart through the years". The picture on the card has a hand holding seeds in it to be planted. If the Lord has used me in planting such special seeds of love into the heart of my grandson; why not pass seeds of love, faith, wisdom and information of the very special lives of our ancestors on down to generations; for years to come as our legacy.

"Tony" is not only faithful in remembering this grand mother; but his mother, Dad and others; He is just one of the most thoughtful young men I have ever known.

You will have the privilege of reading those words that are so very special to me now.

HAPPY BIRTHDAY,
GRAND MOTHER
"A Grandmother shows the love of the Lord to her family
By giving her love so unconditionally"
Long ago, you began planting seeds of faith in the lives
of our family.
Throughout your life, you've watched them grow and
Flourish into a beautiful garden of God's love
On your birthday, I want you to know that my love for
You and my trust in the Lord continue to grow with
Your faithful tending and nurturing.
These gifts you've given me will bloom my whole life
Through

My heart was over whelmed with joy when God revealed to me, as I reread this card from "Tony" and "Trisha"; to use it as the theme for this book. It was perfect! Members of my family began to send in testimony after testimony, memoirs began to come in. God also gave me Revelation after Revelation to write.

"Tony" is the Principal of and elementary school in New York with 350 students; Patricia (his fiancé) is a Little Italian police lady who serves in the courtroom.

Patricia has a beautiful daughter name Natasha by a previous marriage who has just graduated from college; she adores "Tony", I'm sure he will make an excellent father image for Natasha.

Our Paternal Grandparents were of different nationalities. They were the ones to start the Sudduth "Melting Pot" which has continued with interracial marriages throughout the years. The uniqueness about this marriage is that interracial marriages were for bidden in those days. Today it's the norm. There were 12 children born to this union,

8 boys and 4 girls. My Papa, Charles J. Sudduth, was one of the 8 boys, the ninth child born in succession to this union.

I believe one of the reasons God has given me longevity is for this purpose: to get this story out to the off springs of the Sudduth family for generations to come.

I found it amazing (over the years as I searched for, and found so many younger family members; surprisingly enough they were deeply interested in learning about their heritage. This story is so fascinating, I'm sure when others see the title they will be interested in knowing what this story is all about, and will want to read this book, "How the Sudduth Melting Pot Began."

All together a total of 58 grand children were born to the 12 offspring of William and Lucy (Mikens) Sudduth. My Papa Charles, and Mama had 9 children. I am their youngest child.

George Senior, one of my dad's older brothers and Aunt Lizzie also had 9 children also. Lucille (Sudduth) Johnson, who is yet living at 89 years of age, is their youngest child.

In this book you will find a chapter written about 7 of the 12 children born to William and Lucy (Mikens) Sudduth and their children's offspring. There were five of the siblings we have very little information about; however the little information we do have is written in Chapter 4.

My desire is to leave a legacy for descendants in generations to come. Many descendants not even born yet will wonder who their ancestor's were and what they were like, They will get a lot of that information by reading this book. I am one of "Will" and Lucy Senior's younger grand children of the 58 they had; because my father was one of their youngest children. I now am one of the two eldest still living at this time. I can witness with first hand knowledge a lot about our forefathers; whom I came to know even before they passed on to be with the Lord. I am just meeting some of their off springs now, as I have been in the process of writing this book.

In this book you will read memoirs written by offspring of several of William Sr. and Lucy Sr.'s children's children and great-grand-children. I am excited about reading their Chapters, because they have all the latest information about the younger generation. Many of their stories relate to the lives of their fore-parents whom thy have never seen but only heard about. I can testify to the veracity of their oral traditions, because God has so graciously spared me to still be alive with a sharp mind and a young spirit to be on this Planet Earth. It is a Privilege and exciting for me to be the only immediate grandchild left to initiate the writing of this Book.

In my search for interested family off springs to help write this book, I was amazed to find several great-great-grand-children who were excited to gather a lot of information and to write articles and even chapters in this Book.

Our ancestors were people who had great Faith in God. Most Of them were talented, very industrious and were great achievers. There were some very sad tragic things that happened to some of them. You will read those stories also.

The one cousin, Lucille Johnson, I have still living now lives in Akron Ohio. She is the daughter of my Uncle George who is next oldest to my Papa, Charles J. Sudduth. Lucille at 89 years of age is very active in helping others who live in her senior citizen apartment complex. Praise God, for the blessings of longevity!!! Thanks be to our Great Creator Almighty God for her good health; sound mind and Ability to still minister to others. I call her occasionally. She has contributed to this book by putting me in touch with her son, Anthony Johnson, a Minister of the Gospel. She has passed the information she knows on down to him. She also gave me information directly about her immediate family that was very helpful in me writing the chapter about her Father and my Uncle George Sudduth.

I believe God has spared me especially for this time, as some of the prophecies given for me are yet to be fulfilled. My greatest desire is to be able to fulfill my destiny. I can't be Thankful enough that God has given me a sound mind and a young Spirit. Although my body has gone through some challenging experiences with physical illness; all of my vital organs are in good condition for my age the doctors say and others have verified. Today I have the victory and am tremendously blessed.

I believe God is who He says he is, I believe God can do and does do what He says He can do, I believe I am who God says I am and I can do all things through Christ who strengthens me. The word of God is alive and active in me! I believe God!

On the 24th of May 1987 I was out shopping driving my 1976 Pontiac Grand Prix. As I entered 320th street intersection off of 12th Ave South, I had a panic attack at the red and green light. I prayed *"Please God help me to get pass this red light and find a Place I can stop and park"*. When the light turned green I turned left. There was the Federal Way City Library; where I found a place to park. I always carry my small Bible with me, and so I immediately opened it to see what God wanted to say to me. Without hunting for a special Scripture, I opened to Hosea 10:12 which says:

"Sow to yourselves in righteousness, reap in mercy; break up your fallow ground: for it is time to seek the Lord until He come and rains Righteousness upon you."

What a word and revelation this word was to me; a wake up call. I immediately began to seek the Lord to find out what the meaning of this was. As I prayed, fasted, and sought the Lord, the Lord gave me scriptures to claim and meditate on. These have been very special to me through the years. The Scriptures, which I hold so dear given and claim, were:

"Yes even when I am old and gray headed, Oh God Forsake me not, but keep me alive until I declared your mighty Strength to this Generation, and your might and power to all that are to come". Psalms 71:18

Psalms 92: 12-15 the second Scripture I've claimed also; another prayer of David:

"The (uncompromisingly) righteous shall flourish like the Palm tree (be Long lived, Stately, Upright, Useful and Fruitful); he shall grow Like a Cedar in Lebanon, majestic, stable, durable and Incorruptible. Planted in the house of the Lord, they shall flourish in the Courts of our Lord. (Growing in grace) they shall still bring Forth fruit in old age; they shall be full of sap (of Spiritual Vitality) and rich in the verdure (of trust, Love and Contentment). (They are living memorials) to show that the Lord is upright and faithful to His promises; He is my rock, and There is no Unrighteousness in Him"

What shall we say then? Is there unrighteousness with God? God forbid. Romans 9:14.

God has been faithful to answer my prayers through the years; the big things and even little things. I am amazed that even such things as the loss of an ear ring I care about; if I've prayed about it, and forget about it, there it is. My desire has always been to know Him more and to do His perfect will. I want to fulfill my destiny and purpose for living. He has brought me through every test and trial; even serious illnesses with no stroke or heart attack. Every body says, I still look younger than my years, and have a young spirit with a sound and sharp mind. To God I give all the praise and the Glory.

He gave me the desire to write this book as a legacy of the Sudduth family which I have fulfilled and you now have in your hands as proof of his ability to fulfill his promises to me. He gave me a desire also to write my autobiography which I have started.

I love life. Each day now, I look forward to an awesome adventure; this is a really an exciting time to be alive. I can see Gods Mighty Hand upon His People. I know we are living in the end times and there is, yet, more work God wants to do through his people. I see Prophecies being fulfilled daily, famine, plagues, disasters through out the world makes us know our redemption is drawing neigh. There are wars and rumors of wars through out the world. Sin is abounding every where. Yet, at the same time revival is everywhere; through "Trinity Broadcasting" network and "Day Star" and so many other Christian Broad casting stations; God is miraculously working. The gospel and teaching of the word of God is covering the earth. or net works the word of God is being preached all over the Earth.

The movie "The Passion of the Christ", was sweeping the Land in 2003 during the time of this writing (2003-2008). People are flocking to see this movie. They are going to Christian Book Stores to buy Bibles; people that have never read a Bible before. Born again Christians being stirred to pray more and repent. I myself had neglected to pray as much as I should every day for our Leaders. I seldom ever miss a day now praying for not only our leaders; but for the body of Christ also, and all men and women every where, that we my live in peace in all Godliness and honesty.

SO YOU, my son, be strong (strengthened inwardly) in the grace (spiritual blessing) that is [to be found only] in Christ Jesus. And the [instructions] which you have heard from me along with many witnesses, transmit and entrust [as a deposit] to reliable and faithful men who will be competent and qualified to teach others also. Take [with me] your share of the hardships and suffering [which you are called to endure] as a good (first-class) soldier of Christ Jesus. No soldier when in service gets entangled in the enterprises of [civilian] life; his aim is to satisfy and please the one who enlisted him. 2 Timothy 2:1-4.

My prayer for all of you who read this book is; that you may be inspired by God to live ready to meet every challenge in life; By seeking His perfect will for your life; By reading His Holy written word(not just receive the knowledge of His word) that you receive the Holy Spirit for His word is spirit and life.

John 6:63. It is the Spirit who gives life [He is the Life-giver]; the flesh conveys no benefit whatever [there is no profit in it]. The words (truths) that I have been speaking to you are spirit and life.

May God give you Wisdom, Knowledge, Understanding, and counsel And Might.

Isaiah 11:2. And the Spirit of the Lord shall rest upon Him--the Spirit of wisdom and understanding, the Spirit of counsel and might, the Spirit of knowledge and of the reverential and obedient fear of the Lord

The reason I chose the title of this book "How the Sudduth Melting Pot Began" is because my Grandparents on my Father's Side of the family were of interracial marriage. So on down the line the descendants followed suit through the years marrying into different Nationalities. As the interracial marriages increased, we created a "Melting Pot; you will see as you read through this book. My parents were an inter-racial couple, papa was white and mama was black. I married French Creole man. My children's father came from an inter-racial union also. His mother was half French and half black. His Papa was Spanish. My oldest daughter Nesbia Greta's, first husband, Ronnie Lopes, is Portuguese. My only son John Basil's (Johnny) first wife Patricia Saloy is French Creole. "Johnny's" second wife Victoria Lopez is Mexican. My youngest daughter, Paquita Ylonne, married into a family where the Mother was Jewish and the Father was Chinese. The "Melting Pot" continues to grow; going on and on from year to year as each generation continues to marry into different nationalities.

Acknowledgements

Mama said I was a peculiar child. I was a change of life baby, born for her at the age of 39. In those days people thought 40 years of age was old. After my parents had 8 children I as the 9th was a surprise. Mama thought she was through after birthing 8. At my birth she became very ill, even to the point of death. But through the prayers of the Saints, her life and my life were spared. This miracle was a sign to Mama that God must have something special he wanted to do through her life and mine. Mama prophesied over me as a young child. I was very quiet and a child of great faith. I went with her to pray for the sick and even through my childish prayers people were healed. Chapter 10 in this book tells the stories of the phenomenal things God did through her life fulfilling his promises to her.

Some miracles that have happened in my life are revealed in this book. Others will be told in my autobiography. There are many desires and promises God has given me in answer to my prayers; however some of my God given desires I believe will still come to pass. I stand knowing God has promised to give me the desires of my heart if I delight myself in Him. There are still conditions we have to meet. My desire always is to be obedient to Him and to meet those conditions. His timing is perfect. Habakkuk 2:2&3.

If I have accomplished any thing thus far in life; I attribute it to Almighty God, my Sainted Mama and Industrious compassionate Papa; whom God blessed to bring me up in the admonition and fear of Almighty God. He gave them great faith, wisdom, knowledge and understanding. I was an avid reader in my younger years and so I am indeed thankful for the following writers/Authors; who I believe were inspired by God. I read their books through the years, naming only a few; like Kathryn Kuhlman, Madame Guyon, Smith Wigglesworth, CS Lewis, John D Lake, Benny Hinn, Rick Joyner, Tommy Tenny, Francis Frangipayne, Watchman Nee, Oswald Chambers, Jamie Buckingham, and John Osteen. Their writings have been a great inspiration to me.

However, the greatest knowledge and revelations I have received comes from reading and meditating the Book of all books "The Holy Bible"; written by Great men and women, Apostles and Prophets of old, who were inspired by God. Inspired to write Gods Word which is Truth; giving guidelines for every soul of earth to Live by. All Honor and Glory be to God for His Holy Word. It truly has changed my life and prepared me for eternal life; which I received at the time I was born again St John 3:16. All of those who believe on Jesus possess Eternal life; even in this Life (ref; John 3:36 and John 17:3); knowing Jesus is Eternal life. What a revelation! The Word of God is Spirit and Life to all those who Find them; Believe and Receive them. *One day I ask God to show me how much I loved him; because I really do want to love him more than any thing. His answer to me was a question. "Do you Love my Word?" I said yes Lord more than any thing. He said "I AM THE WORD".*

I want to acknowledge those who have inspired or helped me.

Margaret Bigger of Charlotte North Carolina, our instructor; who taught a class of 13 senior Citizens how to write memoirs of their ancestors. She is a Dynamic teacher. We had a special bonding. I learned so much from her teaching. She is truly to be admired for her knowledge and Method of teaching.

Jo Ella Haines was my faithful prayer Partner and a true friend for many years. A confident, one who I Have been able to share so much with, No other friend has been so close in the natural to me as she was. We lost "Jo" on the 19th of August 2006: she went home to be with the Lord. Though we didn't see each other very often, I could call her at any time; she was never too busy to pray with me. She was a woman of faith, whom God gave great wisdom and I have drawn from her wisdom through the years. The greatest reward from our friendship is that God answered our prayers.

Figure 3 – Christina Portillo and Bettye Guillory

Christina Portillo is another person I want to give thanks To for adopting me as her spiritual Grandmother. A beautiful young lady, 55 years of age, that I met about 14 or 15 years ago at North West Church. She is the Christian granddaughter I have needed and longed for; for so many years. She is always very thoughtful, in taking me to church, out to dinner buying gifts and doing nice things for me. She has been there to meet so many of my needs. Her faithful prayers for me have been effective. In my summary you will find a very special tribute to Christina; you won't want to miss it.

Figure 4 - Bettye with Spiritual Grand-daughter Donna Olsen

Donna Olson is another very special spiritual Grand daughter of mine; we adopted each other about 23 years ago. We both were attending the same church in Buckley Washington. Because of the long distance, we had to car pool. Her two children, Nicole and Wayne at that time, were 5 and 2 years of age. Today they are 28 and 25. After grieving their Mother as rebellious teenagers often do, they both have come to know the Lord and are saved today. God answered our prayers in their behalf. Nicole married Brian Hopper, a beautifully saved young man. He is a fireman and real estate broker. They are very active in church. Brian and Nichole have a sweet little son named Trustin. Wayne is a chef and teaches cooking in a Federal Way High School. Donna's husband, a great Father and husband is named Eric Olson. Either Donna or she and Eric together take me to church every first Sunday of each month. On their special family get to gather party days, I am invited as a member of their family; I am Grandma to them. The whole family, even their parents; we love each other, they are my extended family.

Acknowledgments would not be complete with out giving thanks and honor to Almighty God for North West Church; with whom I have been a member for 22 years. I remember in 1991 when Pastor Steve Steffy stepped down as our Pastor; my friend "Jo" Haines and I fasted and prayed for 3 days and visited several churches thinking we would leave NWC. Several of my friends did leave. However, God told me to stay there and pray for the church. That fall God sent us pastor Steve Schell, a true sincere man of God a brilliant and much loved pastor by many thousands. We love his teaching and preaching and he and Mary's lives have shown that they are "True Servant's of GOD"! Pastor Steve Schell and the Staff of NW Church have been so kind to me.

Their prayers love and support through the years have helped to sustain me. I have adopted Pastor Steve. I have told his Mother Helen she birthed him; but I love him like my own son too. He has never failed to take time to talk to me when I go to seek Spiritual advice and prayer. Since I have been a widow for many years; I believe God has placed Pastor Steve as my spiritual covering. Thus, I have gone to him through the years and shared my business adventures when I was active in Cosmetology with it's challenges and accomplishments. He has given me prophetic words of inspiration, and encourages me to continue to press on toward the mark of the high calling of God in Christ Jesus, and to finish my destiny. Even today when he sees me he gives to me a hug and prays for me.

Figure 5 - Pastor Mary and Sr. Pastor Steve Schell, NW Foursquare Church

I use to be active in church when I was younger. When we first built the new church in 1987 I cleaned the bath rooms and taught Sunday school, attended prayer groups and different classes. I don't drive a car any more and am not active now in the church as I used to be. But I look forward to going every first Sunday for communion with the saints and pay my tithes.

Donna Olsen, my precious little spiritual granddaughter, made sure I attend Beth Moore's Teaching classes this year at NWC. The first 10 sessions were on "The Faith of God" and the second 7 sessions on "The Psalms of David".

I thank God for another special friend, confident and Prayer partner who came into my life this past January a year ago 2007. She is from the Steven's Ministry at North West Church my home Church. Carol Reed not only comes and prays with me once a week or does other favors for me: like drive me places, sews for me; and I can call her for prayer any time the need arises. We've prayed much for this book and it's God ordained success. Carol has even helped me a lot in typing chapters in this book for me and is very instrumental in helping me to make decisions on ways to express my self in my writings. What a God given blessing she has been and is to me. We laugh a lot together; which is very healthy. Believe it or not we have cried together as well as laughing until we cried laughing!

Figure 6 - Carol Reed and Bettye Guillory

Carol's beautiful daughter Bethany, a photographer, came with Carol and took pictures of me to put in this book (the picture above is one of them). Bethany has married a wonderful Christian young man since then and I attended their gorgeous wedding reception at North West Church.

I am very thankful to God that I called the church one day. I needed a ride about a year ago and they sent Coy Mc Elderry who drove me to my doctor's appointment. He and his wife Judy took me out to dinner after that and they not only became friends of mine, but I have adopted them as my spiritual children. I praise God for them because any time I have a need for help their hearts are open to help. *Many times Coy has taken me to church and out to dinner. He has given me the money for this my first book. My son-in-law "Jim" has paid for the second book which is to come, my autobiography.*

I have a lot of spiritual adopted children and grand children Praise God! They are very special to me.

I do sincerely love and appreciate all relatives and wish to express my gratitude to the ones who have helped me write this book. Since the older members of our family my age have passed on to be with the Lord I have sought younger relatives who are interested in learning about their heritage to join me in writing this book. About 18 of my younger relatives have joined me and have taken on the responsibility of doing research. They have contacted other members of our family for input. The names of all contributors will be honorably mentioned through out this book.

Forward

To all who enter the spirit of the words communicated between the pages of this book, I salute you and encourage you to drink deeply, to ride the winds of time and to appreciate a heritage of strong God fearing men and women.

Some did not have the global 20th century advantages of learning, of travel and televangelism. Our hardships pale in comparison to what they had to endure for lack of resources.

We are privileged to have the tools and pieces of their lives to help us unlock the secret codes and discover the sometime hidden treasures of the meaning of life. They reinforce and validate us, yet we get to determine who we are. We realize that we don't have to accept the labels that other people put upon us and that what we believe about ourselves will determine our success in life. As we spend time with the Holy Spirit He shows us our purpose and our divine destiny. The beauty is we are all from the same blood line, with a wonderful tapestry of woven and varied experiences. We are at different levels of spirituality and we have chosen different paths to educate ourselves. Can we then allow the fortification of the collective threads of our heritage to inspire us to connect our lives in ways beyond any previous imagination? Time alone will tell.

Some one said "The older I get the less things I believe in; but what I do believe, "I believe more intensely!" I believe that this book will set off a chain reaction not only in our lives; but other lives also. To look with spiritual eyes into our Godly heritage, and to expect the grace that God bestowed on our fore Fathers and Mothers, the favor and mantle of those gone on before us to rest upon us also.

In Jesus Name.
Amen.

I would like to express many Thanks to my Mother, for her long and tedious work over the past few years. Her goal was to compile a book that would bring together a history of genealogy to pass down for generations to come. I was aware of her many struggles that she had to overcome while endeavoring to forge ahead, and make sense of the many gaps that needed to be filled, and to research information on stories sometimes long forgotten. It is because of her tireless efforts, her faith in God, her love for her family and the desire to leave a legacy to her family that she endured.

Authentically
In Christ I remain;

Paquita Y. Wheeler
Youngest Daughter of Bettye G. Guillory

Chapter- 1 - How the Sudduth Melting Pot Began

Written by:
Bettye G (Sudduth) Guillory the youngest Child of Charles J. and Dora (Culpepper) Sudduth.

Figure 7 – William Senior and Lucy (Mikens) Sudduth, my Paternal Grandparents

I, Bettye (Sudduth) Guillory, was at home longer than any of the children with Mama and Papa. I was the last born and a change of life baby for Mama. I didn't get married until I was 24 years old. The other eight children married earlier in life than I did.

I will begin with my Paternal Grandparents, and tell the story as I know it. Mama sat down and shared with me many times, and told me stories about the Sudduth side (Papa's family). I remember only a few things she told me about her side (the Culpepper family).

Both my Paternal and Maternal Grandparents had passed away before I was born; I never saw them, and so all I know about them is what my Mama and other relatives have told me about them. Papa never talked to me much about his family.

1.1 Paternal Grandparents – William and Lucy (Mikens) Sudduth the Senior

My Paternal Grandparents, William Senior and Lucy (Mikens) Sudduth, met one day when Lucy was drawing water from the well. It was in the Country in Tallapoosa county Alabama. Grandpa "William" stopped to ask her for a drink of water. Grandpa was 26 years of age at that time. He was born approximately in the year of 1835. Grandma "Lucy" was a young teenager 15 years of age (the approximate year of her birth was 1846). Guess what? Soon after they met they eloped and got married.

If I remember correctly, my Mama told me Grandma Lucy Mikens (later Sudduth) was German; but other cousins say she was Irish. Since Mikens is an Irish name; I'll go with she was Irish. The picture shown above of Grandma Lucy shows that she had Reddish blonde hair and gray blue eyes.

Grandpa William Sudduth was half Indian and half Caucasian. He looked more Indian than white in the picture of him. To this union was born 12 children; 8 boys and 4 girls.

When I was a girl, we called our parents Papa and Mama, and so I feel comfortable using those terms as I write about them.

My Papa (Charles J. Sudduth) was the 9th child born in their family. There were three Brothers younger than Papa, next to Papa was Elsberry, we called Uncle "Ebb", Uncle Joseph "Joe", and then Uncle John was the youngest child in the family.

1.2 Maternal Grandparents -Benjamin and Molly Culpepper

Although this Book is about my Fathers side (the Sudduth side of the family). It is important to me I think to document the little I know about my Mama's family to be remembered also.

I don't know how Mama's parents met, but Mama's Father, Benjamin Culpepper, was a Black Hawk Indian. He had very dark bronzed skinned with straight black hair. Mama's Mother "Molly" was colored, she was brown skin with kinky hair. Up until the 1950s people were called Colored if they were born of interracial marriages. From the 60s time on, for some reason, they started calling us Black. The saying at that time was, "Black is beautiful". I hated being called black for years; but now I've gotten use to it. *(Smiles)*

I do know that Mama said her Mom, Molly's parents, were born during the time of slavery. My Maternal Grandparents, "Benjamin" and "Molly" Culpepper, had 7 Children. My Mama "Dora" (Culpepper) Sudduth was the youngest of the seven children. Charles and Dora (Culpepper) Sudduth; my parents had 9 children.

I do know that Mama's oldest brother was named Uncle "Doke". Her oldest sister was named Ella. You will find in this book so many children were named after either their parents or Uncles and Aunts. Dora and Ella Culpepper; married two of the Sudduth brothers. Charles, my Father married Dora Culpepper, his oldest brother William II married Mama's oldest sister Ella Culpepper. William "Will" Sudduth and Ella had 9 children. Their children were our double first cousins.

Mama was born in 1873; her next oldest sister was "Aunt Emma". I had a chance to see her when I was a teenager. She and her daughter came to visit us in Topeka, Kansas. My sister "Ella May" was named after my Aunt Ella and my sister Emma was name after Mama's sister Aunt "Emma".

Mama's youngest brother was named Robert. There was a tragic ending to his life. Mama said he was a fine young man and was loved by so many people. He had been given a high position and there were some white people that didn't like that and were envious of him, they hated him. Robert was killed by some of his of enemies. They scalped him because he had sandy red hair; this could have identified him I'm sure they thought. He was wrapped in iron chains and thrown into the river. A couple were fishing one day when there came a bolt of thunder and lightening that brought him up out of the water and dropped in their boat. This was very frightening to the fisherman; but this was an answer to prayers, to find out what happen to him. It was Gods way of finding Roberts body and discovering what really happened to this beautiful, good young man who was greatly loved by so many people.

Grandma Molly (Culpepper) had many talents; she made quilts for her children. She was an excellent cook. My Papa loved her cooking. He liked greens, corn bread and good old southern dishes; like fried chicken biscuits and gravy which were her specialties.

Grandma Molly was a great Seamstress. She made quilts and left them for her children to remember her by.

Grandma Molly was a person that always thought she was sick. There was always something wrong with her; I think you would call her a hypochondriac. The Doctor told my Mama to make her mad one time. He thought this would make her snap out of it. She thought she couldn't even walk and was crawling on the floor one day. The Doctor couldn't find anything wrong with her physically and realized it was just a physiological thing with her. He supposedly gave her some medicine, which was only water mixed with red food coloring and sugar. Grandma Molly said it was the best medicine she ever tasted. So this was the tactic the Doctor used to make her forget about herself. She thought it was the best medicine she ever tasted that cured her.

Grandma Molly was telling Mama what to give her sisters and brothers after her Death. To make her Mama mad she told her she wasn't going to give them any thing. She was going to keep it all for herself. Mama was only 14 years old at that time. When my Mama came home from school that day, Grandma was standing in the door waiting for her with braided switches. Mama got a good whipping that day for talking back to her Mother. Mama said it was worth the whipping to see her Mother all better and up walking.

At first Grandma Molly really didn't want Mama to marry Papa because he only had only a 6th grade education and was white. In those days, it was not popular for whites to marry blacks because of segregation. Grandma wanted Mama to marry a black professor. Mama told me that because she was Black she didn't want her kids to be Black like her. So she thought she would have light skin kids if she married white. When Grandma heard Mama had eloped and married my Papa, Mama got another good whipping from Grandma Molly. In later years, Grandma came to really love Papa. He was very good to her and he loved her very much, too.

My mother, Dora, was a graduate of Langston University, and became a School Teacher at a very early age. She taught school for 15 years altogether. Graduating from Langston University in those days was like Graduating from high school as a sophomore today. In those days, people who went to University were considered a professor with the highest degree.

After Mama and Papa had been married for several years and the first three children were born, Grandma Molly had cooked a delicious dinner one evening, making corn bread, greens, etc. She laid her head on the table as if she were sleepy. Then Papa asked Grandma to let him help her to bed. As Papa lifted her up, her foot drug as he carried her to bed. She had had a stroke.

A few days later when she was dying she heard Angels singing. She said, *"Don't you hear the angels singing? Come on children lets Go."*.

Grandma Molly's favorite song was "I must tell Jesus I must Tell Jesus I can not bear these burdens alone". I love that song too and often sit at my key board; sing it thinking about her and the tears of joy flow down my cheeks. My Grandparent's the Culpepper's were loving parents and God fearing people.

My Mama grew up in the same county as my Papa did. It is so funny that I never knew the name of the town. All I was told is that it was Tallapoosa County. I never knew what the J in Papas name meant. He always signed his name Charles J. Sudduth. Mama related some early stories about them being neighbors in the country with the Sudduth Clan.

She remembers when she was about 4 years old seeing this blond haired 2 year old kid, Charles J, running down the road in his shirt tails. Mama called him a tow head kid *(Smiles)*. Can you imagine a little boy running around in his shirt tails? It must have looked like he had a little dress on. Mama says as a girl she used to chase him down the road.

Six of the Sudduth Neighborhood kids were white and the other 6 were red skinned and looked like Indians. Half of them took color after their Father and the other half took color after their Mother.

1.3 My Dad's Parents and Family

William Senior and Lucy (Mikens) Sudduth had 12 children in the following order: William, James, Olivia, Lucinda, Mathilda, Lucy, Leonard, George, Charles J, Elsberry, Joseph, and John.

1.3.1 "Will "Sudduth Jr.

I remember visiting Papa's oldest brother William the 2nd's youngest daughter "Georgia" Sudduth Taylor" in Los Angeles California. She and Roy her husband had a Parrot that could talk, he would say to "Roy" I want a cup of coffee. Could you believe a Parrot drinking coffee? Cousin Georgia was the youngest of 9 in her family; she is one of my double first cousins. Georgia had a sister named Elizabeth; who we called Cousin "Lizzy" when I was a kid. In later years, she called herself Betty. Velva "Stewart" Moore; who was the same age as me, was cousin Lizzy's daughter. Velva died after having a fall a few years before this writing. I use to call her; as a matter of fact I am the one who would call all my cousins off and on after we became senior Citizens *(Smiles)*. Velva's, Father Nathan Stewart was an Indian.

Mary Lucy (Sudduth) Spann, Uncle "Will's" oldest daughter, a sister to Betty, Larry and Georgia had 10 children. Mary Lucy's oldest daughter was named "Ella May" Spann; her first husband was Alphonso Kingsberry; he was my brother Elsberry's wife Beatrice's brother. After they were divorced she married a man named Eggleson

Ella May Spann and my sister "Ella May" and Cousin Georgia were all Three the same age. (By the way there will be a chapter in this book that will be written by Rasheeda Garner; who is an off spring of "Uncle Will" ; Her chapter will tell more about the Spann family and Uncle "Will's" family.

1.3.2 James "Jim" Sudduth

Papa's next oldest brother was James Uncle "Jim", he married Aunt Mattie. To that union were born; Cramer Senior, Charles, Arie, ILA, Mazie, Jimmy, Ruth and Adolphus. Billie Ruth Parker and Cheryl Points Great grand children of Uncle "Jim's" will be writing about his off-spring in CHAPTER 3. The four sister's were born between Uncle "Jim" and Uncle "Lynn", one right after the other; then the other six boys were born.

I saw only one of my Father's sisters. I was 8 years old when Aunt Lucy came to visit us in Junction City Kansas. My other 3 Aunts had passed before I was born.

1.3.3 Olivia Sudduth

Mama told me Olivia the oldest of my Papa's 4 sisters was 6 feet tall. It was said that when she sat in a chair her hair lay on the floor. Wow! She really had long hair, eh?

1.3.4 Lucinda Sudduth

More about Lucinda Sudduth, she was married to Peeler Burns and they had 4 Children. I talked to my brother Sheldon's wife Margaret in Texas recently; she gave me addresses and phone numbers she and Sheldon had for several years, when they were doing research on family history. From that lead I was able to find connections in Detroit Michigan to my Aunt Lucinda. They were great-grand-children of Lucinda and Peeler Burns.

I just received a little new information about my Aunt Lucinda (Sudduth) Burns, Papa's second oldest sister. After making six long distant calls, trying to find telephone numbers of family members, (by the way) my sister-in-law Margaret Sudduth in Texas gave me addresses; but no phone numbers, I found "Lurlean" Young in Detroit Michigan; believe it or not she is my papa's sister Aunt Lucinda's great-grand-daughter. Wow, what a blessing!

Lurlean is going to make contact with family members. I believe that some one from that side of our family will be writing a Chapter or a manuscript to honor my Father's Sister Lucinda. God answers prayer; Miraculously He has answered our prayers by sending contributors who have been instruments of love by helping me to write this book.

1.3.5 *Mathilda Sudduth,*

We don't have any information about Mathilda Sudduth other than the approximate date of her birth was in the year 1867.

1.3.6 *Lucy Sudduth*

Lucy Sudduth (the youngest of the 4 girls) was married to Joseph Edison and they had 4 children. She visited with us when I was a little girl, her daughter Laura came with her. I visited With Laura and her husband George Thurston through the years. They lived in Akron, Ohio. George died first; but Laura lived to be 100 Years Old.

When "Joe" Edison died Aunt Lucy married Edwin "Ed" Marcus. They had only the one child named "Manch" Marcus. He and his first wife had only one child named "Ruth".

Ruth's Mother died while she was a baby. Edwin Marcus was born to Manch and Grunetta before Ruth was a year old. So Ruth and Edwin are the same age for a month so. After Manch and Grunetta were married they had Evelyn, Deborah, Dorothy and Anita. You will find more information about Aunt Lucy and her family in chapter 5. Aunt Lucy was named after her mother Lucy (Mikens) Sudduth.

Edwin Marcus Junior was the first of Manch Marcus children to die. Then Dorothy died. In the year 2003 Ruth was found dead. She died in her sleep. Her daughter "Pat" and Ruth had not only just a Mother and daughter relationship; but were very close Pals. Pat said she and her Mother talked to each other every day. One day, Pat called and there was no answer. They went to see what was wrong and found her dead just as if she were sleeping. The covers were not even ruffled.

Edwin Jr. and his family moved to the Seattle area in later years. He and I became telephone partners and used to talk often though we never saw each other. I talked to his oldest daughter "Connie" DuBoise not too long ago, and she told me her Dad Edwin Jr. was in the service for twenty years and their family traveled a lot. Interestingly they lived in Akron Ohio for 2 years; where the Sudduth and Marcus side of the family lived. However, they never came to know the Sudduth and Marcus side of their Family.

"Pat" and Anita had only given me the title they had chosen some months ago for Chapter 5, "Mudda the Tie that Binds." The article I was expecting came late so in the mean time I wrote the little I knew about Aunt Lucy and her family and added what I had found out from Eddie Marcus III's daughter Connie Du Boise. Edwin Junior's Sister Ruth's daughter, "Pat" Buckner, and Ruth's sister "Anita" Culp finally did send me a beautiful article to add to what I wrote down *(Smiles)*.

1.3.7 Leonard "Lynn" Sudduth

So far I have no information about my Uncle Leonard's "Uncle Lynn's" Family. All I know is that he was killed working in the mine as a young man. He was married and had a son name Leroy.

1.3.8 George Sudduth

Uncle George was born next. When I first saw him in Akron Ohio he was the Pastor of the "Roberts Street Church of God". He was tall like Papa. They favored with the exception that Uncle George had a more red skinned Indian complexion and Papa's complexion was more white. The story of his life and about his off-spring is being written by members of his family in another Chapter.

1.3.9 Chares J. Sudduth

My father Charles and Uncle George were very close in age, and the last two of the 12 children to go home to be with the Lord. Uncle George died in January 1945. Papa attended his funeral in Akron, Ohio and as he viewed Uncle George's remains. Apparently, He was speaking to Uncle George's spirit when he said (as if he were talking to Uncle George) *"he would follow him soon"*. Six months later in that same year, July 14, 1945, Papa followed his brother George and went home to be with the Lord. Papa died on my sister Ella May's birthday July 14, 1945. Papa and Uncle George were buddies; because of the closeness of their age.

I was 32 years of age when Papa passed.

1.3.10 Elsberry "Ebb" Sudduth

The little known of Ebb is in section 4.5.

1.3.11 Joseph "Joe" Sudduth

The next youngest to Uncle "Ebb" was my Uncle "Joe". The story of his side of our family tree is told in the Chapter 7 which is titled "Remnants of Grace". This was written by his great-granddaughter, Ramel McClelland Eubanks. He had six children. I was in touch with only one of his children, Rose (Sudduth) Parker who lived in Waukegan Illinois. She was the youngest of Uncle "Joe's" 6 children. I used to talk to Rose by phone ever so often. Rose was a Cosmetologist like I was. I had the opportunity to visit her once when she was living in Waukegan Illinois.

1.3.12 John Sudduth

See Chapter 9 for information on John Sudduth.

Chapter 2 - William Sudduth II - "The SUDDUTH Legacy Moves West"

Written by:
Rasheeda Garner A great-great-grand daughter of William 2nd and Lucy (Mikens) Sudduth the eldest Child born to William Sr. and Lucy Sudduth. We called him Uncle "Will". He was a Jr.), Roy Roberson, Eugene Logan, Calvin Spann, ESQ., Megan Spann and Juarezetta Bass.

Figure 8 - William Sudduth II and Ella (Culpepper) Sudduth

The eldest son of William Sudduth Sr., William II was born into slavery at the outset of the Civil War in 1861. He lived the common existence of a member of a sharecropping family in rural Alabama, and became determined to break free of the limitations resigned to former slaves in the South. He left an indelible legacy of westward movement through the continental United States, all while working diligently to ensure the economic and social advancement of the Sudduth family.

William II and Ella Culpepper had nine children together: William III, Robert, Mary Lucy, Aldora, Elizabeth, Larry, Pocahontas, Seth, and Georgia. Three of their children died tragically when they were young: Aldora was born in 1887 and died in 1913 at the age of 26, Pocahontas was born in 1893 died twelve years later in 1905, and Seth, born in 1894 and was killed as an infant in 1896.

As the Sudduth family was traveling west from southwest Alabama to Oklahoma by covered wagon, a fellow traveler accidentally shot Seth, and he was buried on the side of the road.

Only four of the nine children born to William II and Ella Culpepper went on to have families of their own.

William III had two children with his wife Phoebe.

Mary Lucy had ten children with her husband Sumpter Spann.

Elizabeth had one daughter with her husband Nathan Stewart.

Larry Bryan and his wife Sadie had two daughters, Nadine "Dean" and Geraldine "Chick".

The stories of these Sudduth descendants are elaborated further in this chapter, as well as fond stories of Robert, Larry and Georgia.

William Sudduth II union with his wife Ella Culpepper began in southwest Alabama and later on moved west to Oklahoma for the benefit of their family. The next generation continued the ventured westward. Most of William II's descendants reside in Southern California. Each generation of descendants has realized increasingly greater successes, especially in the areas of academics and business careers.

2.1 *William Sudduth III "Doc" Sudduth*

Written by:
Juarezetta Bass, granddaughter of William III

Figure 9 – William "Doc" Sudduth III (1882-1923) and wife Phoebe Anderson Sudduth (1883-1972) with a child

William "Doc" Sudduth III was my (Juarezzeta Bass) Grandfather. Doc was born in 1882 and died around 1923. He was the eldest son of William II and Ella Culpepper. It is said that he was a doctor; thus, his nickname "Doc."

Doc was married to Phoebe Anderson, full blooded Muskogee Indian. As I understand our history, Phoebe Anderson was married to Robert "Bobbie" Sudduth and after his murder; she married Doc Sudduth III. Phoebe had four children, daughter Mamie Island (father Ben Island), daughter Rosetta Sudduth with Robert, and sons William IV and Juarez with Doc. Phoebe died November 11, 1972 in Los Angeles, California. Phoebe relocated to El Centro, California with her children Rosetta

"Rose," William "Bill" and Juarez when they were young adults and teenagers. Rosetta was born in 1901 and died in March 1932. She was married but had no children. William was born March 29, 1907 and died at the age of 67, October 11, 1974. He served in the US Army during World War II in the Asiatic Pacific theatre and received the "Good Conduct Medal" and "Asiatic Pacific Campaign Medal". He was divorced and had no children. He was interred at the Sawtelle Veteran's Cemetery, Los Angeles.

Figure 10 - Juarez Sudduth

My father was Juarez Charles Sudduth. He was born October 26, 1908 in Tulsa, Oklahoma and died July 5, 1952. He married Pansy Liberty Culberson on May 24, 1942. To this union were born two children, Juarezetta Elena Sudduth and Hal William Sudduth. Juarez served in the US Army as a medical technician in World War II. He was interred at the Lincoln Memorial Cemetery in Compton, California, as was his Mother Phoebe. Pansy was born January 25, 1916 and died November 29, 2002.

Hal William Sudduth was born Santa Monica, California, on March 27, 1944 and died after a lengthy illness in Nashville, Tennessee on November 13, 2005. He served in the US Air Force from 1960-1964, and represented the Air Force in Karate competitions. Hal was baptized at the age of 12 and confirmed in the Lutheran Church, and reaffirmed his commitment to Jesus Christ and accepted the call to preach in the 1990s'.

Figure 11 - Left – Juaretta and Husband Ralph(center), daughters on either side, and son Ralph, Jr. Right - Juarzetta and brother Hal Bass

I was born Juarezetta Elena Sudduth in Los Angeles on April 4, 1943. I married Ralph Irving Bass on August 28, 1964, and to this union were born Maliaka Leah, Juonmali Nokwe, and Ralph Irving Jr.

I received two graduate degrees, a Masters of Science and a Masters of Arts. During my 25 years of service employed with Meharry Medical College, I held a faculty appointment for approximately twenty years and held several administrative positions.

After retiring from Meharry, my husband and I became self-employed and provide supportive living for individuals with psychiatric illnesses. We see this as our Christian ministry. My husband Ralph is a licensed minister and holds several graduate degrees.

We will celebrate our 44th wedding anniversary in 2008.

Maliaka was born on January 21, 1966 in Los Angeles, California. She is a cum laude graduate of Spellman College, was a Patricia Roberts Harris Fellow and graduated from the University of Tennessee at Knoxville Law College. She is employed by the State of Tennessee Department of Commerce and Insurance and is the Chief Counsel for Securities and Consumer Affairs. She is single with no children, a collector of African-American and Native American dolls and art, and an extensive traveler.

Juonmali "Nunu" was born on September 6, 1970 in Los Angeles. She is the Mother of my beloved grandchildren, Eden Ani-Hope Hurt, born November 17, 1999 and Thomas Culberson Lee Hurt, born March 16, 2003. She is a striving performer and works in our family business.

Ralph Jr. was born on January 23, 1982 in Nashville. He is currently serving at the rank of petty officer 2nd class and is an Airborne Cryptology Specialist. He speaks Arabic fluently, is a martial arts specialist and enjoys traveling.

2.2 Mary Lucy Sudduth and Sumpter Spann's Family

Mary Lucy Sudduth was born in Alabama in April 1884, and was the third child and the first daughter to William II and his wife Ella. Mary Lucy married Sumpter Spann, a native of South Carolina and together they had 10 children: Ella Mae, Elizabeth (died in infancy), Theodore, Dewey, William, Mathilda, Dorothy, Marcella, Enoch, and Calvin. Mary Lucy and Sumpter initially lived in Wagoner, Oklahoma, and later moved to Muskogee, Oklahoma where they ran a working farm, and she worked as a teacher at a segregated school for black children.

The Spann children were very close, deeply supportive of one another and protective of their parents. One by one, as they reached adulthood, Mary Lucy's children left the confines of segregation and Jim Crow laws in Oklahoma to find better opportunities in Los Angeles, California. Once settled in Los Angeles, they would each send money back to Muskogee monthly, to contribute to the household expenses. In the early 1930s, Mary Lucy, her husband and her youngest children moved to Los Angeles, completing the Sudduth venture west. They lived in a large house on 20th Street in Los Angeles, which became the central location for Sunday dinners and holiday gatherings.

Mary Lucy was a deeply religious woman, raising her children in the Holiness Faith.

Her son Dewey recalled an occurrence when he was approximately 14 years of age and suddenly began suffering from painful swelling and sores to his knees. These inflammations prevented him from walking for several weeks. Doctors were baffled as to the cause, and more importantly the cure needed to relieve his suffering. Mary Lucy was deeply pained to see her son this way, and she began a prayer vigil. For several days, she prayed over him, and as Dewey recounted, on the last day he felt warmth emanating from her hands and when she demanded that he stand up, the sores began to burst and he was miraculously able to walk.

In later years, during her own convalescence as she battled breast cancer, she refused treatment because she believed so strongly that if her faith could not cure her that she was meant to be with the Lord. Her daughter, Mathilda, dutifully tended to her Mother's daily needs as her health declined. Mary Lucy succumbed to her illness in 1934, leaving her three youngest children to be raised by their older siblings. She was interred at Lincoln Cemetery in Compton, California.

The descendants of Mary Lucy Sudduth Spann are primarily concentrated in Southern California. The children that reached adulthood are profiled individually below.

Figure 12 - Children and grandchildren of William Spann on left and children of Calvin Spann on the right

2.2.1 *Ella Mae Spann Eggleton*

Figure 13 – Left- Ella Mae Spann Eggleton Velva Stewart Moore, Calvin Spann Right – Ella Mae

Ella Mae was born in Red Bird, Oklahoma in 1901. She was the eldest of 10 children born to Sumpter and Mary Lucy. She graduated from Manuel Training High School in Muskogee, Oklahoma, and Langston University in Oklahoma. She became the matriarch of the Spann family following the death of her Mother in 1934, caring for her aging Father and becoming a surrogate Mother to her youngest siblings Marcella, Enoch and Calvin.

Ella Mae lived a fruitful life. She was secretary to the Academy Award-nominated actress, Mae Robson, after she moved to Los Angeles during the Depression until Ms. Robson's death in 1942. Her position allowed her to afford a life uncommon to her race and gender. At a time when people of color did not live west of Central Ave., on what is referred to as the "Eastside," Ella Mae bought a two-story house in an upper-middle class, white neighborhood in the heart of the city, which allowed her to send her youngest siblings to better schools, and to guide them to achieve academically.

She was married to John D. Eggleton from 1936 until his untimely death in July 1969.

Although she did not have any children of her own, "Aunt Mae," as she was commonly referred by her many nieces and nephews, was like a Grandmother to them, taking care of them when their parents traveled and hosting regular family gatherings and weekend poker games.

Her personable nature endeared her to all who knew her, and the Spann family was never as close following her death in July 1971.

2.2.2 Theodore "Teddy" Spann

"Teddy" was born in 1906 and grew up on the family farms in Wagoner and Muskogee, Oklahoma. He worked as a janitor at the Max Factor Cosmetics plant after moving to Los Angeles, and eventually he and his brother Bill developed an independent custodial service. Teddy was devastated when Bill was killed in 1949, and died less than a year later by poisoning himself during a family gathering in 1950. The Spann family was shocked and terrified by his suicide, as he seemed to be a jovial man.

2.2.3 Dewey Larry Spann, Sr.

Figure 14 - Top Picture Dewey Spann Sr Family (l-r): Dewey Spann Jr., Dewey Spann Sr., Victoria Spann, Carmen Spann, Ondrey Spann

Figure 15 – Lower Picture Dewey Spann Sr. Family (l-r): Grand daughter Rasheeda Garner, Carmen Spann Garner Rasheeda's Mother, Dewey Spann Jr., Ondrey Spann, Dewey Spann Sr., Monique Roberson

Dewey Spann was born in Wagoner, Oklahoma, on May 1, 1907, and grew up on the family farm in Muskogee. After studying at the renowned Tuskegee Institute, he ventured west in the early 1920s and proceeded to seek employment in various service positions throughout Los Angeles. Dewey literally became a "Jack of all trades," working as a chef, a chauffeur, and an apartment groundskeeper in order to send money to his Mother, and move his parents and younger siblings to California.

He was introduced to Victoria Ball, a young teacher, while she was visiting Los Angeles in the summer of 1936. It was love at first sight, and after a whirlwind 13-day courtship, they were married. During World War II, Dewey built warships and assembled artillery. After the war, was employed in the Parks and Recreation Department for the City of Los Angeles, and was instrumental in the installation of the Exposition Park Rose Garden, which remains a popular site in Los Angeles for brides and grooms to take their wedding day photographs. Shortly after beginning his employment with the city, he was asked to assist in the development of a union of city employees, and diligently distributed literature to co-workers, encouraging them to unionize. Dewey was the first president of the Los Angeles City Employees Union, Local 347, and remained president for 30 years until he retired in the late 1970s.

Dewey and Victoria had three children together: Dewey Jr., Ondrey, and Carmen. Dewey Jr. worked as a marshal for the courthouses in the downtown area for several years and became a salesman thereafter. He is the Father of two sons, Travis and Jared Spann, who have each excelled academically and professionally. Ondrey worked as a receptionist and morning talk show personality at a local radio station, and also worked for a large international import/export company. She has one daughter, Monique Roberson, a graduate of California State University, Dominguez Hills, and an educator. Their youngest daughter Carmen studied at California State University, Los Angeles and the University of Southern California, and receiving a

Master's degree and honorary doctorate degree. She was one of the youngest principals in the Los Angeles Unified School District, and served as the principal of several elementary schools throughout the city for over 25 years. Carmen had one daughter, Rasheeda Garner, a UCLA graduate and an aspiring entertainment attorney and film producer.

Dewey and Victoria enjoyed an enviable lifestyle, and they inspired others to follow their example. After they began traveling extensively throughout Europe, Asia, Africa, and the Middle East, often spending entire summers overseas, their children also became world travelers. While on one trip through Kenya, Dewey and Victoria met a young student and formed an immediate camaraderie. By trip's end, they convinced him to realize his desire to attend college, and sponsored his tuition. They found the experience so rewarding, that in their later years they provided tuition for each of their grandchildren.

Victoria passed away in 1995, leaving Dewey a widower. He spent his remaining years telling stories of his youth in Oklahoma, learning to play CDs in order to listen to his favorite jazz tunes, and riding around the city in his beloved Jaguar.

Dewey was heartbroken by the loss of his youngest daughter Carmen who passed away in August 2002.

His 95 years of life concluded on March 22, 2003, and he is interred with Victoria and next to Carmen at Inglewood Park Cemetery.

2.2.4 *William Spann, Sr.*

William, affectionately called "Bill," was tall, dark and handsome. He was born in Oklahoma in 1909. Bill married young and was the Father of eight children. Whenever he paid visits to relatives, people braced themselves for him bringing all of his children. He was a hard-working man, who worked two jobs to support his large family. Bill was killed at his home during a dispute in 1949, and his death fractured the Spann family.

2.2.5 *Mathilda Ruth Spann Logan*

Figure 16 –Logan Family, the Mother of all in this picture "Mathilda" is in the center with the plaid skirt and white blouse

Mathilda was born September 8, 1912 in Coweta, Oklahoma. She was the sixth child born to Sumpter and Mary Lucy. She attended schools in Muskogee where she met Horace Logan, one of her Mother's students and friend to the Spann siblings. Mathilda and Horace married in 1929, and enjoyed 67 years of marriage.

Shortly after they were married, the Spann family decided that the members that remained in Oklahoma should move west to California. While Mathilda brought her youngest siblings, Enoch, Marcella and Calvin by train, Horace escorted her Mother, Mary Lucy, on the long journey to California by car. The older siblings Ella Mae, Dewey, Bill and Teddy were happy to be reunited with their parents and younger siblings, and the family house on 20th Street in East Los Angeles, became a central location for the family to congregate.

Mathilda and Horace, who had six children together, moved their growing family to 45th Street in 1931, and later to 53rd Street, down the street from her brother Bill and his family. When Mary Lucy became ill, Mathilda cared for two households, nursing her Mother daily and assisting with the upbringing of her youngest siblings until her Mother's death in 1934. Horace Sr. was a finished carpenter, working for Ted Cooper Construction Company in Los Angeles. His expert craftsmanship is evidenced by the improvements he made to the homes and properties of several Spann and Logan family members. Mathilda worked at the Los Angeles County General Hospital as the supervisor of housekeeping for more than 25 years. In their later years, Mathilda and Horace Sr. retired to Riverdale, California, where they built a large, beautiful home that sat on expansive acreage, and grew watermelons and raised livestock.

Horace and Mathilda suffered losses parents should never experience, losing three of their six children during their 67 years of marriage: daughter Mary in 1979, son Robert in 1985, and son Horace Jr. in 1989. Horace Sr. passed away in October 1996, and Mathilda joined him in death in July 1998. Mathilda's warm personality is fondly remembered, as well as her great sense of humor, eccentric gift-giving, and delicious recipes.

Horace William Logan Jr., the oldest of Mathilda and Horace's six children, was born on March 12, 1930 in Los Angeles, California. He attended Hooper Ave Elementary School, George Washington Junior High School and Thomas Jefferson High School. After graduating, he worked for the US Postal Service as a letter carrier in downtown Los Angeles for over 30 years, where his route included the courthouses and city administrative offices. He was married and was a Father of four children, Steven, Anthony, Darrel and Ginger. He died in August 1989 after a brief illness.

Eugene Logan was born December 11, 1931, and has always been very devoted to his family. His parents depended on him to be responsible for his younger siblings when they went to work, and Eugene learned to cook and care for the house as a result. He also served as an apprentice to his dad, and developed carpentry and home improvement skills that he continues to utilize. Eugene enlisted in the Navy following high school, and served four years on the USS Burton Island based out of San Diego, California. The ship was an icebreaker that took supplies to Alaska biannually. He began working at Pacific Bell after being discharged, and worked his way up from a janitor to an installer to a management position. On December 14, 1952, Eugene married Mayhew Ussery, just following Eugene's 21st birthday, and they have enjoyed 55 years of marriage. Eugene and Mayhew had 4 children together, Martell, Sharna, Emond and Sharonda, all successful professionals, 11 grandchildren and 5 great-grandchildren. In their spare time, Eugene and Mayhew travel throughout the country with their 50+ club and Army Reunion groups that meet regularly.

Robert Kenneth Logan was born September 16, 1933 in Los Angeles, California. After graduating from Thomas Jefferson High School in 1952, he enlisted in the United States Navy during the Korean War and worked on the same ship with his brother Eugene at their Mother's request. After being honorably discharged in 1956, he worked as a butcher in Los Angeles. He married Gladys Poindexter, and was the Father of four children, Kathy, Bobby, Kenneth, and Barrett. He died young at age 53.

Only daughter, Mary Ruth Logan was born in 1935. She married Roosevelt Vincent Sapp and together they had 5 children, Marion, Sharon, Gregory, Michael and Stuart. Mary was known for her warm personality and as a loving Mother. She married Bill Harris and died soon after at age 44.

Johnny Dewey Logan was born on June 18, 1936 in Los Angeles. He attended Los Angeles primary and secondary schools with his siblings and attended Santa Monica City College. He was married to his wife Lurline for 21 years, and they had two sons, Anthony and Kevin. He also had a daughter Brenda. He was very loving to his family, and his quick wit made him an expert at telling humorous stories. Johnny always appeared to be having a good time, and was the life of any party. He passed away August 14, 2000.

Thomas Larry Sumpter Logan, the baby boy of Mathilda and Horace's six children, was born on July 6, 1938 in Los Angeles. He worked as a butcher at a packinghouse with his brother Robert. Twice married, he was the Father of 14 children, and was a loving Grandfather to 44 grandchildren and 14 great-grandchildren. He passed away May 17, 2002.

Mathilda, Horace Sr. and four of their children are buried in adjoining plots in Rose Hills Memorial Park in Whittier, California.

2.2.6 Dorothy Spann Roberson

Dorothy was born on April 15, 1914 in Muskogee, Oklahoma. She was the seventh child born to Sumpter and Mary Lucy. After moving to Los Angeles with her parents in 1929, Dorothy attended Manual Arts High School and Langston University in Langston, Oklahoma, where she studied biology. She received her cosmetology license in 1927.

She married Roy Roberson, a successful entrepreneur, after returning to Los Angeles. Together they had two sons, Roy Jr. in March 1936 and Lee in October 1945. Roy Sr. was a talented artisan, able to design and build homes and large structures. He built first black-owned motel in Watts, and later designed and built homes for Dorothy in Pasadena and Los Angeles.

After Roy Sr. became a successful entrepreneur he moved the family to Pasadena, and integrated an all-white neighborhood. Until their move, Roy Jr. had only been exposed to a homogenous environment where he felt safe and his race made him a welcomed member of the community. Pasadena presented the family with the new social challenges. As his Father was building the house, Roy Sr. reflected on experiencing the Tulsa riots of 1921 where 300 blacks were slain and the remainder had their homes burned to the ground. In order to prevent any harm to the house, Roy Jr. and one of his cousins armed themselves, sat up each night and turned away trespassers until the house was completed.

An additional factor that came into play during his transition to life in Pasadena was that his teachers tried to make him doubt his ability to compete academically. Any doubts Roy Jr. had about his ability to compete with white students in Pasadena were dispelled when he received his first "A" on an algebra test. Thereafter he excelled in school.

Roy Jr. was an athlete, playing football, running track and boxing until his dad got sick and he had to return to Watts to run the motel business at the young age of 14. He returned to school in Watts completing high school and becoming a finalist in the Golden Glove boxing competition. He reluctantly became a Father at 17, and raised his son as a single Father after the boy turned 6.

Roy Jr. became very enterprising at a young age, a skill he demonstrated throughout his career. During his three years in an all black company of the United States Army, he utilized his position as the company clerk-the soldier in charge of the company's records-to promote himself every six months. After returning home to Los Angeles with the proceeds of the very successful crap game he ran while stationed at Fort Richardson in Anchorage, Alaska, he leased a motel that he operated and lived in as he put himself through college.

When Roy Sr. passes away suddenly in 1961, his son Lee was in his first year of high school. Thereafter, Roy Jr. and Lee worked together to ensure that their Mother Dorothy became a successful businesswoman. With their Father's motel being as profitable as it was, they made sure she was always immaculately dressed, and had the best of everything until her death in 1999.

At the age of 19, Lee went to work for Pacific Bell, where he worked until he retired as an executive. He is a Father of 4 children, sons Lee Jr., Dale, Ian, and daughter Lomika.

Roy continued to experience racism as he began his career. He was the first black air traffic controller at LAX airport. He remained in the position for 5 years until an overt, racist act forced him to quit. He worked as a math teacher for 5 years until he was offered a counseling position at the College of Letters and Sciences at UCLA-a position he held for 25 years-a position developed to ease the burgeoning racial tension which had reached the campus by the mid-1960s.

During his tenure at UCLA, he had the opportunity to attend speeches, meet and dialogue with many of the leaders of the Civil Rights Movement, including Malcolm X, Stokely Carmichael, H. Rap Brown, Muhammed Ali (during his suspension from boxing), Angela Davis, and Oscar Brown Jr., who would become one of Roy's dearest friends.

Roy retired in the 1990s and enjoys spending time with his beloved wife Clarissa, their son Chris, hanging out with his close posse of friends, working in his enormous garden and regularly planning and executing home improvement projects.

2.2.7 Marcella Spann West

Marcella was born on February 10, 1920 in Muskogee. She attended schools in Muskogee until the family moved to Los Angeles in 1929. Marcella was the only daughter that was an adolescent when her Mother, Mary Lucy, died in 1934. Under her sister Ella Mae's guidance, she was able to return to school and continued her education, which included Jefferson High School and Los Angeles City College.

She relocated to New York City in the 1950s. After returning to Los Angeles, she accepted employment as a Nursing Assistant at County General Hospital, and became a homeowner as a single woman. She married Homer L. West after a short courtship, and he was a devoted husband to her for many years as her health declined. Marcella died in December 1987.

2.2.8 *Enoch Spann*

Figure 17 - Enoch Spann and daughter Enid

Enoch was born in Muskogee, Oklahoma on August 10, 1922, and was the "favorite" Spann sibling-everyone loved Enoch. He moved to Los Angeles as a child. When his Mother passed away a few years later, Enoch, his Father Sumpter, sister Marcella and younger brother Calvin, moved in with eldest sister Ella Mae. He attended Los Angeles High School and was one of the first black students to attend the University of California, Los Angeles.

Enoch worked for the United States Postal Service for 28 years, retiring as the tour superintendent at one of the largest post offices in Los Angeles, the Worlway Postal Center. He was President of the Phalanx Club, an association of postal superintendents, an active member of McCarthy Memorial Church where he served as a leader of a junior high school boys group for four years, and was a member of Alpha Phi Alpha Fraternity, Inc.

He was a devoted family man to his wife, Catherine, his beloved daughter, Enid, and stepchildren, Tana, Isaac and Gregory English. Every Saturday, he took Enid to his brother Dewey's home for brunch, and regularly spent time with his younger brother Calvin. Enoch, a life long smoker, succumbed to lung cancer on April 20, 1969. He was cared for during his convalescence by some of his closest family members, including his niece, Carmen Spann. He is interred with Calvin at Inglewood Park Cemetery.

2.2.8.1 *Calvin Spann: Mary Lucy (Sudduth) and Sumpter Spann's Baby Boy*

Written by:
Jodette Spann, daughter of Calvin Span have heard my Uncle John was a very handsome man and died

The completion of this chapter was achieved by the joint efforts of three generations of Sudduth descendants, including the late Calvin Spann, an extensive researcher of the Sudduth family history who wrote a private memoir of his research for his children; Calvin's daughter Megan Spann, who recalls the vivid stories her Father told her about the Sudduth family; cousins Roy Roberson and Eugene Logan, whose candid accounts of preceding generations introduces the reader to the lives and personalities of relatives that passed long ago; Juarzetta Bass, of Nashville, Tennessee, who independently researched the descendants of William Sudduth III; and, Rasheeda Garner, who incorporated stories told to her by her Grandfather, Dewey Spann, Sr., and put all of these writers works together.

Calvin was born on January 10, 1925 in Muskogee, Oklahoma. He came to California by train when he was 4 years old. After the death of his beloved Mother at age 9, he moved into the home of his sister Ella Mae who became his surrogate Mother.

He attended schools in Los Angeles, graduating from Los Angeles High School where he was an excellent student and athlete. Calvin enlisted in the United States Army in 1943 and was honorably discharged after World War II. He received undergraduate degrees from Los Angeles City College and California State University, Los Angeles, where he was initiated into Alpha Phi Alpha Fraternity, Inc.

Calvin was a very hard worker, working as a special education teacher for the Los Angeles Unified School District by day and working at the post office at night sorting mail in order to support his growing family, purchase income properties and finance his academic aspirations.

After working as an educator for several years, Calvin pursued his law degree at the Loyola University School of Law, and became a prominent attorney in the Los Angeles legal community. He began his legal career practicing in the District Attorney's office, and in later years, started his own successful firm, specializing in real estate law.

Calvin married Lillian Curry in 1954, and together they had six children, Calvin Jr., Stephanie, Leslie, Jodette, Bradley, and Anjanette. In 1973, Calvin married Gloria Vargas, and together they had two daughters, Jizelle and Angelina. Calvin's children are all talented, college educated, and are very family oriented.

Calvin was extremely intelligent, very witty, and could tell a great joke. He was also an avid researcher, spending several years researching the Sudduth family history-excerpts of which are included in this chapter. He passes away on July 22, 2003, and he is interred at Inglewood Park Cemetery with his beloved brother Enoch.

Figure 18 - Calvin D. Spann(Calvin authored "The Saga of the Sudduth Clan")

Lucy Sudduth (oldest daughter of William Sudduth Sr.) married Sumpter Spann many many years ago. Calvin and his siblings were all born in the State of Oklahoma. Calvin David Spann Sr. was born on January 10, 1925 in Muskogee Oklahoma to Sumpter and Mary Lucy Spann. He was the youngest of 10 born to this union. He came to California by train when he was 4 years old. He attended grade school in this area and graduated from Los Angeles high school, where he excelled in academics and athletics. After graduating from high school Calvin enlisted in the United States Army as a private in the Quarter Master Corps in 1943. Upon his honorable discharge he entered college. He received an Associates of Arts Degree in Accounting from Los Angeles City College and a Bachelor of Arts Degree in Elementary Education from California State University, Los Angeles. Calvin furthered his education at Loyola University School of Law, receiving a Juris Doctor in 1962.

Calvin began his career in teaching special education in the Los Angeles Unified School District in the 50's and at the same time worked a second full time job for the United Postal Service. He quit the United Postal Service to pursue his law degree in the evening. He started his law career working for the District Attorney's Office and later went into private practice, where he remained for over 35 years. Calvin also had entrepreneurial endeavors, which included owning and operating the Edge-O-town Motel as well as other business ventures.

Calvin married Lillian Beatrice Curry in 1954. To this union 6 children were born: Calvin David Jr., Stephanie Alida, Leslie Lisa, Jodette Micheline, Bradley Curry and Anjanette Pia. Calvin was recently delighted with the news of his grandson to be born in December to Anjanette. Calvin and Lillian were married for 16 years.

Calvin married Gloria Francis Vargas in 1973. To this union 2 children were born: Megan Amparo and Adriana Mariella. United in this union were his stepchildren Susan Michelle and Christopher Joseph Burg. His daughter Megan blessed Calvin with two loving granddaughters Jizelle Adriana and Angelina Renee. Calvin and Gloria were married for 25 years. Calvin had a love for family, friends, movies and travel. His travels included many destinations in the United States and abroad. He instilled the virtues of education, traveling, gardening and movie watching in all his children. Calvin was an avid reader and a history buff.

Calvin loved to tell stories of the family history. There is the story of how we fled Oklahoma after lynching of one our relative. My Dad pretty much feared the South all of his life because of this historic event. There is the story of how one of his Grandmothers was actually a white child raised by slaves because she was the child of an unwed teenage daughter of a slave owner. This child then wed his black Grandfather. I don't know which side of the family, but I do think it was the Sudduth's. Dad told me more stories of family love affairs then those of significant historic event. He also liked the tragic side of family events and would bring up those dark secrets that should be left untold.

On July 22, 2003 Calvin quietly left this earth in his sleep. His sense of humor, overwhelming generosity and dedication to his family and friends will be greatly missed. Calvin is survived by: His ex-wives, Lovie Wilson Lee, Lillian Curry Spann, and Gloria Vargas Spann; his children, Calvin David Spann Jr., Stephaine Alida Spann, Leslie Lisa Spann, Jodette Michelle Burg; Daughter in-laws Vivian Spann and Julie Burg; his granddaughters Jizelle Adriana Quinones and Angelina Renee Quinones; step-grandchildren Olivia, Julianne, Samantha, Michael and host of nieces, nephews, relatives and friends.

2.2.8.1.1   *About Calvin David Spann Sr. 8 Children:*

Calvin David Spann Jr. is married to Vivian J. Jones. Calvin Jr. and Vivian have no children of their own; but Vivian has three sons Justin, Jeffery and Jon Kistler. Calvin Jr. is a lead sales representative for PPG paints. Calvin loves his job and travels both domestically and internationally for the company and for leisure.

Stephanie Alida Spann is single and has no children. Stephanie has worked in auditing for over 25 years. She currently works for the state of Michigan as an auditor working out of California. Stephanie loves traveling and meeting with friends at Starbucks.

Leslie Lisa Spann is single and has no children. Leslie recently did a career change from the entertainment industry to being an entrepreneur. Leslie's business is dental hand piece repair and maintenance. Leslie loves watch collecting.

Jodette Micheline Spann is single and has no children. Jodette has a career in consulting for Oracle Corporation. She has been with Oracle for over 6 years. Jodette will be a million flyer this year on United Airlines and still loves to fly.

Bradley Curry Spann is single and has no children. He is currently working in the legal field and has inspirations in acting. Bradley loves reading and movie watching.

Anjanette Pia Spann is single and delivered her first child on November 23rd. It is a boy named Alvin Wallace Holmes Jr. (AJ). Anjanette has a career in the aerospace industry and has working for Boeing Corporation for over 15 years.

Megan Amparo Spann is a single Mother with 2 daughters, Jizelle and Angelina. Megan has a career in nursing.

Adriana Mariella Spann married Kory Lombard last October. She currently has no children, but would like to have six children. Adriana's job is selling footwear.

2.2.8.2 *"The Saga of the Sudduth Clan"*

Written By: Calvin David Spann Himself

2.2.8.2.1   *Preface:*

The following story is written for the benefit and affection of the fifth and sixth generations of the Sudduth Clan. Especially for the authors youngest two children, Megan Amparo Spann and Adrina Mariella Spann.

This story has cried to be written before the members of the second generation Aunt Holly Sudduth (John's Wife) and the third generation have passed on. Therefore, the later generations would not be able to put together a cohesive and living story.

I must give special thanks to the following members, who have helped me to write this beginning and will in the future aid in writing a fuller and more comprehensive story, they are;

Ruby Shaw	Third Generation
Laura Thurston	Third Generation
Trudy Robinson	Third Generation
Sally Tolliver	Third Generation
Ruth Rodgers	Fourth Generation
Anita Culp	Fourth Generation
Evelyn Sommerville	Fourth Generation
Depholia Simms	Fourth Generation

Thankfully,

Calvin David Spann
(Fourth Generation)

2.2.8.2.2 *The Sudduth Clan:*

Calvin's Version: written some time before his untimely sudden death.

Originally the family name was Sudduth, but because of vanity or what ever, various branches of the family have changed their surname to Suddeth, Suddieth or Suddith. The saying goes "A Suddeth is a Suddith regardless of what name it is called by."

It must be remembered that most all the family history has been handed down by word of mouth and numerous pictures. Fortunately there are people alive, today in 1981, that have seen all the generations from the first thru the fifth generation.

The phenomenal thing about the Sudduth clan, is that from slavery days to the present they for the most part were religious, family oriented, and proud, Maybe the first generation couldn't read or write; but all the generations there after could, which facilitated communication between the various branches.

The original Sudduth was William the first who was born approximately in 1837 as a slave, in the lowlands of the southwest Alabama Dadeville, Sturtevant and Jackson Gap. He was a house slave; which meant he had more privileges and opportunities than a field hand. He was approximately 17 years old when he was freed. He married Lucy Mikens who was said to be a fellow slave on the same plantation. William II physical appearances was as if he were half black and half Indian.

His wife Lucy Mikens story is very interesting; because she was pure white, but in slaved. The family lore has it that she was born out of wedlock in 1838 to a local white teenager. Her family to hide their shame gave her away when she was a few days old to the cook named Ella Mikens, on the Sudduth plantation. This was a fortunate choice; because she was assured of a proper up bringing, plenty of food and a better chance at life, than a poor whites in Alabama, at that time. To hide her appearance she always kept a bandana on her head to conceal her brown straight hair. She had very fair skin and a prominent straight nose, and a casual inspection would have revealed that she was pure white. So the Sudduth slave owners and all the whites employed there, conspired to keep her enslaved, and to hide her true identity. They even allowed her to get married (by jumping over the broom) to her fellow slave William Sudduth II. Her first child was William the 3rd "Doc" born 1855 before she was freed. She was 14 years old at the time. Grandma Lucy said "she never was sure who the Father of her first born child was". As a reader of this story and of American history, knows the female slaves were at the mercy and convenience sexually of their slave masters. Therefore she had 11 more children and she was positive that William I was the Father of all of them. The names of her children were: James, Olivia, Lucinda, Mathilda, Lucy Marie, George, Charles, Joseph, Lynn Elsberry and John.

It appears that immediately upon being freed, William and Lucy, became sharecroppers to feed and house their multiplying brood.

Apparently all went well in the lowlands while the children were growing. It must be remembered that this was the south, during the reconstruction period, after the Civil War. Blacks held elective office and there was relative freedom for them there, until approximately 1885. By this time William I was forty and Lucy was thirty eight years old. Their first born William II was twenty-four, James twenty-three years old and poor. Olivia had been dead five years.

Therefore, when things began to become oppressive, especially for light, bright, and near white blacks, the Sudduth Clan began to move from the lowlands to the mining camps near Horse Creek, Alabama. Horse Creek has been renamed. It is now Jasper, Alabama. It is believed that all of the brothers at one time or another worked in the coal mines. William II, George I, and Charles I, supplemented their incomes by becoming preachers. This is not meant to be derogatory, but it helps to understand the family drive and their true religious beliefs.

The first family tragedy was the untimely death of Olivia, at seventeen of yellow fever. A family friend, Joseph Edison, was engaged to marry Olivia and helped the family with money and work on the family farm, during those trying times. He became so attached to the family that he pursued Great Grandfather and Great Grandmother Lucy to marry one of their three remaining daughters. She was able to talk her youngest daughter Lucy into marrying him.

William II by 1895 had stopped working in the coal mines and had become a full time preacher. He was doing quite well and altogether even though he was only thirty-four years old. He had fifteen children. Another preacher in the community, Rev. Edward Robinson Sr., began to entice members of William II's church into his. Three years later things came to a head. William II became so enraged thereafter he went to Rev. Robinson's home and shot thru the walls and wounded the good preacher. Rev. Robinson's son, in later years married Trudy, oldest daughter of Charles J.

To escape punishment and after advise from his Mother Lucy, he decided to go back to Oklahoma. After going to Oklahoma, William II decided to go back to Alabama to bring his wife and children to Oklahoma. His wife was Ella Culpepper, and her younger sister, Dora, married his younger brother, Charles.

William II was not arrested for shooting Rev. Robinson, but because he looked pure white, other whites feared that his only purpose in Alabama was to recruit black workers for transport to Oklahoma. Therefore a group of whites severely beat William II and left him for dead near the railroad tracks.

When great Grandmother Lucy heard of this, she went to this group of toughs and told them that he was her son and was not a labor recruiter. They helped her look for him. He was found in a culvert under the railroad tracks, recovering from his fearful beating. William II recovered sufficiently by 1898 to remove his large family to Oklahoma. However, he died in 1906 at the age of forty-five, as an aftermath of his fearsome beating in 1897.

The next brother to leave Alabama was James, then Charles, and finally Ellesbury. They all rejoined their older brother William II in Porter, Oklahoma.

The next tragedy to strike the Sudduth Clan was the early death of James in 1909. This was followed by the lynching of Ellesbury in 1911, in Porter. Family legend believes, that Uncle Ebb (Ellesbury) had a barber shop in town. It was the custom in those days for blacks to step into the street whenever a white approached them head-on walking toward them. Unfortunately a black mentally retarded teenager, unable to appreciate this quaint southern custom brushed against a white "lady" who was accompanied by her male escort. The boyfriend put the teenager in his place by beating this teenage dullard right in front of Uncle Ebb's barbershop. The boyfriend wanted to avenge the honor of his white "lady" friend. Uncle Ebb was in his early thirties and being big and muscular decided to even up the fight. To put it in the vernacular, he thereafter stomped that white dude.

This was very imprudent, because that white dude aroused a lynching mob which descended upon poor outnumbered Uncle Ebb shortly thereafter. Uncle Ebb, to his undying credit, was able to kill two of his attackers, one of whom was the local sheriff.

The only surviving brother in Oklahoma at that time was Charles. The mob prevented him from picking up and burying his brother's body, because his last name was Sudduth.

The risky task was assigned to Sumpter Spann, husband of Mary Lucy Sudduth, daughter of William II. Sumpter picked up Uncle Ebb's lynched body and it was given a religious burial.

Charles Sudduth's older son became the target of threats because of their Uncle Ebb's daring deeds. Uncle Charles decided it was wiser to remove his teenage brood to Topeka, Kansas. He did so within two years.

Fortunately Great Grandfather William and Great Grandmother Lucy were dead before the untimely deaths of William II, James, and Ellesbury.

It is reported that the last contact between the white slave master Sudduth and the black slave descendants occurred approximately in 1913 in West Virginia. Apparently Naomi, daughter of Joseph I, struck up a conversation with an older white couple named Sudduth. They remembered the white slave Lucy and her husband William I.

No one in the Sudduth Clan remembers what happened to Lucinda and Mathilda except that Lucinda married Peeler Burns and had a son named Jessie Burns. Jessie left Alabama and went to live in Detroit, where he eventually died.

Either Lucinda or Mathilda had a daughter named Hattie Aaron. Because of a desire to see her family in Oklahoma and a lack of funds, she decided to walk all the way from Alabama to Oklahoma. She did so, by walking from job to job in the direction of Oklahoma. Eventually she was successful. However, she returned to Alabama in style, as a passenger o the train.

Uncle Lynne had only one child, a boy named Leroy. Uncle Lynne died in a mine explosion which left him buried in the mine. The clan hasn't had any contact with Leroy since approximately 1914. If alive he would be in his nineties. It is presumed that he didn't have any offspring, because his wife was much older than he was, at the time, and they were childless.

Uncle John I died in Birmingham, Alabama in approximately 1915. He is survived by his wife Hollie, a daughter Holly Mae, and many descendants living in Detroit, Michigan.

Uncle Joseph I died in 1917 in Kansas City, Missouri. He is survived by his daughters Naomi, Rose, and Ruby. Tragically Joseph was alive in 1914 and he heard of the death of his only son Raful. The son was killed by poisonous mine gas when he was approximately eighteen years old. Father and son had planned to be reunited in Kansas City, as soon as the boy saved up enough money.

Uncle George was the last brother to leave Alabama. He did so when he was lured by high price jobs in Akron, Ohio in approximately 1916, during World War I.

Aunt Lucy's daughter Laura and her husband George Thurston joined Uncle George and his family in 1918. Aunt Lucy Marie joined her daughter in 1920. Thereafter all of Aunt Lucy's children joined her in Akron, Ohio.

Tragedy struck again when Aunt Lucy's youngest son Leslie was killed in the steel mills in Birmingham at age eighteen in approximately 1919. His body was badly burned by molten steel when hopper carrying molten steel accidentally overturned.

William II descendants are now living in Los Angeles, Calif. It is believed that they were the most prolific and therefore contained the largest number of members of all the sub-branches.

Some of Uncle James descendants are in Berkley, Calif. and its nearby cities. He has three daughters and one granddaughter still living in Tulsa, Oklahoma.

The Sudduth men were extremely tall for their times, intelligent, prolific, and hardworking. They believed in changing occupations and even cities to better themselves. It is believed their offspring follow in that same tradition and most have joined Middle class America and quite a few are upper class. At least three are millionaires and maybe more, but few will admit it. They also chose spouses that were hardworking and as intelligent as they were.

There ware very few skills or occupations that the Sudduth clan have not achieved or possess. This helps to keep the family pride high and the family ties secure. Of the approximately five hundred clan members (living or dead), very few if any have been a disgrace or held the clan up to ill repute.

To emphasize the intelligence, the persistence, and the work ethic of the Sudduth clan, mention must be made here, that in the beginning the members had humble professions, such as janitors, maids, farmers, barbers, and part-time preachers.

William Sudduth III came next; who made an outstanding achievement by becoming the clan's first medical doctor in approximately 1912. In those ancient times, a person could become a doctor by the conventional method of going to college and then on to medical school.

The other method was by being an apprentice to a practicing doctor and taking courses from a correspondence school. The latter method was the one taken by William II. By completion of his studies, he was the Father of four, a part-time janitor and part-time farmer.

The various clan members who have achieved success and distinction in their chosen fields are 1.) William II (grandson of George I) is a chiropractic doctor, 2.) Roy Roberson (great grandson of William II) is a professor of black studies at the University of Calif. in Los Angeles, 3.) Charles Jr. "Jack Sudduth" (grandson of James I) is a principal of an elementary school in Emeryville, California, 4.) Juanita Wilson (sister of Jack Sudduth) is the principal agent of the largest intergraded cemetery in Tulsa. Oklahoma 5.), Carmen Spann (great granddaughter of William II) is a principal of Los Angeles elementary school, 6.) Calvin Spann (grandson of William II) is a practicing attorney in Los Angeles.

We are related by marriage to the Honorable Vaino Spencer (Justice of the District Court of Appeal), Honorable Robert Roberson (A Superior Court Judge), and Honorable Charles Scarlet (A Superior Court Judge). These aforementioned judicial officers, serve in the Los Angeles County area in Calif.

Other outstanding achievements accomplished by the clan were by Enoch Spann (deceased), a Postal Superintendent (grade level XVI) and Dewey Spann (Retired) President of Local 347, Los Angeles City Employees Union.

This essay has been written as a beginning of a written history of the Sudduth clan. Other members of the clan are invited to correct, rewrite, lengthen, improve, or add more anecdotes to this humble beginning. Please do not let this be the last recordation of our recorded family history.

Sincerely,

Calvin David Spann

2.3 Larry Bryan Sudduth

Written By:
Nillus NaDell Justice

Figure 19 – Left – Janice and her 3 children seated, Nadel standing. Georgia with baby in lap Right- Nillus NaDell Justice

Larry Bryant Sudduth is (was) my Grandfather. He was one of the sons of William II and Ella (Culpepper) Sudduth. Larry Sudduth was born in Alabama in 1892, the sixth child born to William II and Ella Sudduth. The youngest and last survivor of William II and Ella's ten children, Georgia Sudduth, was born in Coweta, Oklahoma, on October 10, 1900. Georgia and her brother Larry were especially close, and although Larry was older, Georgia was very protective of him.

Larry married my Grandmother Sadie Ramona (Hill) Sudduth in Vineta, Oklahoma. I do not know the year of their marriage. I called him "Granddad Jack". He was a very good looking man and seemed so tall to me at the time as I was a little girl. I remember him hugging me when he would come to visit and we'd take pictures together. Grandmother Sadie was a short lady, perhaps 5'3" tall with a pretty, smooth brown complexion, and wavy dark hair. She was very pretty.

In 1915 Larry and Sadie had one daughter, Nilus Nadean Sudduth. She was born on February 4, 1915 in Vineta, Oklahoma. On March 22, 1916 another daughter, Ellen Geraldean Sudduth was born, also in Vineta, Oklahoma.

The following information is all I have to present about Larry's younger daughter Geraldine's family:

- James Monroe May 15, 1911, married September 18, 1938.
- Ellen G. Monroe March 22/1916,

- Jimmy Forrest Monroe August 22, 1943???,
- Janice Nadean Monroe Miller May 18,1945,
- Adrian D. Miller 5/11/45 Husband to Janice married April 9/66
- Aaron C. Miller 8/13/70 Son,
- Joel J. Miller 9/26/70 son,
- Ian W. Miller 2/17/78,
- Aaron daughter Ashtyn R. Miller 5/12/93
  son Joel W Miller 7/29/98,
- Ian daughter Destinee R Miller 10/2/98

In the 1940s, Larry was accused of killing a white man during a violent altercation in Missouri. After learning of his incarceration, Georgia, accompanied by her employer, Wallace Beery, went to Missouri and secured his release. Larry returned to Los Angeles with them, and he moved in with Georgia thereafter.

In the late 1940s, while repairing Georgia's roof, he feel to his death.

Larry's sister, my great Aunt, told me that Granddad Jack was a gardener in Los Angeles and did many odd-jobs. He sold ceramic pottery. I have a pair of matching vases from his collection. Aunt Georgia also said that he helped pen the song "Route 66", but never received any credit for it. Granddad died as a result of an accident. He was sweeping rain water from a flat top roof when he slipped and fell from the roof hitting his head on an iron pipe that was protruding from the ground. This was in 1951, I believe.

Nadean (nicknamed "Dean") and Ellen (nicknamed "Chick") were quite young when Larry and Sadie divorced. I know very little about their lives together. Sadie later married Arthur Euell and lived in Coffeyville, Kansas where Nadean and Ellen attended schools and church. The family attended Sardis First Baptist Church. Growing up, they were called "The Euell Girls".

Nonetheless, Larry visited his daughters and stayed in contact with them. I have photos with him and his daughters. Their elementary school was Cleveland, an all Negro (that was the name for blacks in those days) school. The Filed Kindley High School they attended was integrated. Nadean graduated from Field Kindley in 1933 and Ellen two years later. Both Nadean and Ellen graduated from Coffeyville Junior College. Both sisters majored in Education.

My Father, Delmer De'Sire Thompson, was born in Coffeyville, Kansas on October 29, 1913. He and my Mother knew one another for years, having attended same schools and he often helped her with her homework. He was a member of Calvary Baptist Church. Daddy was a musician and a plasterer. At the age of 16, he and a group of young men formed a "combo" and had a fifteen-minute slot playing their music on radio station KGGF in Coffeyville, Kansas and many people tuned in to enjoy their music. Imagine that back in those days!

After high school he moved to Tulsa, Oklahoma where he worked in the Ernie Fields Band. Daddy played the tenor saxophone and the clarinet. In those days the band members dressed very nicely.

On February 10, 1963, Delmer Thompson and Nadean Sudduth were married in Tulsa, Oklahoma. Delmer continued to work in Tulsa and traveled with the band. Mother lived in Coffeyville with her parents and on June 1, 1937 I ,Nilus NaDel Thompson, was born.. I was the only child born to their union.

Daddy later quit the band in order to provide a more stable lifestyle for his family, and worked in Coffeyville, Kansas. He was employed as a plasterer and on the Missouri Pacific Railroad. He as eventually forced to move from Coffeyville due to lack of work, and he moved to Kansas City, MO. He worked in Kansas City as a plasterer, at the Swift Packing Company, and retired from General Motors. Nadean never left 602 East 5th Street there in Coffeyville except when the family lived with Daddy's Mother for a while when I was quite young.

Nadean worked as a domestic in private homes there in Coffeyville, worked as an elevator operator at J.C. Penny Company, and as a presser at Winfield Walker's Dress Shop. She was an active member of the Ladies Civic and Social Clubs. In the later years of her life she was on the Missionary Board at Sardis.

Mother died in church after testifying one Sunday morning.

I attended Cleveland Elementary School as did my parents and their sisters. My cousins, Jimmie and Janice (Ellen's son and daughter) also attended Cleveland. My daughter, Roxann, also attended Cleveland for one year. I graduated from the 8th grade as Valedictorian and received a $10 scholarship from one of the clubs in Coffeyville. I attended Roosevelt Junior High during the 9th grade, and then attended Field Kindly High School for grades 10 through 12. I took business courses (i.e., shorthand, typing, and bookkeeping). I graduated from Field Kindly in May 1955.

I was a member of the first Brownie, and later Girl Scout Group in Coffeyville organized by Earlene Clairborne. Ms. Clairborne had to obtain special Permission from New York to start a Girl Scout Troop since she was not yet 21. I still have the Bible given to me by Mrs. Isham when I was a Girl Scout.

I majored in Business at Field Kindley high School and was a member of the drum and Bugle corps shortly after graduating from Coffeyville Community College in 1957 with an Associates of Arts Degree in secretarial training..

During the summer of 1955 my Daddy and granddad sent me to California as a high school graduation present. Once in California, I decided that is where I wanted to live. I did return to Coffeyville and completed two years of college at the same junior college my Mother and Aunt graduated from. My major was business and I received an AA degree. And several years later, my cousin Janice attended and graduated from Coffeyville Junior college as well.

On February 16, 1958 I married Robert Gene Harmon, in Santa Barbara, California. We broke tradition and became "Catholic." We were concerned for the formal education and Christian education of our future children. On Sunday, August 7, 1960 at 9:10 P.M., our first child, Michael Roy Harmon was born in Inglewood, California, weighing 6-lbs 6 oz., 19 ½ inches long. A handsome fellow! Tuesday, January 23, 1962, we were blessed with a beautiful daughter, Roxanne Geraldine Harmon, born at 5:35 P.M., 6-lbs. 12 oz. and 19 ½ inches long. She too was born in Inglewood, California at Daniel Freeman Hospital. I was in room 453 with both births.

Gene and I divorced when Michael was 5 years old and Roxanne was 2. I raised the children with the help of the Lord, as He saw to it that I was employed on jobs that paid an adequate wage. I was able to take good care of my children. My only regret is that their Daddy did not aid in raising them. I feel both he and they missed out on a lot.

I was a secretary to the girls' and boys' vice principals at Jefferson High School in Los Angeles. I was a receptionist/jewelry worker at a jewelry manufacturing company. I worked as a Deputy Sheriff in Los Angeles County from 1966 to 1977. After disability retirement, I didn't work for several years, and then was hired as a librarian at Verbum Dei High School, an all-male Catholic High School. In 1985 I hired on at Hughes Aircraft Company as a document processor and later administrative secretary.

My daughter, Roxanne, graduated from St. Matthias High School. She attended Southwest Community College for one year and married Milton Roque in Los Angeles, California. Milton and Roxanne have four children, Darvell De'Sire age 25, Milton Francis II age 19, Roxanne Nadean 17, and Mileana De'Sire is in Heaven and would be 16 if here with us. Darvell received his BA degree from Northwest State University in Natchitoches, LA and is working in Louisiana. Milton II is attending Spartan Aeronautical Engineering School in Tulsa, Oklahoma. Roxann Nadean graduated from King Drew Medical High School on June 17, 2004. She had been accepted into Xavier in Louisiana. My daughter Roxann is saved and is a school-community coordinator for the Los Angeles Unified School District. Milton is self-employed as a big rig driver.

My son, Michael, graduated from Verbum Dei High School and attended some junior college classes. Michael has two children with Nitto Bates; they are Michael Jr., who is 22 and is attending college in SE Charleston, West Virginia; Michael Jr. is married to GeorgiAnne. Michelle Lynn is Michael's oldest daughter and will be 21 in March; Camille NaDel is Michael's youngest daughter with his wife Rhonda Nancy. After being separated for several years, Michael has a 9-year-old son, Brian Michael. Michael is currently employed as a computer trouble-shooter. He hopes one day to have his own computer business. Michael is saved now, praise God for that.

On December 31, 1998 I married my current husband, James Willie Justice. We grew up together in Coffeyville, Kansas, and dated for a year before I moved to Los Angeles in 1957, after I graduated from junior college.

All of my grandchildren are very special to me, and I thank God for them. They are all so unique. With 8, it is quite a bouquet. Now that Mileana is in Heaven, I consider GeorgiAnne as mine also, so I still have 8 active, vibrant young people in my life. I am their "Gran." My son and daughter are very special children; we have come through many rough times together. The Lord promised to bring us "through" the bad times. God is truly good and I stand in awe of Him on a daily basis. I thank God for His son Jesus and His saving grace."

On December 31, 1998 I married my current husband James Willie Justice. We grew up together in Coffeyville Kansas. We dated for a year before I moved to Los Angeles California in 1957, the year after I graduated from Junior College.

I retired from the Federal Insurance Co in Overland Park. I am an active Church member as well as an active member in Inner City women's Aglow fellowship

2.4 *Georgia Sudduth Taylor*

Georgia, sister of Larry and youngest daughter of William the 2nd, enjoyed many years of marriage to Roy Taylor until his death in the 1980s.

Georgia moved to Los Angeles in 1923 with her sister Betty and niece Velva. She lived continuously in Los Angeles for 70 years. "Aunt Georgia," as she was lovingly referred to by her host of nieces and nephews, lived a rich life. For decades she worked for Wallace Beery, an Academy Award winning actor, which afforded her a life of luxury. Her home, in what was then the upper class section of South Central Los Angeles, was always immaculate and full of fine furnishings.

Shortly after her husbands death in the 1980s her health rapidly declined due to her bout with diabetes. Although her leg was amputated, she continued to attend family functions and enjoyed regular visits with nieces and nephews. She never lost her sense of humor and maintained her independence despite her limitations. Occasionally, her nephew Dewey would bring his granddaughters Rasheeda and Monique to spend the night at her home and would help her around the house, and they would wake up in the morning to find her preparing breakfast from her wheelchair.

Georgia passed away on April 2, 1993, at Midway Hospital in Los Angeles, and is interred at Inglewood Park Cemetery.

Velva "Stewart" More, niece of Georgia Talyor

Figure 20 - Velva (Stewart) Moore (daughter of Elizabeth) with her Aunt Georgia Sudduth Taylor

Velva was the only child of Elizabeth affectionately called Betty and was Georgia's older sister. "Georgia was born in 1891-the fifth child born to William II and Ella Sudduth. Elizabeth and Georgia were daughters of William II. Betty, a fiery redhead was one of the first Sudduth family members to move west. Her desire for better opportunities outside of Oklahoma, and the successes she realized inspired her siblings, nieces and nephews. After the death of her sister, she became a great influence on Mary Lucy's bereaved children.

For several years in the late 1940s and early 1950s, Betty moved farther west from Oklahoma than any other Sudduth family members, running a boarding house in the East Chester Flats are of Anchorage, Alaska for "colored" travelers. The house was near Fort Richardson Army Base and Elendorf Air Force Base, and she regularly served meals and held events for servicemen on leave from the bases. Her great-nephew Roy Roberson enjoyed his visits with Betty when he was stationed at Fort Richardson.

Betty had one child with Nathan Stewart, a daughter named Velva, who was born in Coweta, Oklahoma on February 15, 1915. Betty moved with Velva to Los Angeles in 1923, where Velva attended primary and secondary schools, graduating with her high school diploma from Polytechnic High School.

Velva, a fair redheaded, married Curtis C. Moore Jr., of Dallas, Texas, and together they has one daughter, Yvonne, affectionately known as "Doll Baby." Velva was a cosmetologist over 30 years, operating several salons in Los Angeles, retiring in 1994. She was a member of several social clubs, but enjoyed being involved with travels clubs, as they encouraged her to love the world of travel.

Always very thoughtful, Velva was known for remembering relatives and friends' birthdays with calls and cards, and family members always expected her attendance at family functions. A devout Catholic, Velva was an active member of the St. Paul Church until her death on January 25, 2004, and she is interred at Holy Cross Catholic Cemetery.

Figure 21 –Yvonne White

Daughter Yvonne was employed by the Foreign Service branch of the State Department, and worked overseas for 38 years. Her assignments ranged from one year to three years, with interval vacations to Europe. After completing two-year assignments, she would return to the United States for her home leave for 4-6 weeks, and then on to another location. After her first 9 months of training commenced in 1956, Yvonne received her first assignment to Paris in 1957 and became very ill with an asthma attack due to an allergic reaction to the numerous chestnut trees throughout the city.

From 1970-1973, she was assigned to a roving communicator assignment, replacing personnel from 1-2 months at a time. The brevity of these positions led to her being assigned to work in 37 countries during the remaining years of her tenure. She was relocated from her last assignment to Islamabad, Pakistan after the embassy was bombed.

Yvonne retired in September 1994, and returned to the US to live with her Mother. She joined 4 Senior Citizen travel clubs, returned to college and received certifications in various subjects. She had also served on the Los Angeles Grand Jury, which brings criminal indictments and hears arguments from district attorneys, and serves the civil function of developing recommendations to improve county operations. Yvonne sought a position on the Grand Jury because her knowledge of foreign governments was extensive, yet she was less knowledgeable of her own country's government system.

Chapter 3 -"James Journey to the Oklahoma Bible Belt"

Written By:
Billie Ruth Parker; Her Grand mother's Grand Parents were William Sr. and Lucy (Mikens) Sudduth. James Sudduth Senior was her Dad's grand father

Figure 22 Left: Billie Ruth Parker; Right: seated (l-r) Billy her dad, niece Qiana, and her mother Lizzie; standing (l-r) sisters Collette, Sherlena, and Angie, brother Orlando, and Billie Ruth.

3.1.1 PREFACE

God chose to devise a plan to create each of us. He brought our family together to share with him all that he is. It gives God great pleasure when we place our faith and trust in him. When we accept him as our Lord and savior we become his children. Our family truly is a wonderful gift from God; though life is temporary and fragile, often broken up by divorce, distance and eventually death; I am so glad our ancestors were spiritual people who loved Almighty God. They have passed down a legacy that will continue throughout generations to come.

God commanded us to Love Him first of all, and our neighbors as our self. I do believe we are a family that loves each other and since we are Gods children every thing he has belongs to us. Our families are made up of very industrious people; extremely busy with working; trying to accomplish goals, and just making a living for themselves; and so we seemingly forget or haven't taken time for relationships with each other; but now we are showing our love for each other by banding together with Bettye to work on putting this book together; so that generations to come will have the opportunity to enjoy learning about their ancestors. Time is a precious gift and although it may seem late; It' never too late when God says now is the time. Bettye's

Mother Dora (Culpepper) Sudduth; whom God gave the gift of healing many years ago; has left a legacy of her ministry with a booklet of her life and work; which will be in this book as one of the chapters. This story is one of the high lights in this book that will bless many people beyond measure. The attributes of love are giving your time, money, energy, comforts, prayers thoughts etc. Bettye and her Mother have given all these and more to put this book together believing it will be a blessing to all who read it and ponder its writings. The family members that Bettye has ask to contribute toward putting this book together; have graciously consented to do so. I believe because we are put together by God, as heirs we are now discovering our purpose in life joined to gather as offspring of the Sudduth family tree. As far as I know, most everyone who are contributing toward writing this book if not all, are born again Christians who Love the Lord, and are doing a lot of research work to find out as much as they can about their side of the family tree.

Here I quote Colossians 2:2&7: *"That their hearts may be encouraged, being knit together in love, and attaining to all the riches of the full assurance of understanding, to the knowledge of the mystery of God, both the Father and of Christ.*

Let your roots grow down unto Christ and draw up nourishment from him as you have been taught, abounding in it with thanksgiving. See that you go on growing in the Lord, and become strong and vigorous in faith and truth. Amen

This Poem is dedicated to: "James, Journey to the Oklahoma Bible Belt"

The Sudduth melting pot boiled with colors of Indian, black and white

These were Ancestors of ours who really put up a great fight

Mixing races was a shame back then; but the truth be told,

this is how the Sudduth family began

So Many secrets were kept till somebody died

Then the stories were told and it spread far and wide

my great grand pa "James", took the journey from Alabama to Oklahoma, to set his family free

This book is for us to learn all about its Sudduth family history

He married a Lady named Mattie; who was strong and tuff like he Because their faith and trust was in God, He brought them through a lot of stuff

By being Mulatto some thought it a shame; thus they passed for white while others black remained

Since the truth is being told, everybody can rest; knowing that now there is no more family secrets, so we can carry on with our Sudduth family crest.

Poem written by:
Billie Ruth Parker
Tulsa Oklahoma
March 1, 2004

3.1.2 INTRODUCTION

Figure 23 – "Jim" Sudduth's Daughters on left and right ends, (1-r) a friend, Melinda, Bettye, and Juanita

I would like to tell the story of my great-Grandfather, James Sudduth and especially his children. One of his daughters, Ila, was my Grandmother. My great-grandpa James (James the first) Sudduth, was born in May 1862 near Chambers, Alabama. He died in Beggs, Oklahoma sometime between 1910 and 1919. His Mother was Lucy Mikens, who was half German and half Irish. She was born in Georgia in 1844 and died in 1903. His Father was named William Sudduth. He was half Indian and half White also born in Georgia. William and Lucy married when he was twenty six and she was fifteen. James had seven brothers and four sisters. Their names were as follows: William II, Lucinda, Leonard, Matilda, Olivia, Lucy, George, Charles, Elsberry Joseph and John. Great-grandpa James was born in Chambers Alabama. A 1870 census report said that by the age of 16 he was living in Tallapoosa, Alabama. He was fair skin and very handsome. In 1885 he met and married his lovely bride Mattie Victoria Lindsey (Price) at the age of 23, she was 15 years old at the time. Mattie was sort, fast moving a hard working young lady. Her Mother was named Jane (a slave) her last name unknown.

Great-Grandmother Mattie was born August 25, 1869 in Dadeville, Alabama and died in Tulsa Oklahoma on August 6th 1956 was buried at Jackson Grove Cemetery in Coweta, Oklahoma. She married James T. Sudduth in 1885. Before they left Alabama they had four children. The 1910 census says that Mattie had 13 children, but only 8 were living. I'm glad my Ancestors paved the way for us; because I feel like they were treated like animals. They had a lot of babies and could not have any say about their children lives. The first four children born in

Alabama were named: 1.Cramer Sudduth born in 1886, 2.Charles born 1892, 3. Arrie born, 4. Ila 1897. The rest of the children were born in Oklahoma. 5. Mazie was born in 1900, number 6. James Jr., born in 1904, 7.Ruth born in 1907, and 8.Adolphus was born in 1909.

James the first, journey started after his oldest brother William 2nd came to Oklahoma in 1898. By the way; about half of the Sudduth Family were white and so some of them passed for white; the other half took their color after the Indian side, and then they started to marry women that were mulatto (mixed with black), and other nationalities. The Children that were born to these unions of course were of many different complexions. My Great Grandfather James came to Oklahoma with his family in 1900. They evidently were living in the township of Van, county Muskogee, Oklahoma in 1910 and moved to the township Shahan, County Wagoner so the 1920 census says. I assume the eldest son Cramer had moved away; because the second oldest son Charles became the head of the household at this point, I was told. By this time Cramer had two sons Cramer Jr. and Thomas living with Mattie too.

My Great Grandpa James at first was a very sweet man until he started drinking. (I was told), then he became very abusive to his wife Mattie. One day Charles became fed up with his Dad's treatment of his Mother and shot his Father, who then died of the gun shot wound. I don't have any pictures of my great grand Father. I sure wish I did though.

Billy Ruth Parker's story.

3.1.3 *The Eight Children of James and Mattie Named above*

**Figure 24 - Mattie Victoria Lindsey-Price Sudduth
born - 8/25/1869 (Georgia) - died - 8/6/1956 (Coweta, Ok) This is James "Jim"'s wife**

James and Mattie Sudduth's first child was named Cramer Sr. born in 1886 and died in 1966; He had five kids. I never met him; but I know his son Cramer Jr. (nick named son) who is now still living at 96 years of age.

3.1.3.1 *Cramer Sudduth Sr.*

Figure 25 – Left:Cramer Sudduth Sr. and second wife Mae, Right: Cramer "Son" Sudduth Jr.

James and Mattie's oldest child was Cramer Sr. born in 1886 and died in 1966.He had 5 children. I never did meet him. His son Cramer Jr., who now lives in Omaha, Nebraska, is 94 years old at this writing. His wife named Dorothy departed this life in 2003. Both she and Cramer were very sweet loving people and very active in their church and community. Cramer Jr. has made many trips to Oklahoma. He is a loving and devoted family man. In 2002, our family went to Nebraska to visit them. We had a very warm visit as they welcomed us with opened arms into their home.

In 2001, Cramer Jr.'s nieces came to Tulsa Oklahoma to visit relatives. I'm sorry I did not get to meet them. My Father told me he was lying in his chair half asleep when the door bell rang. My Mother answered it, invited them into the den where Father was sleeping. Mother said "Here are your kinfolk from Omaha Nebraska to visit you". Dad said "I looked up and saw white folks". It was Cheryl and her sister Debra. They introduced themselves and told him the story. They looked at pictures and had a good time visiting my Dad found them to be warm and friendly. My Dad was surprised that they would acknowledge they had black blood in them. Dad went bragging on his white family coming to visit him. They all were excited about the visit.

When my brother and I heard about our white kinfolks visit, we were excited and decided to go to Omaha to meet them. We already knew Cramer Jr. (Cramer Jr. and Margaret had the same Father; Cramer Sr., but different Mothers.)Margaret's Mother was white, and Cramer Jr.'s Mother was black.

One time we went to Cramer and Dorothy's house. Cheryl and Debra came over. Both of them had been tracing their genealogy. They were quite confused trying to figure it all out. It didn't seem to make sense. However, as questions were asked and stories were told, pictures were looked at, we finally figured it out. We talked all day and laughed as the puzzle came together. They did not imagine they had any black blood in them! Their Mother Margaret only had told them that they had Indian blood. Finally she told them the truth; she had a black brother Cramer who lived in the same town.

Cousin Cramer Jr. told me a story one time about when he went to visit his sister Margaret. His wife (who was dark skinned) had to sit in the car because his sister did not want her in the house.

This is only one of the many stories about what the Sudduth family went through back then, with relatives passing for white and the darker skin could only pass for black. Cheryl and Debra both are beautiful Christians who love the Lord. We love them for wanting to know about their true heritage, loving and accepting us.

Cramer Sr. (Mulatto) married a young white girl named Mae. She was rather short in stature and probably weighed about 300 pounds. She was hard of hearing and very near sighted. Mae was a sweet, loving lady that liked to cook. She would serve you royally whenever you came to visit. They had to leave Oklahoma because Mae's brothers became angry when they found out their sister had married a black man and a lot older than her. They changed their last name from Sudduth to Jones when they left Oklahoma and went to Topeka, Kansas.

My Grandmother told me stories about the distinctions as the races began to divide. There were 5 different Indian tribes. Whites and Indians began to distance themselves from blacks. There were many tears shed as relatives began to move to Oklahoma.

Anyone with African ancestry was subject to segregation laws. Some children were removed from school when it was found out that their kin were Creek Freedman. Another example was when a husband found out a spouse's true race, he immediately sued for divorce.

Children, who appeared to be Indian, would be assigned to the Tribal roll by the commission and those who appeared to be black to the Freedman rolls. Many of our people were incorrectly assigned.

There were lawsuits filed to get names back from the Freedman roll to other rolls, but they had no success. Being mixed races of Mulatto, Tri-racial etc., it was hard to search for our ancestors because of the altered records.

Families were not excited when they saw edited diaries suggesting that they had relatives that were black skin. That is why we are excited and proud of Cheryl and Debra for making the effort to find us. They told us that when you see any name spelled differently that resembles "Sudduth", we are all kinfolk. Some examples would be

Suddath, Suddeth, Suddarth etc. The white side didn't want people to know that they had black blood; hence they changed spelling of their last name.

The picture below shows some of our white relatives. Margaret on the left in the picture below was Cramer Seniors only daughter; her mother Mae was white. Margaret married a white man that was prejudice; they had 10 children, Cheryl and her family below on the right is one of Margaret's daughters; who is very sweet and was so proud to meet her black relatives. Her grand parents Cramer Sr. and Mae have been dead for may years; yet she pursued the hunt for her black relatives when she found out she had some.

Figure 26 – Left: Margaret Sudduth Peavy Right: Points Family: Kent, Cheryl, Kenny. Anna, Amanda, Phil and Kendra

3.1.3.2 *Charles Sudduth*

You will find that as the stories are told many of our fore parents named their children after relatives a lot. Charles J. Sudduth, born 4/17/1892, died 8/2/1978, was the 2nd oldest child born to my Grandfather James and his wife Mattie. He was named after his Uncle Charles J. Sudduth. (His Dad's younger brother who was Bettye's Father.) He was born in Dadeville, Alabama. The family moved to Webbers Fall, Oklahoma in 1900.

Charles spent his childhood years in Webbers Fall, Oklahoma. He finished his schooling in wagner where he met and married a beautiful Cherokee Indian lady named Malinda Flowers. Charles was 20 years old and Malinda was 19 when they married. She was born March 13, 1893, and died July 21, 1986.Charles and Malinda had 4 boys and 3 girls: Juanita, Vernell, Charles Jr. (Jack), John, Joseph, and the 2 youngest children were twins, Betty, and Robert (Brocky).

Figure 27 – The Charles Sudduth Sr.'s Family; standing L-R Joe, Venell, Charles Jr.,Betty, John, Brocky Sitting L-R Juanita, Malinda, Charles Sr. and a cousin John Camp

Juanita's story.

Charles oldest daughter Juanita contributes her story, and I write as she tells it to me.

Juanita speaking here:

My Father Charles brother, James Jr. and I played together as we were growing up. We had a happy childhood. Some of the games we played were: basketball, croquet, marbles, and jacks. At night we sang church songs before going to bed. My Daddy loved to sing with us. One time I said to my cousin "You can tell my Daddy he's not going to whip me". I had a big surprise. He took some sprouts and stung me good!".

My Mother Malinda was a half breed Cherokee Indian. She was very loving, kind, and generous person to us as well as others. She balanced that with being the disciplinarian of the family.

Both of my parents were devout Christians. Our family attended Sunday school and Church regularly. She taught us the golden rule and made sure we knew about life.

Mother was the youngest of 4 children in her family. Being of Indian heritage, her early schooling was acquired as a student at an Indians mission located near Coweta, Oklahoma. She attended Beacon College in Muskogee, Oklahoma after completing high school. She matriculated at the agricultural and normal school, which is now called Langston University. Following Oklahoma's admission to the union as a state, she was a pioneer in the education profession as a teacher. She became the first teacher at Kemper, Mayflower, and Flower schools near Coweta, Oklahoma.

In 1912 Mother married my Father Charles Sudduth Sr. She continued to teach intermittently and at different intervals while raising her family. She was a devout Christian lady who received her religious training in a Christian home environment.

She accepted the Lord Jesus Christ at the Indian mission at an early age. She later joined the Jackson Grove Baptist Church of Coweta, Oklahoma.

Mother not only taught in the public schools, but taught Sunday school also. She saw the importance of education for economical and social survival in our democratic society. Mother and Father both made sure all 7 of their children were highly educated. Our family then moved to Tulsa, Oklahoma in 1930.

They joined the Morning Star Baptist Church at this time, where we all became members. "Great institutions are but lengthened shadows of men and women who built them". Mother made history with her record of service as a Christian leader and witness for Christ that will live as long as Morning Star church shall live. My father was a deacon in the church, sang in the choir, and became president of the choir, taught Sunday school as well as men's bible class in 1940.

As I explore and dig deep into finding out information about our family, there are so many puzzling documents. For example, I was told by my Uncle that my Grandmother Ila Sudduth said "If you see any name that resembles the spelling of our name Sudduth, we are all kinfolk". The white side did not want to let it be known that they had black blood in them. Did you know that around 1879 blacks left Georgia and Alabama for new territories ending up in Oklahoma and Texas?

3.1.3.3 *Arrie Flynn Turner (Sudduth)*

Figure 28 - Arrie Flynn Turner (Sudduth)

Everyone called her Aunt Sis. She was a 5 foot; small framed lady with long straight beautiful hair always neat and well dressed. She was born in Alabama with a purple birth mark on the left side of her face under her eye.

I remember her as a very quiet woman, often just staring at you. She was a very giving person when you visited her. She would not let you leave unless she gave you something of hers.

She had a spectacular garden every year with her green thumb. Everything she planted would grow.

She married Andrew Flynn and had only one child, Annie Mae. When Andrew died, she married a man named Mr. Turner. She died in Tulsa, Oklahoma.

3.1.3.4 *Ila Parker Sudduth*

Ida was the only name I knew my Grandmother by until I started researching and found out her actual name was Ila. She changed her name because she didn't like it.

I got to know my Grandmother when we went to her house in the summer months. When summer came, we knew where we would be going, off to Grandmother's house. I did not stay the entire summer as my sister did. All of the grandkids would come to see her and gather together in her big 3 bedroom house. Grandmother would go to bed after all of us and wake up before we got up. I always wondered, "Did she ever sleep?"

While visiting her, we had something to do every single day. It might be picking berries, fishing, walking to town, or reading the bible. We always played a certain game. She would pick a word and we would try to make as many words as we could out of that one word. She had lots of pencils and paper for us to play school.

Where food was concerned, one of my favorite memories is her homemade pickles. For breakfast every morning consisted of teacakes, brown gravy, and rice, homemade biscuits with homemade jelly, honey, or butter. It also consisted of smothered chicken, bacon, eggs, and sausages.

My Grandmother had a garden where we would pick cucumbers, tomatoes, greens, cabbage, and onions etc. for our dinner meals. It felt so great to go out and pick our own vegetables, the food tasted so good.

I remember she was very calm and quiet. I never knew her to raise her voice.

Grandmother was very picky about her beds. Every night before we went to bed, she would come in and take off the beautiful spreads (that had knots on them), made out of chenille cotton. She made her own quilts. The beds were so high we had to jump to get up on them.

When you awoke in the morning, you had to make up your bed. You were not allowed to sit or play on the bed. Grandma said "The bed was made to sleep on, not to play on".

Grandma was a very fast walker. When we walked to town, we would have to run to keep up with her. She would walk and pick up stuff on the way like handkerchiefs, clothing, or shoes for example. She would pick up anything she thought she could reuse. Sometimes she even found money.

She would sing songs that stick with me still today. One such song is "At the Cross". She said she knew all of the hymns in the hymnal. (There were over 500)

Grandma moved to Tulsa, Oklahoma after Grandfather died. I would come over after work to sit with her. Our favorite show was "The love boat". We would sit and watch that show laughing and just enjoy each others company. She also liked watching television preachers because she was very religious.

She died when I was 31 years old.

My Grandfather, Flavous Parker, changed his name to Frank Parker. He was born in Arkansas on December 6 1889. He died in Okmulgee, Oklahoma on June 7th, 1971.They were married on Christmas day, December 25th, 1912.Grandma was 15 and Grandpa was 23.They had 13 children.

The only thing I remember about my Grandfather was that he had a favorite chair. He would come home and head straight for that chair, sit there and watch TV. While watching TV, he wouldn't say much, he would just smile and bring us candy. He let us do anything we wanted to do.

He had this little round container with a silver top. He would unscrew the top and insert the contents into his lower lip, making his lip look deformed! He would pick up a can that was beside his green chair and spit in it. Then he would wipe the brown juice that was going down the side of his mouth.

Grandpa always wore the same clothes, but they were neat, pressed, and clean. We were so thrilled when he came around; we wanted to cuddle up to him. When we got bored, we went to see what Grandma was doing.

To this union of Ila (Ida) and Flavous (Frank) Parker were born these 13 children. Those with an * are deceased: Herman, Emma*, Ruthy Mae*, Fred, Maxine*, Leroy*, Carl*, Curtis*, Frank*, Eugene, James/JC, Elizabeth*, and Billy.

Thank God for memories.

3.1.3.5 *Mazie Holland (Sudduth)*

Aunt Mazie was born in Oklahoma, but moved to Arkansas after her marriage to Robert Holland. She was a very petite lady, with long straight hair. She wore glasses that were too big for her head. You always saw her wearing an apron; it was part of her dress!

Aunt Mazie loved to go to church. She baby sat a lot of children.

She was a wonderful cook. Some of her marvelous dishes were fried corn, biscuits, and fried salt pork.

She was a funny lady that could keep you laughing all day.

Her granddaughter, Portia, said that they took trips to Arkansas to visit her family. They would have to go through a little town called Sallisaw, Oklahoma. When they went through this town, Aunt Mazie would say "What did Sally see?"

Aunt Mazie and Robert had 12 children: Alfred, Limuel Andrew, Bernace, Stanley Wayburne, Arrie Verline, and Mary Louise, Vernace, Ernestine, Leonard Duboise, Robert McLee, Helen Mareah, and Bettie Jean.

3.1.3.6 *James/Jimmy*

I do not know much about Jimmy. Uncle Fred said that he came to visit him in 1928.Jimmy was very good looking, so all the women liked him. Some Sudduth men liked white women.

While Jimmy was visiting in Oklahoma, he got into trouble with a white woman by flirting and carrying on. He insulted the woman in some way. She went and told her husband. The husband got a posse up to find Jimmy. They came and searched our house, (Jimmy was hiding in our loft).They did not find him. When they left, the family got him away safely.

He lived and died in Omaha, Nebraska.

3.1.3.7 *Ruth*

Ruth was a very lovely beautiful woman. She lived in California and had 3 children: George, Louise, and Trum. She is buried in Crown Hill Cemetery in Tulsa.

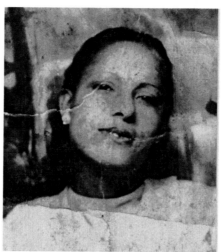

Figure 29 - Ruth Sudduth

3.1.3.8 Adolphus

I don't know much about him. All I do know is that he died at a very young age.

3.1.4 The Grand Children

3.1.4.1 CHARLIE'S FAMILY

Charles Sudduth Sr. the 2nd oldest child of James and Mattie. He married Malinda flowers January 1, 1912.

His entire family valued education. Each child has achieved some sort of degree. They felt education was the key to a successful life. They had 7 children: Juanita, Vernell, Charles Jr., John Dubois, Joseph, Seth, and Betty L and Robert L (twins).

3.1.4.1.1   Juanita's life

Juanita is the oldest and still living in Tulsa, Oklahoma. She was born October 20, 1912 in Coweta, Oklahoma. She attended grade school and high school in Muskogee, Oklahoma.

She loved to play basketball and read.

Church activities were a high priority in her life. Sunday school and choir were 2 of her favorites. In 1930, at 18 she went to Langston University where she received a Bachelor of Science degree in Education in 1940.

Juanita's first teaching position was in Wagoner, Oklahoma.

She married Ray Johnson in 1932, and they have 1 child named Jacquelyne (Jackie) Sue Johnson-Hughes.

Jackie, a graduate of Oklahoma State University, worked for Bell Helicopter for 39 years. Her husband, Bob Hughes Sr., graduate of Tulsa University, had the most wins for a basketball coach in the

United States. Bob Hughes Jr. is a graduate of Texas University and a basketball coach as well in Houston, Texas. He has 2 girls, Robyne and Carlye Juanita. Robyne has a BS-MS PHD. She is a professor at Oklahoma State University. She has 3 children: Grant, Galriella, and Grierre.

Her marriage to Ray Johnson ended in divorce. She then met and married Johnnie Wilson in Columbus, Missouri. In 1946.

Juanita is 92 years old. She is still cooking, reading, and writing. She is the most caring and knowledgeable person I know. I think spelling is her gift to the family. Any word we give her, no matter the length, she can spell it!

Juanita's husband, Johnnie, was a very smart man. He was an inventor. He designed and built their home at 802 E. Pine. Johnnie owned and operated Wilson's TV & Repair where he was known all over the state for his work.

While Johnnie worked, Juanita was a full-time manager of the biggest black cemetery in Tulsa, Oklahoma. She is credited with perpetuation the Crown Hill Cemetery.

She made friends with every person she met; she took personal interest in their welfare. She was House Mother to hundreds of families for 28 years. She retired in 1999, at the age of 87.

3.1.4.1.2   *Vernell*

She was born December 14, 1914. She graduated form Langston University in 1940. She met and married Ellis Pearson. They had no children.

She was a teacher in Berkeley, California.

She died April of 1999.

3.1.4.1.3   *Charles Jr.*

He was born March 13, 1917. He graduated from Lincoln University in Missouri.

He met and married Peggy Fowler. They had no children.

Charles was a teacher and principal in California

He died March 19, 1990

3.1.4.1.4   *John D.*

He was born March 23, 1920. He graduated from Langston University and then moved to California during the war.

He met and married Emelda. They had 2 children; Gary and Kenneth. Gary is a licensed building contractor. He has 2 children; Nicole and Juan. Nicole is at Princeton working on her Masters degree. Juan is studying for his BS degree.

Kenneth is an insurance broker and has 2 children; Amber and Kenneth Jr. Amber has on son, Kevin John Jr.

3.1.4.1.5   *Joseph (Joe)*

He was born January 4, 1924. He moved to California with John where he met and married Tulip. He was inducted into the US services and stayed on until the war ended. When the war ended he returned to California where he currently lives with his wife. They have one son, Darryl Joe, who is vice president of the Williams Sonoma Company. Darryl has 2 daughters, Melinda and Holona. They both attended school in California. Melinda is married and has one son, Kai.

3.1.4.1.6   *Betty L & Robert (twins)*

They were born July 5, 1930 in Tulsa, Oklahoma.

Betty graduated from Langston University. She is a teacher.

Emerson graduated from California University with a BS in Elementary Education and a Masters in Administration.

Betty and Emerson have 2 children, Linda J. Hall and Bryan Chapman. Linda is a teacher in Berkeley, California.

3.1.4.2 *ILA AND FRANK PARKERS 13 CHILDREN*

3.1.4.2.1   *Herman*

He grew up with his Mother. They were the best of friends and played together. When he was born there was a saying "Born with a black pappy is always unhappy."

He went to school at Sunrise School through the 8th grade.

He married Dorothy Shepard in 1834. They have 4 children; Erma Jean, Leanna Marie, Carol Sue, and James Edward.

After Dorothy died, he married Magnolia.

Herman is a tall, slender, beautiful dark skinned man with elegant white hair. He has a gold tooth and when he smiles, it brings out his handsome features all the more.

He resided in Okmulgee on his farm of over 12 acres. He farmed cotton, corn, and peanuts etc. He also did construction work, cement finishing, and carpentry on the side.

I remember when I was little, he raised pigs.

He had a well and you would have to take a bucket on a rope, cast it down in this big hole and fill the bucket with good, fresh, cold well water. We would always take a big drink before we took it into the house.

Uncle Herman loved God.

He was quite a soft spoken man. When you talked to him on the phone, he would always make you laugh. He had positive things to tell you.

His eyesight was bad. Because of this his brother teased him. When women came around brother would say he could see them real good.

He only lived in 3 different places during his lifetime; California, Nevada, and Colorado.

Uncle Herman had a stroke and never recovered. He passed away on October 25, 2004 at the age of 91. He was only 3 days short of his 92nd birthday.

3.1.4.2.2   *Emma*

Aunt Emma was born August 4, 1917 in Beggs, Oklahoma.

They moved from Beggs when she was 5 years old to Sunrise, Oklahoma.

She was a beautiful and very hardworking. She could do just about anything a man could do.

When I was about 10 years old, I looked forward to seeing my Aunt Emma every Saturday. I could hardly wait for that day to come. She would come and pick me up to go fishing. We both loved fishing.

She was not scared of anything. One day we saw a big snake. She slowly walked up to it and killed it with a hoe.

I really looked forward to the lunch that she would bring. She was an excellent cook. Two of my favorites were her pound cake, and her lemon cake.

Aunt Emma married twice. Her first marriage was to Claude Coleman and the 2nd was to Curtis Wilson.

She moved to Tulsa in 1930. She later left Oklahoma, lived in Missouri, as well as California, but returned to Oklahoma in 1957. She had been running from town to town trying to avoid God. BUT in 1959 she was saved, sanctified, and filled with the Holy Ghost. She stayed with God until He called her home.

She had 2 children; Lucille and Ludois.

3.1.4.2.3   *Ruthy Mae*

I did not know Ruthy, but I am named after her.

She was born January 16, 1919. She died in 1922 at the very young age of 3.

3.1.4.2.4   *Fred*

Uncle Fred was born May 18, 1920in Beggs. He attended elementary school at Attuck in Okmulgee, Oklahoma. He finished the 6th grade at Sunrise School.

He was tall, good looking, and smart.

He farmed cotton and corn for 2 years. At the age of 18 he went to the CC camp to help farmers build their farms and then landscaped them for 2 years. At age 21 he was a self-employed yard man. He also painted cars and did body work on them.

At the age of 26 he married Erma Delois Hale on January 29, 1946. They had 9 children; Freddie, Curmay, Sue, Yvoughn, Mark, Jimmie, Gail, Joyce, and Tina.

He owned Parker's Salvage & Junkyard from 1951-1980, retiring in 1981. Needless to say he was a very hard working man.

After Dorothy died, he met and married Opal Green. Then he married Melva Alexander on August 10, 1984. When she passed away he married Ozette Walker in 2000.

He liked to fish and shoot pool.

My Uncle is the kind of person you just love to be around. He always had something funny to say. He loves to tell funny stories.

When he was little there was the family mule named "Old Gin". He got his name from being tough like cotton gin. He was a smart mule that didn't have to be guided. He knew where home was. My dad would tie him up and go drinking. When dad had had too much to drink, "Old Gin" would guide him home safely.

My Mother and "Old Gin" were known to talk to each other. Supposedly the mule had come to the kitchen window and told her "good-bye", trotted off, never to be seen again.

Mother and Daddy were very strict. We were scared of Daddy.

Momma was a good hunter. She never missed what she aimed for, and always brought something back for us to eat.

3.1.4.2.5   *Maxine*

She was born February 8, 1922. She died November 18, 1922.

She died of a fever from pneumonia.

3.1.4.2.6   *Leroy*

He was born July 28, 1923. He died on November 10, 1975 from an asthma attack. He married Myrtle Edd in 1947. They had 2 sons; Leroy Jr. and Paul.

Uncle Leroy was a very big, but handsome man. He was said to have the strength of 5 men. He could walk up a ladder with 100 lbs in each hand, and 100 lbs in his mouth, so they say.

He was known for his barbeque. He could eat a whole chicken with all of the trimmings in one sitting.

He always wore coveralls.

He was a quiet man that loved to fish, and a great story teller.

3.1.4.2.7   *Carl*

He was born April 18, 1925. He died October 7, 1991 in Tulsa, Oklahoma. He enlisted in the Army to fight during World War II. When his tour was completed he met a very beautiful, soft spoken woman, with a big smile, named Inez Hale. They were married in 1948, in a house on Lansing Street, by a little preached that walked all the time.

They never had any children of their own, but in God's plan he became the spiritual Father to a multitude of kids.

He led by example, and as a result many of these children were dedicated to the Lord. My Aunt and Uncle left Tulsa and went to California where they lived with his sister Ruth. In 1950, they did come back to Oklahoma.

He owned Parker's Body and Fender, running it for 35 years.

He was a man of his word. Once he told you he would do something, you could count on it being done. People looked up to him and respected him. They admired his manners and the way he carried himself.

Uncle Carl came to accept Jesus as he personal Savior in 1955. He acknowledged his call to the ministry after receiving the baptism of the Holy Ghost. God led Uncle Carl to build a house where he would be glorified. The first edifice was dedicated to God in the fall of 1963 and was named Tabernacle C.O.G.I.C. The membership increased and God's servant increased in the knowledge that without faith it is impossible to please God. The enlarged sanctuary was rededicated Faith Tabernacle C.O.G.I.C. Two ministries were birthed from this labor. Elder Julius Ballard was one of them. Julius married Uncle Carl's niece. The other ministry was Pastor Rahe Orr, who also married one of Uncle Carl's nieces.

Uncle Carl and Uncle Fred had a lot in common. They married sisters, which they both met at the Tulsa Linen Co. Back then that it where all the black folks could work and get a decent wage.

In the summer of 1974 a new sanctuary was built. The name of the church was then changed to Love Tabernacle C.O.G.I.C. because Uncle Carl loved to do for people.

The church today is a living memorial in Tulsa, Oklahoma, located at 3146 North Xanthus Place.

We truly understand the example of what God meant when he said, "Let the greatest among you be the servant of all". Uncle Carl was a man who served is fellowman well. Dinners were served to the needy on holidays, open air evangelistic services along with many other deeds of charity that only god knows were done. Those that served with him could share his pure joy, the soundness of his judgment, the wisdom of his counsel, the gentleness of his temper, the firmness of his purpose, the affectionate tone of his manner, and the tenderness of his strength as he cared for us. Only those who really knew him could understand the loss of this great servant of God.

Uncle Carl was the one that kept the family together. He always wanted us to get together. I remember one time when I was so "gung ho" to leave town. He sat me down and explained that I had everything going for me here. Why did I even want to leave town?

Uncle Carl died at the age of 66. He had been fasting for 41 days. He had not had anything to eat or drink. He had fasted before and was alright, but he was a younger man then.

He was fasting for faith. We had a family reunion coming in 2 months. I wanted to record his sermon, but he didn't believe in doing that.

I miss him deeply; he truly was one of a kind.

3.1.4.2.8   Curtis

He was born October 29, 1926. He died September 23, 1945.

He was a very handsome man. He married Rosie Mae Purdom at the age of 18.

He was in the Air Force. He came home for the birth of their baby.

After Curtis and Rosie had gone swimming, they got on a train at 5:00 pm to come home to Tulsa where they were going to visit his brothers Frank and Leroy.

Arriving they looked for his brothers in a gambling house, but did not find them. When they were leaving a freak accident happened.

A man's gun fell out of his waist pocket and shot a bullet into Curtis' leg. They took him to Morton hospital to check the leg wound, not knowing the bullet had gone to his bladder. As a result, he bled to death. His wife got the news and fell to the floor. This caused her to have a miscarriage. She lost her baby boy.

3.1.4.2.9   Frank

Frank was born November 28, 1928 and died October 8, 1991.

His brother Carl had died one day before. Uncle Frank had a heart attack. The family actually had the funerals the same day. I myself did not like that. I felt they praised Uncle Carl more than Uncle Frank. It was true Uncle Carl was a preacher and Uncle Frank was an alcoholic, but it taught me you cannot judge anyone's life.

Uncle Frank was a man that would feed you if he thought you were hungry. If you were stranded in the cold or homeless, he would take you in.

Uncle Frank married a very strong woman, Leomia Hawkins. They had 7 beautiful, good looking children: Frank III Daryl Wayne, Richard Lee, Carl Edward, Michael, Curtis, and the only girl, Christy Gail.

3.1.4.2.10   Eugene (Ed)

He was born June 27, 1931.

He was taught how to be a drywall hanger and started his own business in 1963, Parker's Drywall & Construction Co. He was self employed like most of the Parker's (seems like they didn't like working for someone else!). The Parkers' were very business minded. He had this business for over 41 years. It is amazing that at the age of 73, he is still going strong.

Uncle Ed tells jokes that make you laugh. He loves to fish, like all the Parker's do.

He married Jewel Ivory on September 23, 1949. They had 4 children: Coyle, Eddie, Judith, and Joseph. His 2nd wife was Hazel Davis. They were married June 7, 1957 in Gary, Indiana. They had one child, Leatrice.

3.1.4.2.11   James (Uncle Bat or JC)

He was born on January 16, 1933.

Uncle Bat is a true fisherman and hunter. He would go everyday if he could. Both Uncle Bat and Uncle Ed are known for fishing in Mohawk lake in Tulsa. They still fish with fishing poles made out of bamboo trees. They have over 5 fishing poles out at once. They do not like fishing with reels and rods, but they do have a lot of them.

Uncle Bat is a salesman. He likes to set up on corners to sell all kinds of stuff; bicycles, watermelons, golf balls, and tools etc. I think that's where I got my urge to go into sales from.

He carries his Bible everywhere he goes. He loves to discus the Bible with each customer. I have told him, he needs his own church. He certainly could be a preacher. I love being around him to soak up his wisdom.

He is a very active man, so if you see him just sitting around, you would know he is not feeling well.

He married Dorothy Lee Ward in 1954. They had one son James Wayne. Then Uncle Bat's 2nd marriage was to Elmanda Adam. They had one daughter, Miki.

3.1.4.2.12   Elizabeth (Aunt Doolie)

She was born November 8, 1935 and died October 20, 1985.

Aunt Doolie was a lovely, beautiful tall woman who loved God. She was very humble.

Her husband James Thompson was terribly abusive to her.

Her daughter Beverly said "Mother was a praying woman. All of us believe that her constant, continued prayers sustained them.

She believes her Mother lives inside each one of these children. We make Mother proud by making the right godly choices. Our Mother truly lived for God always helping those less fortunate. It was her standard of life. It is not by might or by power that we are what we are today. It is because of our dear Mother.

She was a good cook. There was always something sweet to eat at her house.

James and Elizabeth had 10 children: Linda, Carolyn, Daniel, Ronald,

3.1.4.2.13   *Billy*

He was born on July 28, 1938. This is my Dad. I was named after him and Aunt Ruth.

I recall that when he was growing up, he was a very religious in his early childhood.

He was a big eater. His Mother made sure he had enough to

eat.

He is a big man, very handsome and the best dressed man in Tulsa, Oklahoma.

My father was a very strict and possessive man. We could not spend the night away from home. He always knew where we were at every minute.

He was not the type to show much affection, even to give you a hug, but I would hug him all the time.

He used to drink a lot. We would hate for the weekends to come, but prayers do work. He no longer drinks.

He is a hard worker and has his own business, Parker's Paint & Body.

He used to take us to football games. He walked so fast, we had to run to keep up with him. One time while he was still drinking, and a little tipsy, he took us to church instead of the football game that we thought we were going to. He had "pants" on. Back in those days you didn't go to church dressed in "pants", especially a "Holiness" church. We tried to tell him that we couldn't go because of the way we were dressed, but he said we were going anyway. He made us sit up in front to get prayed for and to be anointed with the Holy Oil. He told us "We could go up to God anytime. It's not what you wear, all you need is prayer.

He met my Mother in 1955, while visiting her Aunt. My Mother was born November 15, 1941. Mother was only 14 when she began to date. Her Mother told her she was not old enough to date. Grandfather finally talked with Billy and gave his permission to date openly, rather than secretly.

Billy's Mother wanted him to go to California. He went and stayed for several months. My Mother and Father were both heartbroken. Billy decided to come back to Tulsa even if he had to walk! His brother Carl gave him money to go back home

On September 29, 1956 they married. They had 5 children: Collette, Billie, Sherlena, Arlando, and Andralique. We also have 6 grandchildren: Qiana, Brion, Brandi, Brooke, Arlando Jr., and Trinity. They also had one great granddaughter, Micah.

Both Billy and I are now self-employed. I graduated from Langston University in 1992 with a BA in Psychology and a minor in Sociology. In 1998 I started "New Beginning Agape Counseling".

Billy has been a great provider and Father. He is the best body and fender repairman. He is remarkable even today.

We have been married 48 years. I feel like we have the greatest children and grandchildren in the world!

3.1.4.3 MAZIE'S FAMILY

Aunt Mazie was the 5th child born to James and Mattie on February 25, 1900. She died in 1985.

She was a petite woman with long beautiful black hair.

She always wore an apron.

To continue the story of her life she has a combination of over 100 children, grandchildren, and great grandchildren. We are very proud of our family.

3.1.4.4 JIMS FAMILY - Leanna's Story

We were born and raised in Okmulgee, Oklahoma. We lived on a farm where I helped with the family's household duties and also with the farming.

My parents were hard workers and excellent providers. My Dad made sure our needs were met. If there were things we wanted, he tried to provide for those also. His example of being a hard worker was not lost on us. We all learned to work hard. I helped plant, chop, and pick whatever our family harvested that year. I was good at driving the family tractor. It was a standard shift vehicle. Let's not forget the team of mules! Hard work allowed us to purchase 10 acres of land, build a new home, which is still in use today.

As a child, I loved to spend time with my dad. I was my dad's pick (I was told).

I married my childhood sweetheart Johnny Goudeau. We had one daughter Janice Marie.

Our family loved to spend quiet evenings at home or taking drives in the country. One family treat was going to Dairy Queen every pay day.

Jan completed high school and married Roderick D. Bagby Sr. They have 2 sons: Rod Jr. and Markeaton. Both of them were active wrestlers and won lots of trophies. My grandsons have families of their own.

I am a very blessed woman. I am retired after 33 years as a cooking instructor and baker at Oklahoma State University. I was married to a wonderful man for 45 years before he passed away Christmas 2000.

My Father James Herman and my brother James Edward live with me. I am thankful for the teaching, love, and care I received from my "Grandma Parker"

3.1.5 *The 58 GRANDCHILDREN OF ILA SUDDUTH-PARKER*

Herman's 4 children: Erma, Leanna, Carol Sue, and Edward

> **Erma-Pastor Oather Todd's** 7 children: Sharon, Joyce, Marsheila, Glen, Oather Jr., Shawn, and Mark
>
>> **Sharon's** 2 children: Alecia and Howard
>>
>> **Joyce's** 7 children: Quinton, Corey, Carmen, Donte, Jamel, Jamason, and Jamesell
>>
>> **Leanna's** 1 child: Janice
>>
>> **Janice's** 2 sons: Roderick Donald, Markeaton Odessar
>>
>>> **3 grandchildren**: Tatyanna, Tiara, and Markeaton Jr.

> **Carol Sue Mitchell Goudeau III –** 4 children: Kathy, Faye, Arlene, and Mitchell IV
>
> **Carol Sue** 2 more children: Sterling Ross Jr. and Sterling Ross III
>
>> **Grandchildren**: Thaddyeuss Thompson Jr., Allyson Faye, and Sterling Ross IV

Emma's 1 child Lucille Goudeau

> **Ludois Lablance – Helen Ward** Anita, Kenny, Dale, Diane, Michelle, Lisa Rashon, and Kris

Fred's 9 children: Freddie Deloise, Sue Perry, Curmey, Mark Allen, Yvoughn, Jimmie, Gail, Joyce Faye, and Tena Mae

3.1.5.1 *Ila's Granddaughter - Yvoughn's Story*

I was delivered without the aid of a doctor or midwife I the middle of a snowstorm. My Mother's sister helped in my birth. My brother, Curmey, was hit by a car and died a few days later at the age of 9.

My Grandmother Ila was a good cook.

We were brought up in church.

My Father hated discrimination. His Mother had instilled in him a general mistrust of white folks.

We all finished high school and 5 went on to attend college.

I married the same year I graduated from high school, we had 4 children: Rahe A, Orr Jr., Minister Timothy Shelton Orr, Christy LaShaun Orr (Rider), and Micheal Erid Orr.

I also have 4 grandchildren and one on the way. They are Cheyenne Michelle Rider, Casian Alise Rider, Kimberly Dawn Orr, and Timothy Orr Jr.

My husband is now in full time ministry after retiring.

Chapter 4 - Memoirs of Siblings of whom Very Little is Known: Olivia, Lucinda, Mathilda, Leonard "Lynn,"& Elsberry Sudduth

Written by: Bettye Guillory:

This chapter is to tell the little that I have heard and know about William Senior and Lucy (Mikens) Sudduth (my grand Parents) five children out of 12 whose names are written above. I have mentioned them earlier in this book.

Several of my cousins have done research on all 12 of William Senior and Lucy's children; but they were not able to find a lot of information about these 5 siblings. We have a lot more information about the other 7, written in separate chapters they are William Senior, James Sr., Lucy, George Sr., my Papa Charles, Joseph, and John. My Uncle's William "Will", James Uncle "Jim" were born first then Papa's 4 sisters, Olivia, Lucinda, Mathilda and Lucy, were born one after the other in succession. Strangely enough – Papa never mentioned them to me; they had all passed before I was born except Aunt Lucy the youngest of his 4 sisters.

4.1 Olivia Sudduth

Mama did tell me that Aunt Olivia, who was the oldest of the 4 girls, was six feet tall. When Aunt Olivia sat in a chair her hair laid on the floor. Wow! That was really long hair. My cousin, Billie Ruth, sent in an article on the family history which said Aunt Olivia was born in 1863 and she died in 1880. She evidently died at the age of 17. No one knew the cause of her death at such a young age. There was no other information about her life.

4.2 Lucinda Sudduth

Aunt Lucinda (Sudduth) Burns was the next oldest of the girls. She married Peeler Burns. They had 4 children their names in their order of birth were: Dock, Ida, Jessie, and Luther. Lucinda and Peeler lived in Carrollton, Georgia where they were farmers. Lucinda died there in 1885.

4.2.1 Ida Sudduth Burns

Ida their only daughter's husband killed her. There were no details given to me about the murder. Believe it or not the law finally caught up with him, and put him in jail. Someone killed him in the jail. That was a case of "You reap what you sow!" This is an ole saying; which is really a Proverb.

Peeler later moved to Jackson Gap, Georgia where he met and married His second wife, Georgia. The Peeler and Georgia had 6 children: Blue, John, Ada, Sallie, Nora and Fred.

Figure 30 - Ida Sudduth Burns

Dock Peeler, Aunt Lucinda's oldest son, married Bernice. They had 6 children: Chum Burns, Harl Burns, Peeler Burns (named after his Grandfather Peeler), Marion Burns, Lela Burns and Jessie Burns.

Jessie Burns and His wife, Carlister, were farmers like his Grandfather and Father Peeler. Jessie and Carlister's children were: Hulet Burns, Anne Mae Burns, Pulliam, Carl Burn, R.M. Burns, Bubba Burns, Hollie Burns, Gladys Burns Rowe, and Myrtis Burns Rowe.

Myrtis, the youngest of Jessie and Carlister's children, is still living at 93 Years of age. She now lives in Camp Hill Georgia. She has 4 boys. One son is a minister who travels for the "Trinity Baptist Church". She had only one daughter, Ada that was killed in an accident.

Ada Burns Bailey's children were: Rose Bell, Adie Mae, Mary Kate, Durie, Rufus, Grady, Daisy and Louis.

4.2.2 Jessie Sudduth

Figure 31 - Jessie Burns

I have met William (Billy Burns) over the phone; whose grand Father was Jessie Burns. Jessie if you remember was one of my Aunt Lucinda's sons. "Billy" his grand son gave me most of this information about my Aunt Lucinda's family. Billy now lives in Detroit Michigan; he gave me his Aunt Myrtis phone number and I called her; she is Billy's Mother's sister, she seemed to forget some things as she is now 93 years old at this writing. She would repeat herself; however she did give me quite a bit of information. I was excite to learn that one of the Older cousins were still alive.

Billy's dad was Carl Burns. Jessie the 1st was Carl's Father. Carl like his Father was also a farmer who tills the Soil and Raised crops.

4.3 Mathilda Sudduth

Mathilda Sudduth was also in the writing that I received From A cousin who had done research on our family history. It said Mathilda was born in 1867; but no further information about her.

4.4 Leonard Sudduth

Uncle Leonard "Lynn" I believe was next. It appears that he was rather young when he married, and had one son named Leroy Born to him and his wife. Uncle Lynn was killed when he was accidentally crushed in the mine where he was working.

Figure 32 – Leroy Sudduth son of Leonard Sudduth

4.5 Elsberry "Ebb" Sudduth

Figure 33 – Elsberry (1877 – 1911) and his wife

Mama said that Uncle Ebb was a fine young man who was very handsome with red hair. He is one of those who died at a young age. He was lynched in Coweta Oklahoma during a riot Mama said. The story about his being lynched is told in another chapter.

Chapter 5 – "Lucy Sudduth Marcus, "Mudda", the Tie that Binds"

5.1 Bettye's Memories of Lucy Sudduth Marcus

Written by:
Bettye Guillory; however Titled by Patricia Buckner Lucy's great grand daughter and Anita Culp her grand daughter; Lucy (Sudduth) Marcus; Lucy was named after her Mother, Lucy (Mikens) Sudduth

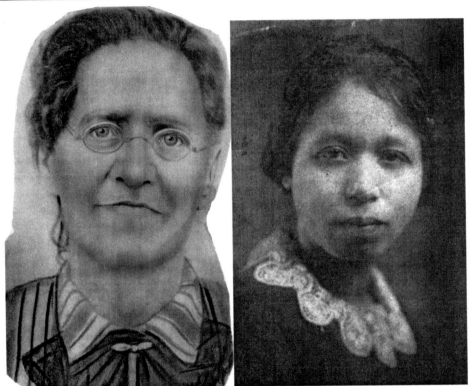

Figure 34 – Left – Lucy Sudduth Edison Marcus Right – Laura Edison Thurston Lucy's daughter

Figure 35 - George and Laura Edison Thurston

This Chapter was supposed to be written by my Papa's sister Lucy Marcus's Grand daughters Anita Culp and Great Granddaughter Patricia Buckner. The two of them chose a title for this chapter; "Mudda" the Tie that binds". I understand the grandchildren called Lucy "Mudda" instead of Grandma. The title was all I received from the two of them and so I have written what I know about this side of our Family tree. I did receive some important information from another grand daughter. Connie DuBoise a daughter of Edwin Marcus Jr.; who is Manch Marcus only son. Manch was the son of my Aunt Lucy.

This Chapter is about Lucy (Sudduth) Marcus. Lucy was named after her Mother (my Grandmother) Lucy (Mikens) Sudduth. She was the youngest of the four daughters born to our grand parents. These four daughters were all older than five of the boys; George, Charles, Elsberry, Joseph and John. Lucy's first marriage was to "Joe" Edison. To that Union, I believe there were five children born. I knew only one of them, Laura Thurston. Laura was married to George Thurston. The only time I remember seeing Aunt Lucy was when I was about 8 years old. She and her daughter Laura visited us in Junction City Kansas. I remember it was very hot that summer and they were trying to keep cool.

Aunt Lucy's second husband was Edwin Marcus. They had only one son name Manch Marcus. Manch married and had a little daughter named Ruth. Ruth's Mother died shortly after she was born. Her dad, Manch, married Grunetta soon after Ruth's Mothers Death. Grunetta gave birth to young Edwin early on after their marriage. Edwin was named for his grandpa Edwin, "Ed" Marcus. Ruth and little Eddie were born approximately 11 Months apart; so that both of them are the same Age for at least one month.

I remember talking to my second cousin Eddie (Edwin Marcus); many times after I found out they lived in this area. Eddie was like his sister Ruth very up beat and funny, we laughed a lot about things. I was surprised to hear of his death. He was not a person that complained a lot about his illness.

Figure 36 - Top - Manch Marcus, son Edwin Marcus
Bottom - Edwin Marcus Sr., Grunetta Marcus, Edwin's wife and their first child Edwin Jr.

Manch had 4 daughters by Grunetta. Evelyn being the oldest daughter had one son named Bruce. Dorothy had two sons: William and "Timmy". Anita had 3 sons. Deborah didn't have any Children. Eddie was the oldest child of Manch; yet there is Ruth the half sister was Manche's sixth child. Ruth had a very fair complexion with red hair and a few freckles. Manch's half Sister Laura didn't have any children of her own and so she raised Ruth as her own child. Ruth grew to be a lovely young lady and surprised every one by marrying Samuel "Sam" Rogers. They had a daughter name Patricia. I remember at West

Middlesex Camp Meeting Ruth told me she thought she had a tumor and she was six months pregnant with Mark. I think "Pat" was a young teenager when Mark was born.

Ruth and I use to have a lot of fun together; she was very up beat and always full of laughter. She was really funny. She looked after my oldest sister Trudy in Trudy's latter years and gave Trudy a royal home-going memorial Service and burial. For that I was and am truly grateful. Ruth was found dead one Saturday by her daughter "Pat" and son in law "Mike". It was a real shock to them and every one; it was so unexpected. I think she was 80 years old. She and her daughter "Pat" were close pals. Ruth's husband, "Sam", I think died several years before Ruth. Ruth did get to enjoy her First great-grandbaby for a short time. I am not sure if "Pat" had the second grandchild before Ruth passed or not. But "Pat" does have the second grandchild now. "Pat" was the image of her Father "Sam", even the same complexion, a beautiful brown skin. If they were the same age, they could pass for twins because of their likeness. Mark was the same complexion as his Mother Ruth, fair skin with reddish brown hair. I know Eddie and his family traveled quite a bit because he was in the service for more than 20 years; in the army for 19 Years and transferred to the Air Force, later retired from the Air Force. After his retirement from the service he and his Family settled in the Seattle area.

Eddie's oldest son named after Eddie is called Chipper. He has been Lieutenant for the Seattle Police department for 35 Years. Consuella "Connie" next oldest of Eddie's children was with Quest Phone company for 28 years and worked as Manager. Connie has 3 sons. Tony has 2 sons. Connie lives in Atlanta Georgia and works as Manager of an Auto Store. I was deeply impressed by talking to Connie today and for The first time hearing of the great successes of her family.

Cliff has retired because of Illness. Howard lives in Atlanta Georgia and is President of a national Insurance Company. He has been with this company for 25 Years. He travels a lot and has a son and a daughter. Debbie works with Freedom Church and finds needy families to help. She Has 2 daughters. I was deeply impressed by talking to Connie today and for the first time hearing of the great success of her family.

I remember talking to her Father Eddie over the phone many times when I found out they lived in this area. I didn't realize how ill he was; because he was very much like his sister Ruth, always up beet and funny. We laughed a lot together and I was very surprised to her of his death; he never complained a lot about his illness. It was a pleasure to at least get some information about some of my Aunt Lucy's off springs.

5.2 Lucy's Grand-daughters remember their Grandmother – Mudda the ties that Bind

Lovingly submitted by
Patricia Rogers Buchner & Anita Marcus Culp (Akron, Ohio).

Lucy Suddeth was our Mother. She taught us to love God, to respect each other, to be strong, to be wise and to never forget our roots. We lovingly called her Mudda and she still lives in our memory and in our hearts.

Life for Lucy began in 1868 in Jackson Gap, Alabama. She was the sixth of twelve children born to William and Lucy Mikens Suddeth. What a beautiful girl she was. She had long flowing brown curls, a creamy, fair complexion and light eyes. As she grew, she attracted many admirers and eventually married a young man who helped the large family of sharecroppers on the farm. He was Claude Edison. While living between Jackson Gap and Brook wood, Alabama, they had three children - Laura Jane, Joe and Claudestine.

Lucy taught her children to love the Lord, to seek an education and to strive to make something of themselves.

Joe Edison was blessed to become a Pastor of several apostolic congregations. He commuted between Sacramento, California, Detroit, Michigan and Cincinnati, Ohio for many years. He was married to Eva Gresham Edison and was the proud Father of Claudestine, Loretta and Gwen. Joe passed away of heart failure while on his knees and in prayer in Cincinnati.

Sadly, Claude died as a very young man of heart failure while walking along some railroad tracks. He left Etta Boone Edison and no children. Laura, however, was blessed with a long and rich life. She lived to reach 100 years old! She was a founding member of the Robert Street Church of God in Akron, Ohio. She and her husband, George Thurston, worked beside her Uncle George Suddeth, the founding Pastor. Laura was the church pianist, founded the Young Ladies Guild and preached many sermons as an ordained minister. She was a talented seamstress, a dedicated missionary and mentor to many.

Figure 37 - Calvin Elsberry Jr, Trudy in front, Bettye Sudduth Guillory, Ruth Rogers, Kathryn Waynesboro, Sam Rogers, Laura Thurston, Beatrice Sudduth, Elsberry Sudduth Sr, seated BeBe Chapman granddaughter of Bea and Ebb

Laura became a health food advocate before it became popular. She read books and self-educated herself about the benefits of carrot juice, lecithin, vitamin E and steamed vegetables. Using a juicer machine, she crushed her carrots into juice which she consumed daily. Her efforts worked! Laura continued to crochet well into her 90's and even exercised by touching her toes without bending her knees!

After Lucy ended her marriage to Claude Edison, she married Edward Marcus in Brookwood, Alabama. Mr. Marcus was quite industrious and entrepreneurial. He owned real estate in addition to his work as a straw boss at the sawmill. Lucy and Edward had three children - Leslie, Honey Ruth and Edwin.

As the rubber industry began to flourish in Akron, Ohio, many people began to leave the south and migrate to the area for jobs and a more prosperous life. Several members of the Suddeth clan did likewise. Lucy and Edward Marcus, Laura and George Thurston, Charles Suddeth and George and Elizabeth Suddeth joined the migration. Edwin, the youngest of Lucy and Edward's children, came to Akron as well. He brought his wife, Grunetta, their baby son, Edwin and baby daughter, Ruth Mary. Sadly, Edwin, Sr. lost his first wife, Eugenia and Mother of his daughter, Ruth, due to childbirth complications. Later, Laura and George Thurston raised Ruth Mary as their own.

There are two stories about Leslie's early death. It was told that he was lost in a mine accident or died from steam as a part of a train accident in Alabama. Honey Ruth suffered a ruptured appendix at the age of thirteen and died en route to a hospital from Brook wood, Alabama to Birmingham, Alabama.

Lucy and Edward Marcus led a comfortable life in Akron. Gramp, as we affectionately called him, owned a car wash in downtown Akron. He also was a parking lot attendant and janitor at the U.S. Post Office. In the 1930's, he worked for the Works Projects Administration at the Akron airport. Grunetta and Edwin lived with them and were blessed with other children. They were Edwin 11, Ruth, Evelyn, Dorothy, Anita and Deborah. The family pet was a large, friendly black and white, mixed breed dog named Cubby. Several members of the Suddeth family resided very near each other on Lucy Street! They were located within walking distance of Goodyear Tire and Rubber, Co. and the Robert Street Church of God where Uncle George Suddeth was the Pastor. This is also where the entire family attended church.

Edwin Marcus was born in 1900 and raised a beautiful and talented family on Lucy Street. He worked at Goodyear for years until his retirement. He never met a stranger and used his personality to great advantage as he helped many who were addicted to alcohol. He mentored them, fed them and counseled them to health and perfect recovery. His picture hangs at the national headquarters of Alcoholics Anonymous in honor of the service he gave voluntarily. Grunetta, whom he affectionately called "Mama", worked tirelessly by his side. Edwin passed away in 1972 and rests in the family plot at Mount Peace Cemetery in Akron, Ohio.

The Suddeth men and women were noted for their erect stature, fair skin and uncommon good looks. There were many instances during those segregated and blatantly racist years when they were mistakenly recognized as white and later demoted or ridiculed when it became known that they were actually black. Lucy relayed a story in which her brother, George, was given a position as a trolley driver at Goodyear. When management called him in and asked him if he was black, George replied that he was. The boss asked, "Why didn't you tell us?" George answered, "You didn't ask."' George was immediately demoted to an elevator operator. Most other blacks were only allowed to be hired in as janitors.

Mudda was a wonderful wife, Mother, Grandmother and friend. As she reached her declining years, she often sat on her front porch and would wave to passersby. As a highly respected member of the neighborhood, she was visited by many after she fell and broke her hip. She was immobile but spirited until the end of her life in 1932. Mudda rests at Mount Peace Cemetery in Akron, Ohio.

Figure 38 – Patricia Rogers Buckner-Michael daughter of Ruth and Sam Rogers

Figure 39 - Anita Marcus Culp

Anita, Lucy's granddaughter and daughter of her youngest son, Edwin Marcus remembers: "Lucy would plans treats for the family by air drying apples on a bed sheet and spreading them in the sun on the roof Imagine the effort that process must have taken, but Lucy wanted the children whom she loved so dearly to enjoy a healthy snack."

Mudda seldom recommended a spanking as a form of discipline for any of her grandchildren. She would council, defend and discuss an alternative plan. She usually favored a mild form of punishment and that approach was adopted by Edwin as well. It is no wonder that her grandchildren dearly love her and remember her so fondly.

The Suddeth saga continues to develop and spread its history in many ways throughout the United States. God has blessed our ancestors and continues to work in the lives of the Suddeth descendants.

•

Blessed be the tie that binds
Our hearts and Christian love
The fellowship of kindred minds
Is like to that above.

Before our Father's throne
We pour our ardent prayers
Our fears, our hopes
Our aims are one.
Our comforts and our cares.

We share our mutual woes
Bear our mutual burdens
And often for each other flows
The sympathizing tear.

When we asunder part
It gives us inward pain
But we shall still be joined in heart
And hope to meet again.

Chapter 6 - George Sudduth, "A Journey of Faith"

Written by:
Bettye Guillory; Lucille (Sudduth)Johnson gave me important information; Lucille is George Sudduth Senior's youngest daughter

Figure 40 – L-R Charles J Sudduth, Lucy Sudduth Marcus, and George Sudduth

This chapter is about George Sudduth Senior and his descendants. George is next oldest to my Father, Charles J, in age. I am waiting on a manuscript from Anthony Johnson; who is writing about the George Sudduth side of the family tree. The dead line has been set to have all material for the book to be in by November 1, 2007. That is the special cut off date; hopefully no family member will be left out. I decided to write what I know about this family in case I don't receive Anthony "Tony's" information in time. I just stopped to call "Tony's" Mother and she told me he had had a stroke and had to give up his Pastors position in Cleveland Ohio and the stroke had impaired his member some what. Right now I pray for his complete recovery.

George Senior was married to a young lady named Ada for a short period of time and to that union one son was born named John. John grew up to be a very handsome young man. He married a young lady we called Lila. I had the opportunity to visit their unique home when I visited relatives in Akron. I was a young girl then. Their son, John Sudduth, became the first colored policeman in Akron, Ohio. John and his wife, Lila, never had any children.

John Sudduth lived to be about 91 years of age; his wife died before he died. John was in World War I, and before he died he lost one of his legs.

John's Mother Ada died when he was very young.

His Father, George Senior married Ada's cousin, Elizabeth Powers. We called her Aunt Lizzie. George and Lizzie had 8 children together 6 boys and 3 girls. John the half brother of them made Uncle George have a total of 9 children.

Figure 41 - George Sudduth's Family; his wife Aunt Lizzie seated on right, 5 sons & 2 daughters with grand children

George Sr. had deceased when this picture was taken; Aunt Lizzie's oldest child was named Sally who married a man named Tolliver. My cousin Sally and Tolliver had two daughters and one son. Their only son William died at a fairly young age. Their oldest daughter Lucy Marion married a man named Larry Roberts. Lucy's husband Larry became a high Ranking Officer in the Air Force. Lucy and Larry had Children 4 Children, a daughter named Robin who is very popular and became a television anchor. Their youngest daughter was named Detholia .

George Sr. and Lizzy's oldest son was named Thomas "Tom". He was fair skinned, tall handsome, stocky, and well built.

I mention the complexion; because I think it is interesting how children turn out who area born of parents who are of different nationalities. The melting pot's affect is talked about through out the book; because that's somewhat of what it's about. It bears mentioning something on how this affected the children produced from these marriages.

The next oldest son was James, "Jim". He was the short son, brown skin and very out going. Jim was the only one of the nine children that finished College; and had an executive career, he married;, he and his wife had two children

William "Bill" was tall, dark brown and thin. He was athletic, a basket ball or foot ball star, if I remember correctly.

Henry was tall dark and handsome also. He was not as tall as Tom or Bill.

But all these boys had beautiful hair.

Now the there was George Junior, their youngest son, who became a minister like his Father. George Jr. married a girl named Lena. They had two children: a boy and a girl. The daughter is named Barbara. Barbara was a beautiful lady who took such good care of her Father, George Junior, during his last days on this planet Earth.

Mary, their next youngest daughter, married James Lott of Detroit Michigan and had 4 children. They had only one daughter named Caroline: a beautiful girl who loved the Lord, Mary Sudduth Lott her mother died, and I'm sure Caroline died of a broken Heart. Caroline was only in her fifties. She and her Mother, Mary, were Very Close Pals.

Mary played the piano for her Dad's Church, The Roberts Street Church of God in Akron Ohio. She also played for the church she attended after moving to Detroit.

Lucille was Uncle George's youngest daughter. She is still living at 88 years of age. Lucille married James Johnson and bore 3 children: 2 boys and a girl. One of her sons was Anthony "Tony" a minister. Tony has 3 children also. Roger the other son is living in Houston, Texas and works with audio/vision. Roger has 1 child. His daughter, Cheryl, has 2 children, a boy and a girl

Chapter 7 - Legacy of "My Papa" Charles J. Sudduth & His Multi talented Family

Written by:
Bettye G. Guillory. Charles J Sudduth was the 9th child to be born to William Sr., and Lucy (Mikens) Sudduth.

7.1 Mama and Papa: Their Early Years

Figure 42 –Papa Charles J. Sudduth and Mama Dora (Culpepper) Sudduth

7.1.1 Their Courtship

Papa was born on November 25, 1876 in Tallapoosa County, Alabama. I don't know if Tallapoosa County is the name of the town or not.

Mama, Dora Culpepper, was born in June 1874 in the same town where my Papa was born.

I will tell the story as Mama told it to me.

Evidently the Sudduth's and Culpepper's were neighbors in the country. and the first time she saw Papa was when she was 4 and he was 2 years old.

Mama speaking said; *"I saw this little tow head white boy in a shirt tail."* By the way little boys wore short tails instead of long pants in those days. Mama said she chased him down the road.

From this first episode I have no information as to Mama and Papa's relationship until the time they got married. She was 19 and he was 17 years old.

Papa's Mother was Irish; she had reddish blonde hair and Blue green eyes. I have a picture of my Grandma and Grandpa in Chapter 1. Papa was about 6 feet tall and with a white complexion. He could pass for white.

I wish I had a picture of my Mama's father and mother. I never saw them. My mother told me her Father was Black Hawk Indian with a jet black complexion and with straight black hair. Mama said her mother had brown skin with kinky hair. So my Mama was born with a black complexion rather dark skin. She was short about 5 feet tall.

They had to elope because Grandma Mollie Culpepper (Mama's mother) wanted her to marry a black professor. Grandma was opposed to Mama and Papa's marriage because he wasn't a professor. Grandma actually whipped Mama for getting married to Papa.

Mama's told me a little secret on why she married Papa. "*Schuss*", she said. She didn't want us kids to be black like her *(Smiles)*. She figured her children would be light skinned. This is why she didn't marry the black Professor her mother wanted her to marry and why she married Papa.

I think Papa only had either a 6th or an 8th grade education. Mama was considered highly educated in those days because she graduated from Langston University. Graduating from Langston University then was like graduating from college today. Today academically speaking it would be like finishing your sophomore year in high school.

Amazingly enough Grandma learned to love Papa as if he were her own son, he grew to be very close to her through the years.

Here's a little nugget I've injected; in fact this chapter has a few nuggets I don't have in any other chapter. I would like for you to know we, Sudduth's, are human and have had our problems. Thank God we are over comers through the Power of the Blood of Jesus Christ. In our younger years, we went through things like every one on this planet earth goes through; but by the Grace of God we learned a lot by our mistakes, and over came as we have sought the Lord and endeavor to die daily to the flesh by Gods help.

Mama had real concerns when Papa was a young man she said. Women would chase after him; because he was very tall and handsome. Papa was friendly and very hospitable, kind and appealing. I remember Mama telling me a story about when Papa went to do some work on a woman's house. She invited him to have coffee and a piece pie with her. Mama thought she had put something in the coffee; because Papa said he was drawn to this woman. They had to even move away from that town to get rid of her. Papa was loyal to Mama. He loved her very much. I remember Him saying one time "The blacker the berry the sweeter the juice *(Smiles)*. They were married 52 years when Papa died. I can honestly say, I never remember them having any argument.

It's amazing why people marry certain people. Like me, I Married John Guillory because he was, valedictorian of his class, and was handsome. I thought I would have pretty kids too *(Smiles)*

Another reason for marrying was because my parents were so strict on me I wanted to get away from home. I thought I would be free to do as I pleased. I couldn't wear lip stick or slacks; I wasn't allowed to go to movie's etc. Right here I would like to tell all Single people who might read this book; stop pray and make sure you allow God to make your choice when choosing a soul mate.

Knowing the Lord and truly hearing the Holy Spirit speak to you Heart and mind makes a difference; I believe God gives us the desire of our heart, if we ask him Psalms 37:4 delight ourselves in Him and have faith; yet wait on Him; then the right person will come and our spirit will agree. I have learned from my mistakes.

7.1.2 *Making a Living*

Mama taught school for 15 years – teaching before and after her marriage. She later gave this up to raise her growing family.

Papa and Mama worked in the fields during the time they were raising their young children. Mama said, some time she would have a little one walking along beside her while she was hand plowing. She would at times be carrying one child on her back and one in her stomach all at the same time.

Papa was a good provider, a "Jack of all Trades", for his family. He made around $58.00 a month. When I was a girl, that amount was good wages in those days. The reason I called him a "Jack of All Trades" is because he worked (before and after World War I) as a carpenter, glazier, paper hanger, painter, and a stone mason. Papa was also a minister of the gospel.

Mama baked pies and opened a pie shop. She was a good cook, especially pastry cook. She and Papa also had an eating place in Camp Funston, Kansas. Camp Funston was an Army base. They had a shooting gallery. The soldiers came and played games for fun.

Mama and my older sisters cooked and served meals to the soldiers.

7.1.3 The family home

**Figure 43 – Top Row Left Trudy, Buck, Ebb, Emma, Ella
2nd Row Maude, Dora (Bettye 3 on Mama's lap), Polly, Charles J with Trudy's baby Freddie, Sheldon with rabbit**

The house Papa and Mama bought when I was 3 years old cost $1800.00. It was located in Topeka which was the "Capital of Kansas". This is where all 9 of us kids grew up. The family owned and lived there for approximately 45 years.

I don't really recall too much about my oldest sisters and brothers living in that house. I do have memories of Napoleon (7 years older than me), Maude (5 years older than me) and Sheldon (3 and half years older that me) at home when I was growing up. I remember my two oldest sisters living at home for awhile after one being divorced and the other one separated from their husbands.

As you can see from the picture above most of my brothers and sisters were considerably older than me. I am the youngest.

7.2 Mama and Papa: Their Children

My parents had 9 children 5 girls and 4 boys. The first being a Girl, then a boy, girl until they got to me a girl being the 9th and the youngest.

Figure 44 - Charles J. and Dora (Culpepper) Sudduth's 9 Children L-R
stand Ella-Mae, Bettye Gyle, Bonnie Leonard "Trudy", Maude Esther,
Emma Lou, L-R Squatting: Napoleon "Poly", Elsberry "Ebb", Nathaniel
"Buck", Charles Sheldon Sudduth Sr.

7.2.1 *Bonnie "Trudy" Leonard Sudduth Robinson*

My Mama and Papa wanted to name their first child Leonard after
Papa's brother whom they called "Lynn"; evidently they were fond of
Lynn; who was killed at a young age working in the mine. I'm not sure
but I think Lynn was in his early twenties, because he was married and
had one young son. So this is how Bonnie got Leonard as her middle
name *(Smiles)*.

Through out this whole book you will notice that people had a
habit of naming their children after parents or an Uncle or an Aunt.
They love to honor relatives by naming their children after them, I
Guess.

"Bonnie Leonard" we called "Trudy". She was born in February 27,
1894 in Alabama. As an adult "Trudy" had long black hair that almost
touched the belt of her dress. when she was a girl and broke her right
elbow falling through a Train trestle. It was not set properly, so she
could never completely straighten that arm out all her life.

She married Fred Murphy when she was 18 years of age. With Fred
she had a baby, name "Freddie" who died when he was 2 ½ years of age
with Pneumonia. Her husband, Fred Murphy, was hit by train and was
killed instantly.

A few years after her first husband's death, Trudy married Alfred
Bryant. They lived in Los angles California. Alfred was a tall very

handsome man; but their marriage did not last very long for some reason.

Trudy was known for her beautiful voice, she became a very popular and was asked to sing almost every where she went. In Los Angles, California, she sang in "Bethel A M E choir". It was a 75 voice choir in which she sang the obbligato parts.

I remember I called her "Trud". She came home to visit from California one time when I was in high school. I was surprised to see her with a shingle hair cut. Her hair was so beautiful and always longer than any of us five girls wore our hair.

After Alfred, Trudy married a man named Earl Johnson. Mama prophesied that this marriage would be a mistake. Mama saw this coming in a vision and it came to pass just as Mama predicted. That marriage lasted even shorter that her marriage to Alfred Bryant.

Many years later when she was in here sixties she moved to Akron, Ohio and met Eddie Robinson, a Church of God Minister. Eddie had been married to a Christian Lady whom I believe was from India. Before she died, Eddie and his 1st wife had 10 beautiful children.

Brother Eddie asked Trudy for her hand in marriage several times before she finally consented. They had almost 30 years of a good marriage before he died.

I remember going to visit her when she was 89 years old. She was living in a senior citizen home. I couldn't believe my sister looked so old. She had beautifully mingled gray hair. I took her to a beauty salon; a salon that belonged to one of the members of her church. They graciously allowed me to do Trudy's hair in their salon because I had been a licensed beauty operator for many years. I did her hair and dressed her up. She looked so beautiful.

Trudy died in January 1989 and would have been 95 years of age the next month (February 27, 1989).

7.2.2 *Nathaniel "Buck" Sudduth*

Nathaniel (Buck) born in 1895 in Alabama. He changed his name because he decided he liked the name Nathan better than he did his given name Nathaniel, He was the second oldest child, born in Alabama.

He was blessed with Great musical talent.

As a matter of fact our whole family was born with musical talents. Mama sang duets with Papa in church and played the accordion, piano and mandolin guitar. The greatest gift God gave her were her Gifts of Faith, Prophecy, and healing. She also had gifts of Vision and Dreams. There is a chapter later in this book that tells about her healing ministry you will really enjoy. Mama was also an artist.

"Buck" played the big bass drum in Jackson's Band in Topeka Kansas. I remember him also playing the base tuba in parades as they marched down Kansas Avenue for special holiday celebrations. He also played: the guitar, piano and saxophone. The Sudduth brothers often sang in a quartet together, "Buck" sang tenor, "Polly" sang lead, "Ebb" sang baritone and Sheldon sang bass. "Buck" was really great in knowing harmony. Sometimes the girls and boys would sing together.

"Buck" married Lela Hickman. They both were 18 years old at the time of their marriage. Lela was always plump even as a young girl and had Rheumatoid arthritis. She was not able to bend her wrists and her ankles were stiff when she walked. She was a real good cook and "boy oh boy" she made the best sweet potato pie I've ever tasted. She was the first person I ever saw that liked to chew ice cubes.

Roxie was the first and only child they ever had. She was a beautiful girl. She was the spit and image of her Dad, Buck. Roxie played the piano beautifully and could play by ear and improvise; which I have never been able to do. Roxie taught me to play "Smoke Rings". The one and only song I learned to play by ear. I have to have the music when I play any thing else. I have a key board my children bought me and when I sit down even now to play my key board I end up playing "Smoke Rings".

My Mama and Papa were very strict on all of us. I was very sheltered and even though I was eighteen people always thought I was younger than my years. Roxie and I were pals even though she was five years younger than me. Roxie taught me a lot of things; because she could go to movies and dances where I couldn't go. She taught me how to dance. I loved dancing.

Roxie married Bryan Harris "Deane" who was her childhood sweetheart. She fell in love with him when she was 15 years old and he was 18 years old. They married when he finished college when she was 20. They had a beautiful, but short life together. She developed TB and she passed away at Christmas time in 1939 at the age of 22. They were living in Chicago at the time.

When my son John Basil was born (July 19,1939), I was staying at Mama's recovering from the birth. Mama had brought my bed down stairs; so I wouldn't have to climb the stairs to go to my bed room. It was in July and very warm out doors. Roxie came to see John Basil and wouldn't come in. She just peeped through the screened window since the window was open. I wanted her to name him and she suggested naming him after his Daddy, John Louis Guillory.

Roxie was 5 years younger than me but you would have thought we were the same age.

"Buck" divorced Lela I believe when Roxie was about 18; which was devastating to both Roxie and her mother. I don't think Lela or Roxie ever got over it. Lela passed when she was 46 years. The only thing I could think of why they were divorced is that she was very religious and probably she had become to religious for "Buck". They weren't spending enough time together and thus grew apart.

Mama and Lela ministered together in praying for the sick. Mama loved Lela they were very close. Lela died after Roxie died. She was only 47 years old. I am sure she died of a broken heart after losing Buck by divorce and her only child Roxie by death. She had moved to

California; was in ministry there. Friends missed her at church one Wednesday night and found her dead on the couch as if she had just fallen asleep.

He married Isabel Ware who was of American Indian descent. Isabel had two daughters; Dorothy and JoAnne by a previous marriage. Buck was married to Isabel Ware for about 30 Years before he died. He retired from the Santa Fe Shops after many years. He lived a long and good life and died at the age of 78 Years.

Isabel died a few years after he did.

7.2.3 *Ella Mae Sudduth Lucas*

Ella Mae, the 3rd oldest child who was born in Alabama in 1896. There were 4 years between her and Bucks births; this was the longest period my parents ever waited between any of their other kids Births. All of the others were 1½ to 2 years apart.

Ella Mae was beautiful and very sweet. Ella Mae, Emma and Buck had noses like Papa. The other six of us had "roaming noses" like Mama. You could tell when you saw one Sudduth, because we all favored.

Ella was very special to me; if I could have a favorite sister, she was the one. She, Trudy and Maude were very good to me; as a matter of fact I think all my sisters and Brothers spoiled me; since I was the baby.

Ella married Eugene "Gene" Lucas and they only had one baby named Marvin Eugene, who died when he was 7 months old. The baby weighed 25 pounds. He was so fat his little throat closed up on him. The doctors operated on him but he died anyway.

Eugene the dad was an alcoholic; this grieved my sister Ella Mae, as she loved him dearly. He was a cigar smoker and would have tobacco juice running out his mouth sometimes when he was high.

He wrote a newspaper which was pretty popular in Topeka at that time. Ella was cashier at the Ritz Theater for a number of years. It was the only black Theater in town. It was located on Fourth Street in the black section of town where blacks had their restaurants and business places.

Ella Mae was the first of the children of Charles and Dora's to die at 55 from a hemorrhage of the brain. Papa died first in 1947 then Mama in 1949 and then Ella in 1955.

Eugene died many years later with a stroke. He was in his late Seventies. I was living in Spokane Washington at the time. Gene was so sick. I had visited him in the Veteran Hospital in Kansas some time before. One day I just felt led to call him and the Nurse put the receiver to his ear. I led him to Jesus. He repeated the sinner's prayer as best he could after me, because He couldn't speak clearly on account of the stroke. This was on a Monday the nurse told me the following Thursday he called her into his room; ask to be baptized (sprinkled) and then he died.

7.2.4 Calvin Elsberry "Ebb" Sudduth

Calvin Elsberry, was next oldest, born in 1900 in Oklahoma.

We called him Ebb. He liked playing foot ball. Mama thought it was too dangerous; because he got his shoulder blade knocked out of place one time playing football.

Ebb taught school in Oklahoma and met his bride, Beatrice Kingsberry, while teaching school. She had one brother named Alfred Kingsberry who was married to our cousin Ella Mae Spann.

Ebb and Bea had six children: Calvin Junior, Dora Adella, Benjamin, Louis "Puggy", Kathryn Ann, and Elizabeth "Beth". Dora Adella was named after her grandmothers Dora (my mom) and Adella (Bea's Mom). Benjamin was named after his mother's dad.

Beth was married to Bill Petersen and had 3 children: William "Bill" III, Michelle and Bruce.

She divorced Bill and married Michael "Mike" Lewis. They had a beautiful baby girl named Melissa. Beth died of cancer when she was only 43 years old. "Mike" who is white was a wonderful husband and father. He did not remarry until Melissa had grown up.

I was very close to my brother Ebb. My brother Ebb's wife Bea was like a sister to me.

His story below reflects what a special man he was to me and others. I hope it will touch you.

7.2.4.1 Children's Memory of Ebb - Twin Oaks, A Quiet Strength

I, Elizabeth Jean (Waynesboro) Rattray, am a granddaughter of Calvin Elsberry and Beatrice Louise Sudduth. I am the third of four children born to their daughter, Kathryn. At the time of this writing, I am forty eight years old. By the time I was born, Grandpa was in his late fifties. He and Grandma had been working together diligently, and planning for a comfortable retirement. The preceding text, so meticulously researched by my eldest cousin, Harry, provides genealogical lineage of our Grandfather. In the rest of the chapter, I endeavor to give insight to Calvin's heart, his legacy and a peek at his branch of the family.

Calvin Elsberry Sudduth, had fiery heart. He loved the Lord Jesus and he loved his wife and family passionately. Physically, Calvin was tall (around six foot), lean and handsome. He had sparkling gray-brown eyes and a slanted smile. He was an articulate man with fair skin and wavy hair, making it difficult to peg his ethnicity.

Ebb, as Grandma Beatrice called him, was simply charming. He could sing smooth as a lark and was an apt story teller. He charmed Beatrice away from a "would be" suitor while she was attending Wiley College, in Marshall, Texas. Their courtship is legendary in our family, proving Ebb (a country school teacher at the time) to be quite the romantic. He read aloud to her the classic Ivanhoe. They wed on May 10, 1922 in what was then the Oklahoma Indian territory.

Not long after, Ebb took a job in a coal mine in Albuquerque, New Mexico. There Beatrice gave birth to their first born son, Calvin Jr. He continued mining work in Lester, Colorado, through the birth of their second child, Dora. In the late 1920s, Ebb was injured in the mine, resulting in the loss of one kidney. At one point he was given up for dead. He bore a scar that wrapped nearly half way around his torso.

They moved to Ohio in 1928, where work was more abundant and eventually had six children, three boys and three girls. Although they were raised during the Great Depression, they wanted for nothing.

Initially, Grandpa worked outside the home and Grandma (Beatrice) held down the fort. She was an amazing cook, and a seamstress who kept their girls impeccably dressed. To help meet the needs of their family, Beatrice did sewing jobs from home. As times grew lean, they both worked for a short time in the B.F. Goodrich rubber factory. In the early 1930s, Ebb suffered a heart attack, Beatrice and their children stayed in Akron, while Ebb went to convalesce with cousins (the Spanns) in California for almost a year.

On his trip home, he stopped to visit family in Topeka, Kansas and took sage advice from his brother Sheldon regarding work at the nearby Boys Industrial School. That proved to be a strategic position that set the stage for the remainder of their lives. At first, Ebb worked with the youth and Beatrice worked in the laundry. Over time, they began to work as a team, directly parenting delinquent boys for whom the school was home.

In the summer of 1951, a great flood wrought devastation to Topeka, Kansas. According to National Weather Service records, the Kansas River crested at 36.4 feet, rising in some areas to just below the second story of buildings. There was no electricity and drinking water had to be brought in by boat. Grandpa recounted when some of the boys begged him to let them jump out the window for a swim. Grown weary of their petitions, he grabbed a mole that had made its way to higher ground and tossed it into the murky flood water. The mole was instantly electrocuted. It stretched out flat as a board, thereby quenching all further pleas to swim.

The destruction of the flood drove thousands of people from their homes and businesses and Calvin and Bea back to Ohio. There, they continued in the same work, serving as cottage parents at the Cleveland Boys Industrial School (CBS) until their retirement in 1970. The school, located in Hudson, Ohio, it was a working farm that offered delinquent boys education through high school and training in industrial trades.

I fall somewhere in the middle of the Grandchildren, so my account of my Grandfather's life and history are fairly limited. But what I can tell you is that they had a profound influence on the lives of many people, some family, some friends and neighbors. The number of boys for whom they cared must number high into the hundreds. The boys referred to Calvin and Beatrice as Mom and Pop. They were loving, but firm with high standards of expectation. My memories of their service begin in the Lincoln cottage at CBS. (All of the cottages were named for former U.S. presidents.) There were strict rules for us not to interact with the boys. It was made very clear to us that most of them were living there because they were delinquent kids in need of intense supervision and reform. Grandpa and Grandma poured out of their abundant hearts a divine grace for each boy to see their own worth. The grounds of CBIS are now the Cuyahoga County Youth Development Center. It is now co-educational and still residential.

We used to play baseball with Grandpa on the immense lawn and he helped me learn to ride my bike on the long gradually sloping driveway. Staying overnights with my Grandparents was the only true peace I ever felt as a child. There was a quiet strength and stability that seemed to follow and draw people to them. I can still close my eyes and experience the familiar smells and sounds. Grandpa sang a lot. Sometimes hymns, sometimes silly songs about nature or people. During the day, there was usually something savory on the stove and at night, I would often fall asleep to the murmur of prayer coming from their bedroom, coupled with sound of a train in the nearby distance.

We had access to a baseball diamond and an indoor gymnasium with a basketball court. What that meant was, you could play until your heart felt like it was leaping from your chest! There was no end to our imagination. Grandpa and Grandma lived in the perfect place to gather all of their children and grandchildren at the same time. In the hallways outside their living quarters, we played a game called "fire". Each kid would guard one entrance to one long hallway. The object was to get the ball past each other. It might get rolled through your legs or hurled past your head, but you had better get it out of your hallway and back to your guard position before everyone counted to ten. If you didn't, it meant that your house had burned down and you were out of the game. You were almost sure to lose if you were guarding the hall that had the stairs at the end that led to the empty shower room. That ball could bounce from stall to stall quicker than any ten count would end.

Baseball was Grandpa's favorite game. He was usually all time pitcher for us. His favorite players were Larry Dobie and Cal Ripkin. For years to come, following their retirement in 1970, and even after they passed away, those now grown men from CBS would show up at the door of the Sudduth home on Barlow Road in Hudson. They came to share stories of what Mom and Pop Sudduth meant to them and where they had gone in life since. Some appeared with wives and children in tow all different times of the year. All were filled with gratitude. I especially loved going into town to pick up the mail with Grandpa at Christmas time. There was far too much mail to fit in the box at home, so it was bagged up and waiting for them throughout the season. Sometimes, Grandma would make hot cocoa and we'd sit for hours reading letters and looking at pictures they'd receive from around the country and beyond.

Grandpa and Grandma built what was their retirement home in Hudson, Ohio while they were still working at CBS. My parents, Theodore and Kathryn Waynesboro (their second youngest daughter of

Calvin and Beatrice), were the first to live there. The house at 380 Barlow Road became home to most of their children and grandchildren at various times throughout our lives. It was a place of refuge and healing for countless people over the years. There was always plenty to eat and room for one more at the table.

It was there that we lived again after my parents divorced. My Mother moved in with older brother, Howard, my younger sister, Kathy and I in tow. My oldest brother Ben had grown up and moved out on is own by then. Our cousin Louis (Aunt Dora's youngest) had already been living with them for several years. It's a three bedroom house with one and a half bathrooms. No matter which family was in residence, the same separate rooms were designated, one for the girls and one for the boys, with the parent's room in the middle. Sometimes, when a thunder storm would come at night, we would grab our pillows and blankets and slip in to sleep on the floor in their bedroom. Once, Grandpa got up to go to the bathroom and accidentally stepped on my little sister, Kathy. He jumped, groused a bit and then we all laughed until we fell asleep.

When I was in high school (1972-76), Grandpa still got up every morning, to turn up the heat and make our lunches. He would stand in the front door and peer out the window giving a goodbye wave when the school bus arrived to pick us up. One day I came home from school to find Grandpa waiting on the front steps with tears in his eyes. When I sat down beside him, he put his arm around my shoulder and began with a quiver in his voice, "I'm waiting for your little sister's bus. I have some bad news to tell her." As we were leaving for school that morning, Grandpa spied a mouse in the house. It ran under a bed in our room. He grabbed a broom and pummeled the poor thing to death. As he swept up the carcass, he got a better look. It seems that Kathy had left the cage door open after the morning feeding of her gerbil, Tootie. Grandpa gave him a decent burial in the back yard. When Grandpa told Kathy, she felt so bad for him that she just hugged him and said, "It's okay Grandpa."

Grandpa could stave off boredom like nobody else. He would pay us to pick up sticks in the yard so he could cut the grass. He might also assign you to walk the length of the driveway, picking and tossing the gravel back from the yard, so it didn't fly up and cause injury during mowing. Sometimes he would let us steer his riding lawn tractor. It was especially rewarding to help him pick blueberries. Because we knew that Grandma was going to bake some "to die for" confection. He would let me eat raw green beans right out of his garden. (I detest cooked green beans.) Time flew by so quickly when I worked with him that I forgot about being bored. Not only would he teach us silly songs, he could make any bird call known to man by cupping his hands to his mouth. He was a human juke box of hymns. My favorite time to hear him sing was (First at Robert Street Church of God, then later Arlington Church of God) on Sunday morning. The best seat in the house to me was right between both of them. Grandma would give me a stick of gum to keep me from being fidgety, reminding me with a gesture to chew mouth closed. I would look up at Grandpa and wait for the concert to begin. His voice rose straight to heaven.

Grandma Beatrice grew up in a very rigid religious family. Although the Sudduths have strong evangelical roots, she and Calvin did not to require their children to attend church regularly. With sporadic church attendance, the kids usually chose to go to church where ever most of their friends attended. For them, church was a merely a social attraction. All six of their children strayed from relationship with Jesus Christ. Although Ebb and Bea were together for sixty years, every one of their children divorced at least once. As adults, only two of their daughters, Dora and Kathryn, developed strong relationship in the Christian church community. Ironically, those same two sent some of their children to Catholic grade schools (myself included) where we were taught many unscriptural principles quite characteristic of other world religions. Thankfully, not one of us are practicing Catholics.

In the process of gathering information for this chapter of the book, I spoke with my siblings, including my brother Ben (now deceased), who was raised primarily by our grandparents. Ben confirmed for me that Grandpa and Grandma had a "quiet" walk with the Lord. Their hearts and home were open to so many people over the years. They were highly regarded, respected members of their church and community. Both strong in character, living out the scripture, *"A good name is rather to be chosen rather than great riches, loving favor rather than silver or gold." (Proverbs 22:1)*. Calvin and Beatrice surely had the favor of the Lord on their lives and we the beneficiaries.

I am blessed beyond words, thanks in great measure to the steadfast commitment of Grandparents to our family and to our Lord, Jesus Christ. I have the memory of peaceful days in their house, seeing Grandpa pour over the scriptures as if he were enjoying a sumptuous meal. Many are the times since his passing, I have wished for conversation with him about the Word of God. If only I knew then how valuable his insight and heart would be to me in this life. I have wished I could apologize to him for having the foolish heart of a child, with no care for such things. What I can share are snippets of the testimony of just one of their grand-daughters.

For me there was always money to be made off of a common disdain for housework. Uncle Calvin (my Mom's oldest brother) paid me to wash dishes. I don't remember how old I was when I started that job, but I had to stand on a chair to reach the kitchen sink. All I needed was one of his famous peanut butter and banana sandwiches, a radio blasting top forties and a few quarters for incentive. My Aunt Dora seemed to have an aversion to organization. She paid me to clean out her kitchen cupboards and linen closets. She paid handsomely in money and sometimes jewelry, which she had an enormous collection.

In high school, I rode the bus to Auntie Beth and Uncle Mike's house after school two days a week. I think she and my Mom went to the same cooking class, called *"How to use every dish and utensil known to man for one meal."* I used to think she was letting the neighbors leave me their dishes to wash as well. Another two days of the week, I cleaned for my big brother Ben. I tried to make sure I worked for him on his pay day. That is when he was exceptionally generous. I would sometimes wait downtown Hudson on the village green and catch him on his way home from work. Then there was sure to be a free dinner.

My childhood was filled with every material thing a kid could want. But seemingly out of reach were the things I really needed, to feel respected and purposeful. I had been molested from the time I was seven years old, started smoking pot at the age of thirteen and cigarettes long before. As a teenager, I sought comfort in marijuana and promiscuity. I was raped twice at the age of seventeen in two different situations. At age 18, I didn't know the Lord, but I thought I knew all I needed to know. So I dropped out of the University of Akron, Speech Communication degree program after one year.

I hopped on a bus bound for St. Paul Minnesota where my brother Howard, cousin Bill Petersen and his wife Sharlene lived. Howard had been in a serious motorcycle accident, severing the tendons on the inside of his left knee. Growing up, we never had a healthy relationship. He just never seemed to have much use for me except to inflict pain and humiliation. We got separated in my parent's divorce for a while. But his accident brought us together like nothing ever could. I spent the better part of a year, nursing my brother back to walking. We fought, laughed, cried and I did some growing up.

I arrived in St. Paul in August of 1978. I left from Auntie Beth's house (Mom's baby sister who I am named for), hitching a ride with her daughter-in-law, Sharlene, who was on her way back from Massachusetts. Auntie Beth had been battling breast cancer off and on for a couple of years by then and was in a time of remission. Her youngest daughter, four year old Melissa, had recently recovered from open heart surgery to repair a heart murmur. On my way out the door, I looked her square in the eyes and said, "I love you. Thank you for everything you have done for me." It was the last time I saw my Auntie Beth. She took care of my hair in high school.

Mom was a single parent at that time and it really helped her to have a sister who could tame long nappy hair. During those beauty sessions we would talk about school and boys. I would share my dreams with her. She was good at giving advice without judgment. And her face could express disapproval without ever opening her mouth. Two months after I left home, the cancer returned with a vengeance. Howard, cousin Louis Chapman (Aunt Dora's youngest. He is ten months my senior), and I, were sharing an apartment in St. Paul. We, along with Bill (Auntie Beth's oldest son) and his wife Sharlene, were in constant contact home.

A final update came to Bill from my Mother, "If you ever want to see your Mother, you should come home now." I arrived home from work, just in time to see Bill, Sharlene and Howard (sideways in the back seat with a full leg cast) driving away from our building. Louis ran out of the house and fell to his knees with a loud wail. I knew they were leaving us behind to make the thirteen hour drive back to Ohio.

Louis and I clenched each other in a teary heap in the front yard. We eventually were able to borrow a raggedy car from a girl I had only known at work for only six weeks. On the way to Ohio, we got caught speeding in Angola, Indiana. Louis was thrown in jail because he was driving without a license and the car was not registered to either of us. Auntie Beth died on November 7, 1978, her son Bruce's 23rd birthday.

On the day Grandpa was burying his youngest daughter, he wired money to me at a truck stop to bail Louis out of jail. We missed Auntie Beth's funeral. She was the second of my Mother's siblings to precede their parents in death.

After the death of my Uncle "Benny" (who my brother Benjamin is named for), in the early 1960s they returned to regular church attendance, but I don't think they ever recovered after a second loss.

While still living in Minnesota, I met our paper boy, John Walker, who had a side business of selling stolen goods around the neighborhood. This guy was bad news. He liked to hang out with Howard sometimes, but he made me uneasy. He started stopping by when neither Howard nor Louis were home and I would turn him away every time. I once happened upon him in the basement laundry room of our building. He was sitting on top of clothes dryer smoking pot. One day, when I opened the door to him he brushed past me before I could react, flopping himself on our sofa. I held the front door open and repeatedly insisted that he leave. When he refused, I calmly walked to the back of the apartment to grab a broom from the kitchen. Returning to the living room, I repeatedly struck John, herding him out the open door and locking it behind him.

Several weeks later he made the news by killing a young girl, stabbing her thirty seven times with a screw driver. When asked why he did it, he replied, "Because she laughed at me." He was initially sent to a mental hospital, from which escaped for a few days. Needless to say that was a nervous few days for me. I kept looking over my shoulder thinking, if he stabbed a girl to death just for laughing at him, what must he want to do to me? He was soon recaptured and placed in a maximum security facility.

Later that summer, on a hot St. Paul night I heard the ping of rocks on the french doors of my apartment. I opened the door to my brother Howard and his friend, Victor Mercado. The friend sought refuge from someone whom he had seen take a life. Victor camped out on my couch for a while, but a couple of weeks later, he was gunned down leaving a wife and toddler son behind. It was no secret that Victor had named a guy named Jimmy Salazar as the one he was hiding from. But it was never proven who murdered him.

I sent a letter to my Grandparents telling them how blessed I was without realizing it. It was the beginning of my reality check, learning what it took to maintain the stable lifestyle to which I had grown accustomed. And I thought it only fitting that I send them a grateful acknowledgment. Their reply was a letter which included a picture of themselves standing arm in arm in their front yard, with one of the twin oak trees in the background. Grandma had written on the back, "From your Grandma and Grandpa who loves you very much." That picture is displayed in a prominent place on the mantle of our dining room, right next to our wedding photo. Of my few prized possessions, that photo is tops.

Less than three years after Auntie Beth died, both Calvin and Beatrice also passed. Grandma (Beatrice) said, "It's un-natural for a parent to out live their child." Grandpa (Calvin Elsberry) passed first in January of 1980. He suffered a stroke on Christmas morning of 1979. I don't think St. Thomas Hospital had seen a waiting room so packed for one patient ever.

I had come home (from Minnesota) for Christmas and so had most everyone else. It came my turn to go into Grandpa's room. He had lost the ability to speak, but he was definitely lucid. I leaned in to kiss his cheek. I gently stroked his hair for a moment and told him, "I love you Grandpa" and noticed a single tear fall from is right eye that soaked into his pillow. Two weeks later, Calvin went home to be with the Lord.

It was later that spring, gazing up at a clear blue sky through their kitchen window, Grandma told me how much she missed Grandpa. "I've had a full life." she said. "I've raised my children and some of theirs. I am truly blessed...But I just don't need to be here without my husband." In that moment, I saw the ache of her heart and the fullness of her joy at once. She was bidding goodbye to life this side of heaven. I still lived in Minnesota, but visited often and kept constant contact home. In April of 1981, Grandma was hospitalized with complications of colon cancer. In a call to her hospital room, my Mom held the phone to Grandma's ear for me. She could barely speak any more, so I did all the talking. I told her how much I missed her and that I loved her very much. In May of 1981, at the age of seventy eight, Grandma passed away.

Although both had a fierce love for their family, Grandma Beatrice's strength was not always "so quiet" as Grandpa Calvin's. She had quite a reputation for being a sharp shot with a rock. She once knocked a neighbor out with a blow to his head, before he could strike Grandpa sneakily from behind. On another occasion, she beaned a neighbors dog square between the eyes to avert an attack on one of her children. That single shot stopped the dog dead in his tracks, literally. I don't ever remember her raising her voice.

I got robbed and became homeless briefly at age twenty. I hid things well with good jobs, making good money, living in pretty decent places most of the time. I was of course always tastefully dressed and perfectly coiffed. At twenty one, I began a ten year relationship with a junkie from St. Paul who became my live-in boyfriend. He was a nice guy who worked hard, had low self esteem and not much ambition. I worked while he went to school to become a certified electronics technician. Grandma always said, "You can't make a silk purse out of a sow's ear." But I tried. I was desperate to create a "good life". I knew what it should look like because I had seen my Grandparents example. I had no idea how to get there. In 1988, I moved back to Ohio.

When I thought I had enough and had reached the end of me, I cried out to the Lord to show me what direction He would have for my life. I remember praying for a husband like my Grandpa and picturing myself being the kind of wife that Grandma was. Not long after those prayers, I met my husband, Kirk Rattray.

In the fall of 1989, I was carrying the weight of the world and leaving a deadbeat boyfriend behind. I called my Uncle Mike. (Auntie Beth's widower) I wish I had thought of it sooner. He cleared out a spare bedroom for me by the end of the week. I enrolled in a trade school, the now defunct Ohio School of Broadcast Technique (OSBT). Kirk, was in the class ahead of me. I wanted to learn to write news and he was actually thinking of battlefield reporting. We became fast friends who spent hours talking and enjoying the company of each other. Sometimes we would talk all night, then hop on his motorcycle to seek the perfect sunrise. There was something so shiny and real about him. I was irresistibly drawn to his countenance. One afternoon we left school to grab lunch. Waiting out a down pour in his car on the shore of Lake Erie, Kirk began to share the gospel with me. My spirit, now ready to hear, began to receive truth for the first time. It seemed as though there wasn't a question about life to which this guy couldn't find an answer. He answered from the Word of God, with and without his open Bible, as if he knew Jesus Christ Himself. The only other man I had ever seen delight in God's Word was my Grandfather.

Kirk invited me to church and we began to attend regularly. On a Sunday morning in the spring of 1990, we attended Christ The King in North Olmsted, Ohio. The speaker that morning was an East Indian Christian evangelist named, Mahesh Chavda. His words came straight from God, piercing my heart and drawing me to the most compelling sense of purpose my mind could not have dreamed. On that day, convinced of my sin and separation from the one true God in Christ, I was born again. I began a life long journey of transformation in the hands of God.

Kirk courted me as we dated over the next year. We had one spat over continued phone calls from his ex-girlfriend. He put an end to it, letter her know that it was no longer acceptable for them to have any contact. Kirk asked permission from my oldest brother, Benjamin, to marry me. He whisked me away for a weekend to propose in Greenfield Village at the Henry Ford Museum in Michigan. By this time, I was so in love with him but growing impatient with the status of our relationship. We were refraining from physical relations, and here we were on a trip alone at a hotel. We spent just two nights there, but by the first morning I got down on my knees while he was out of the room. I had a serious conversation with God, deciding in no uncertain terms that I was ready for Kirk to "do it or get off the pot" so to speak. That afternoon, on bended knee under a willow tree, next to a duck pond, Kirk popped the question to which I gave a teary "Yes!" When we returned to the hotel I discovered where he had gone while I was praying. There were a dozen red roses waiting for me in our room. It was eight weeks to the day that we wed. Just as I had always dreamed, my brother Ben walked me down the isle.

The devil got busy right away as he feared our union (and rightfully so). We were so poor when we got married. I lost my job at Cleveland's ABC Television affiliate about two weeks before the wedding. Kirks' Father had a heart attack, then my car broke down. On our wedding day, my Father was kidnapped from a nursing care facility by his brother (a story for another book), so he couldn't attend the service. My brother Howard, one of only two wedding ushers, was having issues that are to this day not fully known. He didn't show up until the reception. During the ceremony, the lit unity candle fell on the floor and rolled under the train of my dress, but caused no damage. The childhood friend, who was in charge of rallying folks to set up tables and chairs for the reception, got drunk and did nothing. When we entered the reception hall and realized that nothing was set up for our guests, we searched "arm in arm" for a place to cry. Within fifteen minutes all of our loved ones joined together, setting up tables, chairs and warming food. There was a fire in the kitchen at the reception hall, that was quickly contained by friends with vast homeless soup kitchen experience. Kirk's nephew left the reception with his honeymoon suitcase still in his car. I had placed my wedding dress in a large garbage bag which mistakenly got filled with dining trash. When I panickedly pulled it from the bag, not one morsel had stained my gown. I'll recount the story when I pass it on to my daughter.

One year after we were married, we bought our house. We got the keys on my 32nd birthday, December 21, 1992. We packed as much as we could fit of our necessities into Kirk's Volkswagen Rabbit and prepared to spend our first night in our new (old) house. After about two hours, we looked at each other and I asked, "Are you cold?" to which Kirk replied, "Yeah, pretty much." We soon discovered that the furnace did not work. We gathered what we needed and headed back to our raggedy apartment in Cleveland. We had our house blessed by one of the senior Pastors from our church (Faith Fellowship at that time). We went from room to room, praying and anointing the doors with oil. The Pastor and his wife spoke words of prophecy over our house. They said among other things, that it would be a welcoming place of healing. This year on October 19, 2007, we celebrate our sixteenth anniversary. It has been an amazing journey of prophetic fulfillment so far.

My Father was an alcoholic who dropped out of our lives for a while not long after my parents divorced, when I was twelve years old. We maintained sporadic contact over the years always connecting over the Christmas season Daddy suffered a stroke that caused short term memory loss. So he lived in a nursing care environment for the last few years of his life. That is where he was kidnapped from on the day of my wedding. For two weeks, we had no idea where he was and I prayed for his safety and to find him daily.

One morning, while sitting at my desk at Baldwin-Wallace College, a family came in for their admission appointment with their daughter.

They were accompanied by a family friend who I recognized right away. It was retired Judge, Joseph Roulac. I introduced myself and told him that my family was well acquainted with him as well. The Judge knew my Grandparents, my Mother and other Sudduth family members. He even remembered me as a child. We exchanged pleasantries and I went about my work, making sure their visit was well managed. Everything went off without a hitch accept for one thing. The student's Mother, Mrs. Evedge decided not to take the tour, but chose instead to remain behind in my office and grill me. She was pleasant enough, but seemed to have some underlying agenda. About two hours after they left the campus, she called me back. When I asked how I could help her, she said, "Are you any relation to Nelson Waynesboro?" To which I replied, "Yes. He's my Father's brother." "And your Father is Ted Waynesboro?" she asked. "Yes Mam. He is." I responded. Well I have to tell you that your Father is in my care." she revealed. She apologized for not telling me while she was on campus and confessed that she was taken aback by who I was. It seems she had been told that Ted's children were drug addicts who abused him and should be kept away from him.

Mrs. Evedge is the owner of the nursing care facility to which my Uncle unwittingly moved my Father. That move proved to be the greatest blessing of the last years of Daddy's life. The Evege's are Christians who cared for Daddy as if he were their own family, including him in their social events and showering him with genuine affection.

Daddy came to stay with Kirk and I several times in the last years of his life. The first time he came to visit was for about a week. He had many good days of lucidity and he was able to get to know my husband. We took him to church with us during his visits and he began to ask me questions about why I could want relationship with him. We talked about the lost years and how it was that I could not only forgive him, but care for and enjoy him. I got to share the Gospel of Jesus Christ with my earthly Father. One Sunday morning, flanked by Kirk on his left and me on his right, Daddy gave his life to Christ and became born again! I saw God take what the devil meant for destruction and use it for His glory.

We foster parented for a couple of years, led our Vineyard church middle school ministry for five years, took in a husband separated from his wife and nursed a sick friend after knee surgery. Kirk lost his job of twenty five years due to plant closing, then was rehired by the new company that took its place. In 2004, we cared for two small children who lost their Mother, my dear friend Molly, to a deadly illness. All while my oldest brother Ben was fighting what became a losing battle with cancer. Six weeks after Ben passed away, Kirk's brother, Brian died suddenly of a viral infection. For about the next eight months I spiraled down at break neck speed to a pit of angry despair. I have often compared the loss of my brother to having my four limbs ripped from my body, leaving me to bleed to death. Through it all, the Lord showed me how much I needed Him. That He was the only one who knew the whole picture and He alone is in control, not me. In every circumstance we could not out give God. I am divinely impacted by each experience.

Kirk currently hosts a men's Bible study group and I a women's group twice a month. By the grace of God we are raising two amazing adopted children, our mortgage is paid in full and we have belonged to the same beloved church family for about nine years. I am an at home mom and just finished our second year of home schooling with our first grade daughter, Morgan who is smarter than me. Then again so is her four year old brother, Carson.

Maybe because we are so much alike, my Mom and I often locked horns. I pushed a lot of parental boundaries and always liked a good party. Still do. My Mom was the first Black Cheerleader in the city of Akron, Ohio and I was the first Black dancing majorette in Hudson, Ohio. We both prefer to speak our mind in the face of injustice and we are fearless fighters for our loved ones. It is with great joy that our fiery spirits are now united in Christ. As time passes, the fervent prayers of my Grandparents are being answered. I cannot stress this enough. While I am a beneficiary of their obedience to the Lord, I can also recognize and learn from their biggest mistake. Their Christian walk had been a quiet one, so I grew up thinking that they were "good" people. I had no idea they were living in relationship with God. I will not make the same mistake. You can argue theology all you want. But you can not deny my testimony. Jesus protected me when I was in harms way countless times. He sustained me through tragic times and continues to transform me daily. To date, four of the six children of Calvin and Beatrice Sudduth have children who are born again Christians. We war in prayer on behalf of our families and live in hope that our faithfulness will bear fruit in the hearts of our siblings, cousins and children unto the salvation of every single one.

I confess that after the death of my brother Ben, I lost heart and sight of my place in the Great Commission. I pondered conversations with Ben after he had come to know the Lord. Ben made it clear that, he too would not continue a quiet walk with Jesus. That is an inspiration and a great comfort to me. The bond our Grandparents created among us is truly remarkable. So many people don't even know their cousins and aren't very close to their siblings. As cousins, we are as close as siblings. We live far and wide, but manage to keep up with one another pretty well.

It has been a number of years since we were under one roof. But the last time was a spontaneous riot. As I recall, my husband and I talked with Cousin Bruce Petersen on the phone (we in Ohio, he in North Carolina). Bruce remarked what a shame it was that we would not be together for Thanksgiving. Kirk and I began to consider the idea of driving to spend the holiday with Bruce and his family. We mentioned it to my Mom, who immediately said, "Boy, I'd like to go too." The next thing we knew everyone, was burning up the phone line. Bruce cleared it with his wife, reserved a block of hotel rooms, and off we went. Cousins came together that year ('98, '99 ?) from five different states.

Mom and Aunt Dora stayed at Bruce's house. The rest of us stayed at the same hotel. We partied like crazy for the whole weekend. There was a ton of food, a karaoke night (caught on tape).

In one scene, siblings Bill, Michelle and Bruce are joined by my husband Kirk in a Beatles song. Kirk is playing a broom. There was also plenty of hot tub hoppin' goin' on. I snapped a classic photo of (seventy something) swim suit clad sisters, Mom and Aunt Dora.

Both have champaign glasses raised while relaxing in the Jacuzzi. Bruce even booked a hotel that allows pets. My brothers, Ben and Howard each brought their dog.

For a brief moment, we tasted days of old. It is added to the memories it conjured. Like hanging out in Michelle Petersen's room, pouring over her Beatle card collection, sampling the colognes on her vanity, or running behind her with a jump rope around her waste as she pretended to be a horse for me, and playing dress up in cousins Beatrice and Carol Chapman's clothes and shoes. (We all have a shoe fetish.) At the end of the weekend, we gave the Petersen house a once over, packed up our car and piled into the TV room to view footage of the preceding days. It was hard to leave. Hosting gatherings is our coveted honor. Getting one on one time with a relative is equally prized. We only wish it could be more often.

Calvin Sudduth Jr. used to go on an annual fund raising bicycle trip that started out from right across the road from our house. The 'Pedal to the Point' was a weekend long excursion from Berea to Sandusky, Ohio. Calvin spent time with us at the close of the event a few times. The trip was grueling, so I always tried to have something to feed him when he returned. Following one particular trip, we found ourselves in need of some assistance to move a large steel dog cage into our house. Calvin (Tootie, he is affectionately called) could have just said, no. But instead he helped Kirk unhinge doors, hoist and maneuver only to receive a single slice of home made apple pie for his trouble that day. I had truly forgotten he would soon be passing through.

These days, I make it a point to always have plenty to choose from for even an unexpected guest. (Just like Grandma.)Of the six children of Calvin and Beatrice Sudduth, all but Dora and Kathryn have passed on. Aunt Dora, who is virtually never sick, had a heart attack this week and received a pacemaker. She turns eighty three in about three months.

Since February 8, 2007, my Mother Kathryn is battling back from a massive stroke. Her progress is slow and steady as she learns to walk again. Her faith is unwavering even in the midst of her greatest trial. I appreciate her so much. I am grateful to her that she valued our family enough to make sure that my siblings and I knew as many of them as possible.

How many other family members can say they got their ears pierced by Dr. William 'Uncle Billy' Sudduth? What a joy it is to have grown up experiencing the wealth of my enormous (maternal) extended family. It is a rare gift that enriches my life and I cherish deeply.

Kirk and I enjoy traveling to visit various family members. It began when we were dating when we took our first road trip to Florida to visit the Petersen brothers, and Louis Chapman, as they all lived there at that time with each of their wives. My sister Kathy accompanied us on my first long drive through the south. We stopped for gas in the wee hours of the night somewhere in Georgia. There, we met a guy who had planted himself next to the microwave and made it his business to find out as much as he could about every passing stranger. I never caught his name, but we have always affectionately referred to him as "Darryl" (the hillbilly other brother from the Newhart Show.) We all three needed to use the bathroom. Kirk went in first, but returned in seconds to make the announcement that still garners laughter today, "I think you ladies should rethink your bladder situation." Just then, a pungent odor hit our noses. We looked around to assess the source and discovered the woman in line ahead of Kathy had a terrible bowel explosion in the bathroom and all over her pants! She was buying cigarettes as if it were the most natural thing in the world. Kathy interrupted my conversation with "Darryl", made me put back the Krispy Kreme doughnuts and get in the car. We managed to hold our bladders to the next stop.

Once in Fort Lauderdale, the Petersen's rolled out the red carpet. At first, they would not join us in the pool. I guess mid-seventy degree temperatures are cold to Floridians. But they eventually couldn't stand seeing us having so much fun without them. This visit was the first time that Cousin Bill and my husband Kirk had ever met. But you wouldn't know it as they played who could stand on the inner tube the longest without falling off, (while they pummeled each other) like two little boys. We took a lot of pictures, but half were lost when Kirk accidentally dropped his camera in the Atlantic Ocean from his parasail. Our day trip to Miami was the first time I saw nude sunbathers. Since then, we have visited the Petersens in North Carolina, Harry Chapman and family in Virginia, his daughter September and family in Virginia, Louis Chapman in Arizona and Seattle, Washington (also got to see Aunt Bettye Guillory and cousins Nesbia and Gina Lopes on that visit.)

We've been to Chicago and Montana to visit with my brother Howard, who is living his dream of being a cowboy. In Montana we became part of the food chain as we were stalked by a cougar. We attended my first rodeo. I was all "cowboyed up" taking pictures when the flash of my camera drew the unwanted attention of a raging bull. He had thrown his rider and charged me at the fence. He spun and thrust his hind hooves, missing my face. But I got the message.

My first visit to Montana was with my Mom. There on a mountain top in Glacier National Park, we discovered that Mom is afraid of heights. She wanted to go down on a road that only goes up until you reach the top. There was no way to turn around once you committed. That was my first taste of bison. I learned how to cook it, low and slow. Kirk, Morgan and Carson love it too. It's pretty much the only beef I eat.

The reunions, near and far, the holiday gatherings, the summers of endless fun are too numerous to count. Folks have moved far away from each other and our lives are busy with things the world says are important. *"...do not be conformed to this world, but be transformed by the renewing of your mind, that you may prove what is that good and acceptable and perfect will of God."* Sadly, gone are the days when we gathered nearly every Sunday at Grandma and Grandpa's for fun, food and fellowship; all the more reason why this book is so important. To the older female cousins who influenced my style and shaped my feminine heart, and the male family members who set the standard for my dream life partner, I thank you. You are indelible parts of me. I would like to thank Aunt Bettye, (my Grandpa's baby sister) for her commitment and guidance to see this family book project through.

Thank you, Jesus, for placing the call in her heart and granting her longevity to draw us together to complete this project. It is my honor and privilege to be a part of this immeasurable treasure.

7.2.4.1.1   *Calvin Elsberry Sudduth*

Figure 45A - Calvin Elsberry Sudduth and his wife Beatrice

Figure 45B – Front (L-R) Puggy, Calvin Sr., Beatrice, Calvin Jr.

Back (L-R) Katherine, Beth, Dora Della

7.2.4.2 *Calvin Elsberry Sudduth - A Genealogy*

Calvin Elsberry Sudduth (1900 to 1980) was born in Oklahoma territory at the turn of the century. He was one of nine children born to Charles Sudduth and Dora Culpepper Sudduth. Calvin was the grandson of William Sudduth and Lucy Mikens Sudduth.

He was married to the late Beatrice Louise Kingsberry (1902 to 1981) for fifty eight (58) years and they had six children; Calvin Elsberry Jr., Dora Adella, Benjamin, Louis Nathan, Kathryn Ann, and Elizabeth. He lived in Oklahoma; New Madrid, New Mexico; Lester, Colorado; Topeka, Kansas; Akron and Hudson, Ohio. Calvin worked as a Chotokoa Instructor, miner, painter, and a factory worker. For many years he and Beatrice were cottage parents to troubled youth at the Boys Industrial School in Topeka Kansas and the Cleveland Boys School in Hudson Ohio.

Great Grand Children of William Sudduth and Lucy Mikens
Grand Children of Charles and Dora Sudduth
Children of Calvin Sr. and Beatrice Sudduth
Calvin Elsberry Sudduth Jr

Calvin Elsberry Sudduth Jr. (1923 to 2001) was born in New Madrid, New Mexico and moved to Akron, Ohio with his parents at an early age. He married the late Mildred Loftin of Akron, Ohio and they had three children; Cheryl Ann, Gayle Lorrette, and Calvin Elsberry III.

After divorce Calvin Jr. and Jessie Wallace had two children Laurie and Charles. Calvin married Patricia Eaton and they had one child Patrick. After serving in the Navy during World War II Calvin lived in Akron, Ohio. He was a welder at Babcock and Wilcox LTD. P. (1)

Dora Adella Sudduth (1924 ....) was born in Lester, Colorado and moved to Akron, Ohio with her parents at an early age. She married the late Harry Edward Chapman of Portsmouth, Ohio. They had five children; Harry Payne, Beatrice Lynn, Eric Dean, Carol Ann, and Louis Sheldon. After divorce Dora married the late Jodie Harris and adopted his grandson Jodie. She lived in Topeka, Kansas; Cleveland and Hudson, Ohio. She now resides in Hudson, Ohio. Dora worked as a housekeeper, hospital attendant, activities director and for many years as a Job Developer and Employment Counselor for the State of Ohio. She retired from the state in 1997.

Benjamin Sudduth (1926 to 1964) was born in Lester, Colorado and moved to Akron, Ohio with his parents at an early age. He married Evelyn Carter of Akron, Ohio and they had one child Saundra Carter. After divorce Benjamin married Victoria Johnson of Akron, Ohio and they had three children; Benjamin Jr., Susan Carol, and Alison Leigh. After Benjamin's death Victoria married the late Charles Norman and they had one child Charles Jr. Before his untimely death Ben was a barber and construction worker.

Louis Nathan Sudduth (Puggy) (1928 to 2000) was born in Lester, Colorado and moved to Akron, Ohio with his parents at an early age. He married a lady named Laura from Topeka, Kansas. They had no children. After divorce Louis married Marie Cahill of Cleveland, Ohio. They had no children. Louis also lived in Topeka, Kansas; Akron and Cleveland, Ohio. He was an Army Air Corps Veteran, cottage parent to troubled youth, and a Security Officer.

Kathryn Ann Sudduth (1930 to 2007) was born in Akron, Ohio and also lived in Topeka, Kansas. She married Benjamin Simpson of Akron, Ohio. They had one child Benjamin. After divorce Kathryn married the late Theodore Waynesboro of Akron, Ohio who adopted Benjamin and they had three more children; Howard Gordon, Elizabeth Jean, and Kathryn Ann. After divorce Kathryn married the late Raymond Thomas. They had no children. Kathryn was a homemaker, elevator operator, retail supervisor, engineering blue print clerk, social services counselor, dog breeder, and executive housekeeper for many years.

Elizabeth Sudduth (1934 to 1978) was born in Akron, Ohio and also lived in Topeka, Kansas; Cleveland and Hudson, Ohio. She married William Petersen of Topeka Kansas and they had three children Michelle Edith, William Paul, and Bruce Craig. After divorce Elizabeth married Michael Lewis of Topeka, Kansas and they had one child Melissa Ann. Before her untimely death, Elizabeth worked as an Employment Counselor and Job Developer for the State of Ohio.

Great Great-Grand Children of William Sudduth and Lucy Mikens
Great Grand Children of Charles and Dora Sudduth
Grand Children of Calvin Sr. and Beatrice Sudduth

Cheryl Ann Sudduth (1945....) was born in Akron, Ohio. She married the late Keith Wayne

Johnson of Akron, Ohio. They had no children and after his untimely death Cheryl married Charles Thomas of Akron, Ohio. They had one child Damien LaShawn. Cheryl lives in Akron, Ohio. She worked for Babcock and Wilcox LTD and retired from B. F. Goodrich Tire Co. after many years.

Gayle Lorrette Sudduth (1946....) was born in Akron, Ohio. She married Bennie Lamar Davis of Akron, Ohio. They had two children Derrick Allen and Matice DeNon and five (5) grand children. Gayle lives in Akron, Ohio. She has a BS Degree and a Masters Degree in

Education from the University of Akron. She has worked as a records clerk at B & W Construction, a reservationists at Babcock and Wilcox LTD. For many years she has been a school teacher in Akron, Ohio.

Calvin Elsberry Sudduth III (1948....) was born in Akron, Ohio. He married Carolyn Davidson. They adopted two children Jonathan Ayers and Sayrah Loftin. After divorce Calvin married Valerie Cox. They have no children. Calvin worked for and after many years retired from Babcock and Wilcox, LTD. He lived in Akron, Ohio and now resides in Fayetteville, North Carolina where he is a Security Officer.

Laurie Wallace (19??....) was born in Akron, Ohio. She now lives in Atlanta, Georgia and has worked for Delta Airlines for several years.

Charles Wallace (Chucky) (19??....) was born in Akron, Ohio. He has also lived in Los Angeles, California and now resides in Atlanta Georgia. Chucky has been an executive chef for many years. Patrick Eaton Sudduth (19??....) was born in Akron, Ohio. He is still in his twenties and is the youngest grandson of Calvin Elsberry Sr. and Beatrice Sudduth. Patrick resides in Akron, Ohio.

Harry Payne Chapman (1942....) was born in Akron, Ohio. Harry married Betty Mae Singleton of Akron, Ohio. He adopted Betty's daughter April Lynn and they have another daughter September Dawn. He has lived in Topeka, Kansas; Cleveland and Hudson, Ohio; Lakehurst, New Jersey; Norfolk , Virginia Beach, and Alexandria, Virginia; and now lives in Fredericksburg Virginia. Harry has a BS in Business Administration and a Masters Degree in Communications from Norfolk State University. He also earned a Masters Degree in Aeronautical Science from Embry Riddle Aeronautical University. Harry holds a Commercial Pilots license with Instrument and Multi-engine endorsements and an Airport Control Tower Operator's license. Harry retired from the Navy as a Chief Air Traffic Controller. He was a Vice President of Defense Programs and a Systems Engineer. Harry is now semi-retired and works as a Loan Officer for a mortgage company.

Beatrice Lynn Chapman (Bebe) (1946....) was born in Akron, Ohio. She has one child Aryka Lynn and a grand daughter Anais Gabriella. Beatrice has also lived in Hudson and Cleveland, Ohio; Norfolk Virginia; Phoenix Arizona; and Washington D. C. She now resides in Atlanta, Georgia. Beatrice has a BS in Nursing from Kent State University and a Masters Degree in International Business and Marketing from American International University. Beatrice has worked as a medical laboratory assistant and a Registered Nurse. For many years she Managed Home health Care Agencies around the country

Eric Dean Chapman (Ricky) (1950 to 1989) was born in Akron, Ohio. He married Renee Haywood and they had one child Carman Nicole. After his divorce Eric and Sue Marion of Supperton, Georgia had three children Preston, Melissa Adella, and Amanda. The late Eric Dean also lived in Topeka, Kansas; Hudson and Cleveland, Ohio; Norfolk, Virginia; Supperton, Georgia; and Washington D. C.

Carol Ann Chapman (1953 ....) was born in Akron, Ohio. She married Neal Troy Howlett. He adopted Carol's daughter Alexis Lauren and they have a son Christopher Neal. Now divorced, Carol Ann worked for many years as a Program Developer in the Mental Health Field. She attended Kent State University. She is presently a Loan Officer for a mortgage broker. Carol Ann has also lived in San Diego, California; Cleveland, Ohio and presently resides in Hudson, Ohio.

Louis Sheldon Chapman (1958 to 2008) was born in Hudson, Ohio. He married Ann Haggerty of Cleveland, Ohio. They have no children. Louis has also lived in Cleveland, Ohio; Plantation, Florida; Mesa, Arizona; and now resides in Seattle, Washington. He attended Kent State University. Louis has worked as an information analyst, retail clerk, and a therapist in the health care industry. He passed away after a short illness in 2008.

Saundra Carter Sudduth (1946 ....) was born in Akron, Ohio. She is the daughter of Benjamin Sudduth Sr. Saundra was raised by her Mother Evelyn Carter. She has not been in touch with the family for many years.

Benjamin Sudduth Jr. (1960 ....) was born in Akron, Ohio. He has two children Samantha and Frederick. Ben has lived in Chicago and now resides in California. He attended the University of Akron. Benjamin has worked in automobile sales and presently works in customer service.

Susan Carol Sudduth (1963....) was born in Akron, Ohio. She married David Watkins. Susan has two children Stephanie Nicole and Jessica Daniel. She is now married to Jamil Mitchell Mount. Susan's step children are Deja and Jamil Jr. Susan has lived in Germany and now resides in Cleveland, Ohio. She attended the University of Akron. Susan worked for many years in customer service and is now a homemaker.

Alison Leigh Sudduth (1964 ....) was born in Akron, Ohio. She and Derrick Lockhart have a child Derrick Lockhart Jr. Allison married Mitchell Lee and they have two children Justin Lee and Mitchell Lee. She is the grand daughter of Calvin Elsberry and Beatrice Sudduth. Allison resides in Akron, Ohio. She has a Degree in Nursing from the University of Akron. Alison has been a Registered Nurse for many years.

Benjamin Waynesboro (1949 to 2004) was born in Akron, Ohio. He is the grandson of Calvin Elsberry Sr. and Beatrice Sudduth. Ben was married to Lisa Mauptin. They adopted a daughter Hanna Michelle. Ben also lived in Topeka, Kansas and Hudson, Ohio. Benjamin attended the University of Akron. He worked for a local utility company for many years.

Howard Gordon Waynesboro (1956....) was born in Akron, Ohio. He is the grandson of Calvin Elsberry Sr. and Beatrice Sudduth. Howard has also lived in Hudson, Ohio; Minneapolis, Minnesota; Washington D. C.; Chicago, Illinois; Montana; and he now resides in Spokane, Washington. He attended a local trade school. Howard has worked as a cable installer, horse trainer, equipment operator, and he is a presently a long distance truck driver.

Elizabeth Jean Waynesboro (1959....) was born in Akron, Ohio. She married Kirk Rattray. They have two adopted children a girl Morgan Taylor and a boy Carson Reece. Elizabeth Jean has lived in Hudson, Ohio and Minneapolis, Minnesota. She now resides in Berea, Ohio. Elizabeth Jean attended the University of Akron. She has worked as a corporate trainer, educational aid, free lance writer, and a writer for the local ABC news affiliate. Kathryn Ann Waynesboro (Kathy Ann) (1962....) was born in Akron, Ohio. She is the grand daughter of Calvin Elsberry Sr. and Beatrice Sudduth. Kathy Ann resides in Akron, Ohio. She has an Associates Degree in Social Sciences from the University of Akron. She has worked for many years as a nanny, drug prevention counselor, and a Children's Advocate at Social Services.

Michelle Edith Petersen (Mickey) (1952 ....) was born in Cleveland, Ohio. She is the grand daughter of Calvin Elsberry Sr. and Beatrice Sudduth. Mickey married Alfred Leroy Nagy and they have no children. She has also lived in Topeka, Kansas and Hudson, Ohio. Mickey now resides in Aurora Ohio. She has a BA Degree in Sociology from Muskingham College. Mickey worked for many years in Administration and recently retired from General Motors.

William Paul Petersen (Butch) (1953 ....) was born in Cleveland, Ohio. He married Charlene Cobb. They have adopted a child Deonte Benjamin. Butch has also lived in Topeka, Kansas and Hudson, Ohio. He now resides in Ft. Lauderdale, Florida. Butch has a Bachelors Degree from Macalister College. He has worked in the sales field for many years. Butch is presently employed by Home Depot.

Bruce Craig Petersen (1955 ….) was born in Topeka, Kansas. He married Janice Lynn Williams. They have a daughter Elizabeth Lucresia. Bruce has also lived in Hudson, Ohio and Ft. Lauderdale, Florida. He now resides in Raleigh, North Carolina. Bruce has a BA Degree in Psychology and Economics from Denison University. Bruce has also earned a Master of Business Administration Degree from Washington University in St. Louis. He has worked for Exxon and Eastman Kodak. Bruce is currently a Manager for Fed-Ex Kinkos.

Melissa Ann Lewis (1974 ….) was born in Hudson, Ohio. She married Brian Widowski. They have a son Benjamin. They presently reside in University Heights Ohio. Melissa has a BS Degree in Psychology from Kent State University, a Masters Degree from Columbia University, and a Doctorate Degree in Child Psychology from Kent State University. She is a Child Psychologist and works in Cleveland, Ohio.

Great Great Great Grand Children of William Sudduth and Lucy Mikens
Great Great Grand Children of Charles and Dora Sudduth
Great Grand Children of Calvin Sr. and Beatrice Sudduth

Damien LaShawn Thomas (1978....) was born in Akron, Ohio. He is the grandson of Calvin Elsberry Jr. and Mildred Loftin. Damien has a BS in Business Administration from the University of Akron. He has worked for the U. S. Federal Government for many years. Damien resides in the Nation's Capital, Washington D. C.

Derrick Allen Davis (1967 ….) was born in Akron, Ohio. He is the grandson of Calvin Elsberry Jr. and Mildred Loftin. Derrick has three daughters Fonnel Jones, Desiree Jones, and Sherita Jones and one son Tazon James. Derrick resides in Akron, Ohio.

Matise DeNon Davis (1971 ….) was born in Akron, Ohio. Matise is the grand daughter of Calvin Elsberry Jr. and Mildred Loftin. Matise has a son Tahj Lomarr. She works as a Certified Master Nail Technician. Matise resides in Akron, Ohio.

Jonathan Ayers (1979 to 1995) was born and lived in Akron, Ohio. The late Jonathan Ayers Sudduth was the son of Calvin Elsberry III and Carolyn Davidson. He lived in Akron, Ohio.

Sarah Loftin (1984 ….) was born in Akron, Ohio. She has two children a girl Cali Jonette and a boy Calvin Jonathan. Sarah is the grand daughter of Calvin Elsberry Jr. and Mildred Loftin She lives in Akron, Ohio.

April Lynn Chapman (1962….) was born in Akron, Ohio. She married Eric Stevens. April had two children Antony Levant and Autumn LaDawn. After a divorce, she and Clinton Smith had a daughter Ariyan Lanae. April also adopted a foster child Anthony Taylor. She is the grand daughter of Dora Adella Harris and Harry Edward Chapman. She has lived in Buffalo, New York; Lakehurst, New Jersey; Cleveland Ohio; Norfolk and Virginia Beach, Virginia; and Prince Georges County, Maryland. April has an Associates Degree in Social Sciences from Tidewater Community College. She worked as a data entry specialists for Giant Foods and the National Automobile Dealers Association. April is currently a substitute teacher in the Norfolk Virginia School system. She has also been a foster parent for more than twenty (20) children.

September Dawn Chapman (1963....) was born in Lakehurst, New Jersey. She married Winfred Sanderlin Jr. They have one child Christian Payne. September is the grand daughter of Dora Adella Harris and Harry Edward Chapman. She has also lived in Cleveland, Ohio; Norfolk and Virginia Beach Virginia. September and Winfred now reside in Suffolk, Virginia. September has a BA in Sociology from Mary Baldwin College and a Masters degree in Occupational and Technical Studies from Old Dominion University. She has worked for Nations Bank and Nauticus Maritime Center. September is currently Associate Director of Human Resources at Old Dominion University.

Aryka Chapman (1974 ....) was born in Cleveland, Ohio. She and Rafael Gravada have a daughter Anais Gabreilla. Aryka is the grand daughter of Dora Adella Harris and Harry Edward Chapman. She has also lived in Norfolk, Virginia; Phoenix, Arizona; and she now resides in Washington, D. C. Aryka attends the University of Maryland, University College. She has worked for many years as an AIDS Counselor. Aryka is presently an Executive at an AIDS Outreach Program.

Carman Nicole Chapman (1969 ....) was born in Cleveland, Ohio. She and David Slaughter had one child Joshua David Slaughter. Carman is the daughter of Eric Dean Chapman and Renee Haywood. Carman is the grand daughter of Dora Adella Harris and Harry Edward Chapman. She has lived in Cleveland, Ohio; Aurora, Ohio; and now resides in Marlow Hills, Ohio. Carman has worked for an area utility company for several years.

Preston Chapman (1972 ....) was born in Norfolk, Virginia. He has three children. Preston is the son of Eric Dean Chapman and Sue Marion. Preston is the grandson of Dora Adella Harris and Harry Edward Chapman. He has lived in Norfolk, Virginia; Georgia Cleveland, Ohio and now resides in Pontiac, Michigan. We have been unable to contact Preston for more information about him and his three children.

Melissa Adella Chapman (19??....) was born in Cleveland, Ohio around 1975. She has one child. Melissa is the daughter of Eric Dean Chapman and Sue Marion. Melissa is the grand daughter of Dora Adella Harris and Harry Edward Chapman. She has lived in Cleveland, Ohio and now resides in Pontiac, Michigan. We have been unable to contact Melissa for more information about her and her child.

Amanda (19??....) was born in Pontiac, Michigan around 1985. She has one child. Amanda is the daughter of Eric Dean Chapman and Sue Marion. Amanda is the grand daughter of Dora Adella Harris and Harry Edward Chapman. She resides in Pontiac, Michigan.

Alexis Lauren Howlett (1980 ....) was born in Cleveland, Ohio. She is the daughter of Carol Ann Howlett and was adopted by Neal Troy

Howlett. Alexis is the grand daughter of Dora Adella Harris and Harry Edward Chapman. Alexis has lived in Cleveland and Hudson, Ohio and now resides in Akron, Ohio. She attended Kent State University. Alexis has held several positions in retail sales.

Christopher Neal Howlett (Chris) (1982 ….) was born in Hudson, Ohio. He is the son of Carol Ann Chapman and Neal Howlett. Christopher is the grandson of Dora Adella Harris and Harry Edward Chapman. He now resides in San Francisco, California. Chris has a BA in Linguistics from Antioch College. Chris is a Retail Sales Analyst.

Samantha Sudduth (1982 ….) was born in Akron, Ohio. She is the daughter of Benjamin Sudduth Jr. and the grand daughter of Benjamin Sr. and Victoria Sudduth Norman. She attended the University of Akron.

Frederick Sudduth (1986….) was born in Akron, Ohio. He is the son of Benjamin Sudduth Jr. and the grandson of Benjamin Sr. and Victoria Sudduth Norman. Frederick attended the University of Akron. He lives in New York City.

Stephanie Nicole Watkins (1984 ….) was born in Akron, Ohio. She is the daughter of Susan Sudduth Mount and the granddaughter of Benjamin Sudduth Sr. and Victoria Sudduth Norman. Stephanie is a student and attends the University of Akron.

Jessica Daniel Watkins (1990….) was born in Germany. She is the daughter of Susan Sudduth Mount and the granddaughter of Benjamin Sudduth Sr. and Victoria Sudduth Norman.

Daja Mount (1993 ….) was born in Cleveland, Ohio. She is the step daughter of Susan Sudduth Mount. Daja is a student and resides in Cleveland, Ohio.

Jamil Mount Jr. (2003 ….) was born in Cleveland, Ohio. He is the step son of Susan Sudduth Mount. Jamil Jr. resides in Cleveland, Ohio.

Derrick Lockhart Jr. (1986….) was born in Akron, Ohio. He is the son of Alison Leigh Sudduth and Derrick Lockhart Sr. He is the grandson of Benjamin Sudduth Sr. and Victoria Norman Sudduth.

Justin Lee (1989….) was born in Akron, Ohio. He is the son of Alison Leigh Sudduth and Mitchell Lee. Justin is the grandson of Benjamin Sudduth Sr. and Victoria Sudduth Norman.

Mitchell Lee (1999….) was born in Akron, Ohio. He is the son of Alison Leigh Sudduth and the grandson of Benjamin Sudduth Sr. and Victoria Sudduth Norman.

Hanna Michelle Waynesboro (1992...) was born in Hudson, Ohio. She is the daughter of the late Benjamin Waynesboro and Lisa Mauptin Sudduth. Hanna is the granddaughter of Kathryn Sudduth Waynesboro and Theodore Waynesboro. She is a student and resides with her Mother in Hudson, Ohio.

Morgan Taylor Rattray (2000 ….) was born in Berea, Ohio. She is the daughter of Elizabeth Jean and Kirk Rattray. Morgan is the grand daughter of Kathryn Sudduth Waynesboro and Theodore Waynesboro. Morgan resides in Berea, Ohio with her parents.

Carson Reese Rattray (2003 ….) was born in Berea, Ohio. He is the son of Elizabeth Jean and Kirk Rattray. Carson is the grandson of Kathryn Sudduth Waynesboro and Theodore Waynesboro. Carson resides in Berea, Ohio with his parents.

Deonte Benjamin Peterson (2000 ….) was born in Ft. Lauderdale, Florida. He is the great grand son of Calvin Elsberry and Beatrice Sudduth. Deonte is the son of Butch and Charlene Peterson. He lives in Ft. Lauderdale, Florida with his parents.

Elizabeth Lucresia Peterson (1988 ….) was born in Ft. Lauderdale, Florida. She is the daughter of Bruce and Jan Peterson. Elizabeth is the great grand daughter of Calvin Elsberry and Beatrice Sudduth. She is a student and resides with her parents in Raleigh, North Carolina.

Benjamin Widowski (2005 ….) was born in University Heights, Ohio. He is the youngest great grand child of Calvin Elsberry and Beatrice Sudduth to date. He resides with his parents Melissa and Brian Widowski in University, Heights Ohio.

Great Great Great Great Grand Children of William Sudduth and Lucy Mikens

Great Great Great Grand Children of Charles and Dora Sudduth

Great Great Grand Children of Calvin Sr. and Beatrice Sudduth

Cali Jonette (2000 ….) was born in Akron, Ohio. She is the grand child of Calvin Elsberry III. She resides with her Mother in Akron, Ohio.

Calvin Jonathan (2003 ….) was born in Akron, Ohio. He is the grandson of Calvin Elsberry III. He resides with his Mother in Akron, Ohio.

Fonnell Jones (1986 ….) was born in Akron, Ohio. She is the grand daughter of Gayle Lorrette. Fonnell works as a Massage Therapist. She resides in Akron, Ohio.

Desiree Jones (1989 ….) was born in Akron, Ohio. She is the grand daughter of Gayle Lorrette. Desiree is a student. She resides in Akron, Ohio.

Sherita Jones (1992 ….) was born in Akron, Ohio. She is the grand daughter of Gayle Lorrette. Sherita is a student. She resides in Akron, Ohio.

Tazon James (2000 ….) was born in Akron, Ohio. He is the grand son of Gayle Lorrette. Tazon is a student. He resides in Akron, Ohio.

Tahj Lomar Davis (1995 ….) was born in Akron, Ohio. He is the son of Matise Davis and the grandson of Gayle Sudduth Davis. He lives in Akron, Ohio.

Antony Levant Chapman (1992….) was born in Prince Georges County, Maryland. He is the grandson of Harry Payne Chapman and Betty Singleton Chapman. Antony is a student and lives with his Mother in Norfolk, Virginia.

Autumn LaDawn Chapman (1994….) was born in Princes Georges County, Maryland. She is the grand daughter Harry Payne Chapman and Betty Singleton Chapman. Autumn is a student and lives with her Mother in Norfolk, Virginia.

Ariyan Lanae Chapman (1998….) was born in Norfolk, Virginia. She is the grand daughter of Harry Payne Chapman and Betty Singleton Chapman. Ariyan is a student and lives with her Mother in Norfolk, Virginia.

Anthony Taylor Chapman (Tony) (1986 ….) was born in Norfolk, Virginia. He is the adopted son of April Lynn Chapman. Tony is the grandson of Harry Payne Chapman and Betty Singleton Chapman. Tony resides in Norfolk, Virginia.

Christian Payne Sanderlin (1996….) was born in Virginia Beach, Virginia. He is the grandson of Harry Payne Chapman and Betty Singleton Chapman. Christian lives with his parents in Suffolk, Va.

Anais Grabreilla Gravada (1992 ….) was born in Washington, D.C. She is the grand daughter of Beatrice Lynn Chapman. Anais is a student. She resides with her Mother in Washington, D. C.

Joshua David Slaughter (1987 …) was born in Cleveland, Ohio. He is the grandson of Eric Dean Chapman. Joshua is a student. He resides with his Mother in Marlow Hills, Ohio.

Makayla Nicole Petersen Jones (2006 ..) was born in Raleigh, NC. She is the granddaughter of Bruce Petersen and resides with her mother Elizabeth Petersen in Raleigh.

The three (3) children of Preston Chapman should be listed here in the order. They are the grand children of Eric Chapman and Sue Marion. They are students and live with their Father in Pontiac, Mi.

The daughter of Melissa Adella Chapman should be listed here in the order. She is the grand daughter of Eric Chapman and Sue Marion. She lives with her Mother in Pontiac, Michigan.

The daughter of Amanda Chapman should be listed here in the order. She is the grand daughter of Eric Chapman and Sue Marion. She is not yet a student and lives with her Mother in Pontiac, Michigan.

Summary:

Calvin Elsberry and Beatrice Sudduth's linage outlined above include; six (6) children, twenty four (24) grandchildren, twenty nine (29) great grandchildren, nineteen (19 great great grand children, or a total of seventy eight (78) total descendents. I know they would be proud of their achievements. Twenty three (23) pursued higher education. Six (6) attended Trade Schools or earned Associates Degrees. Eleven (11) earned Bachelors Degrees. Seven (7) earned Masters Degrees. One (1) earned a Doctorate Degree. The decedents occupations were in private and public sector pursuits including government and the military. I am sure that these achievements can be traced to the love, family values, strong moral fiber and fortitude passed down by Calvin Elsberry and Beatrice Sudduth from generation to generation.

7.2.5 *Emma Lou Sudduth Larkins*

Emma Lou was the fifth Child born to Charles and Dora Sudduth in 1903 in Oklahoma. I believe she had the fairest skin of us all. She was one of 3 with a nose like Papa.

None of my parents children were as white as Papa or as dark as Mama. We were all brown shin or mulatto, different shades of brown.

Emma also taught school in Oklahoma. You only had to have a high school education in those days to teach grade school. She taught in a rural school that only had one big room. The students ranged from the first grade through eighth.

I remember her getting married to Albert Larkin. The Larkin family lived out in the Pierce Addition which was out in the country east of town. Emma and "Al" only had one child named Raymond. They moved to Akron, Ohio when Raymond was a small child.

Many family members (including my Brother Ebb) and friends moved to Akron at that time; because the Good Year Tire Factory had opened up in Akron and was hiring. They were offering good pay and great benefits that drew so many people there.

Mama and Papa drove 1000 miles to visit family and friends in Akron every summer. We went to Sharon Pennsylvania about 69 miles from Akron to West Middlesex Camp Meeting every summer. I remember driving an old Willis Night car Papa owned. I wanted to drive the whole trip by myself. We would stop on the road side to rest and sleep at night. It took a long time to drive to Ohio from Kansas because the speed limit in those days was 35 miles per hour. Papa liked my driving; but thought I was speeding when I reached 35 miles an hour *(Smiles)*.

Albert divorced Emma and married again.

Raymond, their only child, went into the service when he was 18 years old. He started shooting up dope which broke his mother's heart.

She died at the age of 59 in 1961 with cancer. Her favorite song was "It is no secret what God can do." I think of her every time *I* hear that song now. Raymond was very good to his mother while she was so very ill. Whenever she was in excruciating pain and he was called, he would even leave work to come and give her morphine shots.

Raymond was living the gay life style and had a partner that he lived with for over 50 years until the man died. Kathryn Anne, Ebb's daughter and Raymond's cousin, and her daughter Elizabeth Jean were always very kind to Raymond.

I remember calling Raymond on the phone ever so often and would talk to him about his soul. But I never could get him to except the Lord, until about two weeks before he passed. The Lord led me to call him. It seemed urgent. Elizabeth Jean (his grand niece) was by his bed side and handed him the phone, and I led him in the sinners Prayer. He accepted the Lord Jesus Christ, Praise God! What a blessing! He was 72 years of age when he passed.

7.2.6 *Napoleon Bonaparte Sudduth*

Napoleon Bonaparte, "Poly" was born next in 1905 in Oklahoma. My brother had a dark reddish brown Indian color with beautiful black hair and high cheek bones. Poly was considered one of the two black sheep of our family because he smoked, drank and was not faithful to his young wife Marie Payne Sudduth.

He worked at the Santa Fe Shops, made good money. I remember one time Marie told Mama "Poly" had gambled all his check off. She had no money to buy food for herself and their first baby. Mama braided some switches up and went over and gave "Poly" a good whipping. He was 19 years old at the time. Mama was a little woman, but mighty.

"Poly" and Marie ended up with 7 kids. The oldest was a girl, Donna Jean Sudduth Kidd, who left a legacy second to none. Hopefully you will be able to read the story of her career in this book later; she lived an extremely rewarding life.

Marie was an industrious person and worked for more than 20 years at the State hospital.

Marie was a High School graduate and was in love with my brother "Poly". My brother "Poly" who went to school 8 years and only got a fourth grade education. He and Roosevelt Sneed would play hooky and go fishing. "Poly" couldn't read well; however he was good in Math. He earned good money building box cars at the Santa Fe shops from which he retired.

There were six boy's born after Donna. The boys were Napoleon Junior, Jack, Bill, Roy, Dale, and Howard. "Jack" and Howard became ministers of the Gospel. Howard is still living today at this writing. "Bill" became a boxer. Roy who was retarded had an impediment of speech. Believe it or not Roy married a girl who was retarded too. They had a son named Roy Junior. That was adopted by an elderly couple who did a beautiful job of raising him. He graduated from College.

I was living with my daughter Paquita, her husband Keith and their 3 children; when Donna, "Poly's" daughter, sent for me to come to pray for him because he was very sick with cancer of the lungs. I spent time in the hospital sitting by his bed side to comfort him and was the last one to see him alive. He accepted Jesus Christ before he died, received the Holy Spirit, and spoke in tongues. The night before he passed I stayed with him until midnight. Sheldon picked me up that night; as I was staying with him and Margaret. The next morning about 8:00am they called from the Hospital and said he had passed. He was 67 years old. What a blessing to be able to pray with him that night.

His wife, Marie, lived to be 96.

7.2.6.1 Donna Jean Sudduth Kid - Legacy of Life

Figure 46 - Donna Jean Kidd (1977), Daughter of Napoleon

Donna Jean (Sudduth) Kid, born November 25, 1925 entered in to eternal rest on October 4th 2003. Donna was the grand daughter of Charles J.; the eldest child and only daughter of Charles's his son Napoleon and Marie Payne Sudduth. Since her childhood she attended the Church of God on 12th and Lane Street, now called the Capitol City Church of God. She was also an active member of the Asbury Mt Olive United Methodist Church in Topeka, Kansas. Donna was also an Associate Member of the Central Congregational Church in Topeka, Kansas. She attended Buchanan Elementary School and graduated from Topeka, High School. Donna received her Bachelors Degree from Washburn University and her Masters Degree in Social Work from Emporia State University.

In 1966, Donna served as a catalyst in motivating several local Pastors in forming the organization called Doorstep, Inc. housed at Central Congregational Church. She severed as the only paid staff person for several years, organizing volunteers to operate a food and clothing bank, offering assistance with utilities, developing youth summer camps, a day care center, and assisted in providing scholarships for two medical students as well as educational funds and intern sites for social work students. She was and advocate in providing assistance to underprivileged. She also volunteered at the Door step's Dovetail Shop.

In 1976, Donna was hired as the Executive Director of the Jayhawk Area Agency on Aging she was a champing at serving seniors in hr community. Her accomplishments were many during her 20 year tenure at

JAAA. When the agency began, there was one program for seniors in Douglas and Jefferson counties and two in Shawnee county, all funded under the Older Americans Act. Donna conducted public hearings, gathered input and worked to plan and implement programs to address the needs of seniors. Two of the most rewarding programs were in the rural areas of Jefferson County that addresses health needs, with one involving a physician residency program for the rural area, imitated with the assistance of Congressman Bill Roy. A program offering heath screening services through the Jefferson County health department won Nation award. Although the residency program ended, the health-screening program continues today as well as thirteen other providers and six teen services in Shawnee, Douglas, and Jefferson Counties. Donna was also instrumental in starting "meals on wheels" for seniors citizens in the Topeka areas.

As the Executive Director of JAAA, Donna served on several community boards, including the Stormont Veil Advisory Board, Kansas rehabilitation Hospital Advisory Council, and the Kansas Coalition on Aging. Kansas Governors Mike Hayden and Joan Finney appointed Donna to the Citizens Utility Rate payers Board (CURB). Donna was an Adjunct Professor at Washburn University for three years and at Kansas City Kansas Community College for two years. In the early 80's, she traveled with Ghandi's grand daughter to Kingston, Jamaica to work with the Jamaican Consulate to assist in their programs for the elderly.

Retiring in 1996, she was elected a Nation Silver Haired Senator for Kansas, served as the Chair of Shawnee County Advocacy Council for aging, and was President of humankind Inc until hr death. Several of the many organizations she was affiliated with were the Topeka Chapter of Links, of which she was a member for 32 years. Delta Sigma Theta Sorority, and Church Woman United. She also gave her time to her community, by teaching Bible study to young children and volunteering for the Rites of Passage.

On May 23rd 2003, the JAAA presented her "The Donnas J Kid Award" for her outstanding community Service and her tireless efforts to serve seniors in our community. Prior to her passing the Soroptimist International of Topeka honored her with the Woman of Distinction Award on September 26, 2003.

Her husband, Wilbur Kidd, died November 11 1972 and her son, Chalmus Kidd who died October 2, 1998 two brothers Jack Sudduth and William 'Sudduth preceded her in death. Mrs. Kidd is survived by three sons, Rudy Dyer, Michael A. Dyer and Linton S. Kidd, all of Madison, WI., three daughters Judy Dyer and Lynette Kidd both of Houston, TX. Karla McClelland Jackson, of Topeka Kansas, four brothers, Napoleon Sudduth Junior, was of Topeka Ks.; but has deceased since Donna's passing, Roy Sudduth of Topeka Ks., Dale Sudduth, Denver CO., Rev. Howard Sudduth, McClouth, Kansas, two Aunts Corrine Henry, Chicago, Ill. Bettye Guillory Federal way, WA., 10 grand children and 11 great Grand children.

Because of Donna's Love, Devotion to her family, friends and community, she was a *Phenomenal Woman.*

Figure 47 – Top Row – Lanette Kidd, Judy Dyer, Rudy Dyer, Donna Jean Kidd, Carla Jackson Lower Row – Michael Dyer, Linton Kidd, Chalmus Kidd

7.2.7 *Maude Esther Sudduth Lawton*

Maude Esther was born next in line to Charles and Dora Sudduth. She was born in 1907 in Oklahoma. She has quite a history.

She was the second of the two that were called the black sheep of the family; because she had such a temper my two brothers "Poly" and Sheldon called her "Maude the Mule".

Maude was leaving for school one day and Mama called her back to put suitable clothes on for the cold snowy weather. She had her bosom all open. I think Mama must have hit her because she hit Mama over the head with her books.

She got pregnant by Richard Lawton a man who had been married before; he was 20 years older than her. She was 18 and he was 38 at the time. He had reddish brown hair with blue green eyes, and was a contractor, built homes for the rich people, made good money, and gave her every thing she wanted. He had the most beautiful sisters I think

I've ever seen. He came from a large family in a little country town not far from our home in Topeka, Kansas.

I believe Maude had 12 pregnancies; but only nine of the children lived to grow up. She had six of them in succession; then 8 years later Carol Kay, Victoria and Marvin were born.

She ran with a woman named big Dorothy. The two of them became shop lifters. Maude was jailed for selling dope. She and her oldest son Richard Junior "Sonny" spent 5 years in jail. However, the greatest part of her history is that she was miraculously converted before she passed at the age of 80.

Maude was a giver and was kind to me and my 3 children. Whenever she bought for her children, she would buy for mine too. The sad part of the story was that at the age of 42 her oldest son, "Sonny", was shot and killed but by one of his gambler rivalries. I was visiting with Maude the Monday before he was killed. I asked him if he wanted to be saved. He said he wasn't ready yet. As they say, you never know when the hour will come. We need to be prepared. I am concerned about his soul; that he may lost.

7.2.7.1 *Children's memory of Maude*

Figure 48 - Maude (Sudduth) Lawton

7.2.7.1.1.1 Testimony of Gloria Williams - Maude's Daughter

Figure 49 - Gloria Williams

My name is Gloria M Williams. I was born May 2, 1934 in Topeka Kansas. I had wonderful Parents, Richard Lawton and Maude Lawton, whom I loved dearly. I am one of 9 children raised in the church of God. When I was 5 years of age I gave my heart to Jesus, sang in the choir and was also a soloist. My Mother prepared me to be a star, at the age of 5, I began piano lessons, dance ballet and majorette.

Through my early years these were great responsibilities for one so young. At the age of 13 I stepped down from the choir and made my confession to the church that I was no longer saved; but not to worry about me, for one day I would come back to the Lord and it would be forever. I did have a chance to go to Hollywood to be in Rochester's school of dance when I graduate from high school.

In the mean time I met a wonderful young man who was in the Air Force, his name was Joseph L Williams Jr. After one year we decided to get married. He asked my parents for their consent and they said yes, we were married May 25 after my 18th birthday. What a beautiful wedding we had.

Unto us were born five beautiful children the eldest Joseph L. Williams the 2nd, Reginald O. Williams, Kim I. Williams, Mario D. Williams, and baby girl, last but not least Tara D. Williams. After 29 years of marriage, Joseph and I decided to divorce.

From the back ground I received in my early days in the church; I was blessed to be able to raise my five children knowing that God was helping me even though I was not saved.

God has blessed my family tremendously. I along with four of my children have been saved and called into the ministry. I am a licensed missionary/evangelist along with my daughter Tara. Three of my sons were ordained as elders to preach this great gospel of Jesus Christ our Lord.

We were all saved in revival meetings at different times, but under the same evangelist Elder Forrest Lowe from California. {Except for Tara, who accepted the Lord under Mother Jackson in Rome New York}. What a dynamic preacher Elder Lowe was. We received the baptism of God's Precious Holy Ghost which is our power, keeper, and teacher leader into all truth. What a mighty God we serve.

I was 48 years young when I came back to the Lord. I still have one son Reggie and his family that need to be saved. So we are praying and believing God for his salvation. I have 38 grand children and 12 Great Grandchildren all of which are great blessing in my life.

My spiritual parents are Bishop Augustus and first Lady Barbara Stovall; great preachers and teaches in the precious word of God. They have been great examples of true holiness; not only an example, but also in precept. They let us know that you must live this life of holiness every step of the way.

My Grandmother, Dora Sudduth was my greatest inspiration. I always believed that there was no one else that walked as close to God as she did. In those early years of my life, I was truly grateful for my Grandmother. I am blessed to be able to worship with my daughter Tata and her husband Elder Ronald Day, my son elder Kim Williams and his wife Linda together under the teaching of Bishop and first lady Stovall at first Tabernacle Pentecostal Christian Center. My son Pastor Joseph and his wife Linda Williams are in Gainesville Florida. My son the elder Mario and Renee Williams are in Binghamton New York Church of God in Christ where he is the state Evangelist.

God is good to us all, we thank him in every trial and tribulation, for we know in them we will become stronger in Him. It pays to serve Jesus every step of the way. I love Jesus because He first loved me. He paid the price for us on Calvary's cross that we might be redeemed and washed in his precious blood. What a mighty God we serve.

Love in Christ

Missionary Gloria Williams

7.2.7.1.1.2 Marvin Lawton - Lawton Family Tree

Written by:
Teresa Lawton wife of Marvin Lawton, the youngest child born to Maude E. Sudduth Lawton (daughter of Charles J. Sudduth) and Richard W. Lawton Sr.

Figure 50 — Maude Sudduth Lawton and Marvin Lawton

I am the youngest of nine children born to Maude E. Sudduth and Richard W. Lawton, born on August 16th, 1949 in Topeka, Kansas at a hospital then known as Vail Hospital. I am the youngest boy of four boys and five girls.

My brothers are: Richard Jr. "Sonny", the oldest and now deceased], Bernard (who resides in San Diego, California), and Calvin R. (who resides in Topeka, Kansas). My sisters are: Constance Patillo (now deceased), Phillis "Tillie" (resides in Topeka, Kansas), and Victoria Benson (also resides in Topeka, Kansas).

I grew up in Topeka in 1422 Munson. I attended school in Topeka until graduating from Topeka High in 1967. I played basketball there. The next year, I attended Washburn University and played basketball in 1968. Later, I transferred to Butler Jr. College in El Dorado, Kansas. There, I also played basketball and ran track. I graduated with an AA Degree in Business Administration.

I migrated to Wichita, Kansas where I met my first wife, Wendy Wofford. We were married in November 1969. I was employed by the City of Wichita at the time and worked in the Street Maintenance Department until I was drafted into the armed forces in April of 1970. I spent 2 years in the service as a Military Policeman in the 560th MP Company that was deployed into the Republic of Southeast Asia where I spent one year in country until I was honorably discharged in December 1971. Upon my return from Vietnam, I was decorated with a Bronze Star of Valor for saving the life of a 2nd Lieutenant while in combat.

During my time in Vietnam period our first child, Cyndrya Dawn was born on June 13, 1970. We had another child, Marvin M. Lawton II, on September 29th, 1972.

The following next year, 1973, my brother Sonny was murdered on April 19th. The story remains a mystery until this day. God only knows who was responsible for this tragedy.

Upon my return to the States, I also began to work for my wife's Father, Henry Wofford. He was the first black man to do oil exploration in the State of Kansas. I worked for him until 1976 when I left for Los Angeles, California. During that time I also separated from my wife Wendy. We later divorced in 1977.

I became a limousine driver for Jackson Limo Service in 1979 until 1981 when I relocated to San Diego, California. There I met my 2nd wife, Rene Tate. We were married the same year and had a son named, Remar Amir, who was born on July 23, 1981. I started my own limo service, LaCreme Limo Service, the same year and operated it until 1984. In 1984, I began to drive privately for a Vahe Karapetian until 1992.

In 1988, I met my 3rd wife Saundra Carr and we were married on March 4, 1988. We had a son, Christopher J., born on the August 16, 1989 at approximately the same day and time I was born on. We were later divorced in 1994.

My Mother, Maude E., passed on June 19, 1988.

I became saved and born again on July 11, 1988. I was called into the Ministry in June 1996 and attended Masters College Seminary. I was ordained in the AME Faith in that same year. I was ordained in the non-denominational faith where I remain to this day.

During that time period, I also maintained my own business called Marvin's Notary and Auto Registration Service until I moved back to my home town in Topeka, Kansas in February 1999.

I met and married Robin Render-Brown in 1996 and married her in the same year. We would later divorce in 2000 while I was living back in Topeka, Kansas. Later after I returned to Topeka, I met and married my present wife Theresa Smith. We wed on November 21, 2001 and reside in Topeka at the present.

I am a Servant Leader of Have Jesus Will Travel Ministries. We have Bible Studies in the local prison daily and two services on Sunday's at Topeka and Rolling Hills Convalesant Home. We travel to many parts of the country to spend the gospel of Jesus Christ as the Spirit leads us. I have 4 grandchildren: Tremaine and Kahil Hopkins by Chydrya and Bishop and Journey Lawton by Marvin II with one more expected in May 2008 (to be named Adian).

I praise God for my Aunt Bettye Guillory (my Mother's youngest sister) who resides in Seattle, Washington. She was instrumental in bringing me to Christ. We love you Auntie and thank you for this opportunity to be part of your book. We are praying for you and I know the Lord will richly bless you in all your endeavors. We do hope to see you at the reunion in August.

7.2.7.1.1.3 *Victoria Jean Lawton Benson*

Written by:
Victoria Jean Lawton Benson child of Maude E. Sudduth Lawton (daughter of Charles J. Sudduth) and Richard W. Lawton Sr.

Figure 51 - Victoria Lawton Benson

My name is Victoria Jean Lawton Benson. Eighth in line of the nine children born to Maude E. Sudduth Lawton and Richard W. Lawton Sr. I was born on VJ Day August 14, 1945. I have two biological children: Traci M. Downing and Jeffrey D. Benson. I have a son in law Kevin A. Downning, and a nine year old grandson Jarin K. Downing. I have also have two great nieces who reside in my home who are like daughters to me: Miss Sheena S. Selby, 23 years old and Miss Myriah D. Hold, 14 years old. These children are the great grandchildren of Maude and Richard Lawton. All reside in Topeka, Kansas, except for Jeffrey. He is a resident in Palo Alto, California.

Each of has us have been saved by the grace of God and are faithful servants at Capitol City Community Church of God. Our Pastor is Robert D. Marshall Sr. Jeff attends church in San Francisco. Traci serves with the children's ministry, secretary for the Women of the Church of God (Women's Mission), Motion Praise, and she is an Usher as well as being employed at Blue Cross Blue Shield. Kevin serves with the athletic ministry, Men of the Church of God (Men's Mission), and Usher, and is employee at Kellogg's. Sheena plays the trumpet and piano and is also an artist, and employed by Stormont Vail Hospital. She serves with the Children's Ministry, Youth Ministry, Motion Praise, choir, Nursing Home Ministry, and an Usher. Myriah is a student at Topeka Collegiate, plays piano for Youth and Adult Choirs, and also plays the cello, part of the Nursing Home Ministry, phone ministry for Youth, Motion Praise, and an Usher. She likes to play all sports. Jarin is a student at Ross Elementary. He also plays the piano and violin. At 9, God has blessed him with a voice to bring him Glory. Jeffrey travels extensively and sells computer software to law firms. He has been gifted to play the saxophone, and sing to exalt the name of our Lord and Savior. God has allowed me to humbly serve him and my brother and sisters in Christ and in my community as a Trustee, Deaconess, Usher, Sunday School Teacher, Director of the Children's choir, Friendship Coordinator for the Women of the Church of God, Pastors Aid Committee, Evangelism Committee, Kitchen Committee, and Church Janitor.

I have written poetry, two plays (one of which has been produced and a 3rd one in the works). God will exalt His children as we lift his name. I am also a Cosmetologist of 37 years. God has given me a job where people in need of The Savior can be witness to, and His children can be encouraged.

If Grandma Sudduth, my mom, and my dad, could see us, they would know there are many prayers that are being answered. We are still a work in progress, but I don't believe any of us would change this way of life for anything in this World. To God be the Glory great things He has done.

My dear Aunt Bettye Guillory, at 95, is an inspiration to all of her family and people across the United States. What a task of writing a book sending letters of encouragement to Pastors, and a Warrior in Prayer. The Joy of the Lord and the Love of God is exhibited in her daily. May God continue to richly bless her.

7.2.7.1.1.4 Crystal Nevada Thornton

Figure 52 - Crystal Nevada Thorton

Crystal Nevada Thornton, an award winning journalist is a native of Topeka, Kansas and is a direct descendant of "Brown vs. Board of Education Plaintiffs". Her Grandmother Maude Esther Lawton was one of the original 12 plaintiffs, while her Mother Carol Kay Lawton and Aunt Victoria Jean Benson were child plaintiffs in the landmark case. Recently Crystal received the 2008 National Award for Leadership from the Brown Foundation in commemoration of its 20th anniversary. She holds a Bachelor of Arts degree in Telecommunications and Film from Eastern Michigan University with a minor in Musical Theater and was honored by Eastern Michigan University with the prestigious Alumni Achievement Award in 2006.She interned in studio and film production at the Disney MGM Studios in Orlando, Florida and began her television career as a news anchor in Eastern North Carolina.

Crystal's career as a Primary Television News Anchor has moved her from coast to coast for more than a decade. She returned to North Carolina in 2002 to become the Primary Co-Anchor for FOX 8 WGHP-TV where she hosted the Friends of Fantasia watch parties leading up to her win on American Idol in 2004.

Crystal came to WGHP-TV from KDAF-TV in Dallas, Texas where she was one of the original anchors to launch WB33 News@Nine on January 11, 1999.She also produced and hosted the station's Community affairs program "DFW Close Up," for which she was honored with two Emmy Nominations.

In addition, Crystal has worked as a Primary News Anchor in Portland, Oregon, Corpus Christi, Texas and Washington, North Carolina.

Crystal became a new mom in 2005 and recently became an Independent Sales Director with Mary Kay Cosmetics just 10 months after signing her agreement. This latest accomplishment places her in the top 2% of the company's sales force, out of more than 1.7 million consultants worldwide.

Crystal also is an accomplished Vocalist and recording artist who has worked with some of gospel music's finest, including The Winans, The Clark Sisters, BeBe and CeCe Winans, Donnie McClurken, Edward and Walter Hawkins, Vicky Winans, Fred Hammond, and Karen Clark-Sheard. Her first solo CD is self titled: Crystal Thornton "A Little Lower than the Angels."

Crystal has had the honor of performing throughout the country singing the National Anthem for the Portland Trail Blazers, The Dallas Mavericks, The Texas Rangers, The New York Yankees, The Seattle Super Sonics and the Los Angeles Lakers. Her talents have also been heard internationally through The Trinity Broadcast Network. She hosts "The Master's Music" on Total Christian Television seen in over 170 nations. She has been a guest on Bishop T.D. Jakes "The Potter's Touch," featured as one of "God's Leading Ladies" and was honored with Greensboro's "Women of Faith Award" in 2004.

Crystal is an active member of the National Association of Black Journalists, the National Academy of Television Arts and Sciences, Alpha Kappa Alpha Sorority Incorporated, the Links, Incorporated, The Society and the Junior League. She serves as a board member for several local organizations including the High Point Chamber of Commerce, the Winston Salem State University Child Development and Lab School, the Salvation Army of High Point and the Carl Chavez YMCA. Crystal has a passion for the arts and has used her celebrity to promote the importance of keeping the arts in public schools. She has over twenty years of theater and dance experience and continues to share her talents with young artists. Crystal is married to Lt. Col.

Ronald Stephen Thornton, Jr of the United States Marine Corps. Ronald is also a commercial airline pilot. They have a son Ronald S. Thornton, III.

Figure 53 - Crystal, Rock, and Ron Thornton

7.2.7.1.1.5 Phyllis Haber Lawton Williams

This is a Short testimony of Phyllis Haver (Lawton) Williams, grand daughter of Charles J. and Dora Sudduth.

We call Phyllis "Tillie"; she was born July 11, 1929 in Topeka, Kansas. She left home when she was 16 years of age; she has 3 children, Monique, Ciji, and Christi; who have blessed her with 7 grand children and two great grand children. "Tillie" spent most of her life working in a laundry and led a very simple life. At some point in her younger life she developed a habit of smoking and drinking. Her Mother was Maude Lawton, one of Charles J's four daughters and sister of Bettye'.

Maude went home to be with the Lord in 1988. "Tillie" was very close to her Mother; even like best friends too. Her grief was so deep she said she would not be able to attend her Mother's funeral without a drink. I, her Aunt Bettye; was in Topeka for my sister Maude's; Tillie's Mother's going home celebration. I remember persuading her to trust God, He would take the appetite of smoking and drinking away from her if she would give her heart to Christ. She didn't think she could give those habits up on her own.

Phyllis gave her heart to Jesus sitting on the porch where her Mother had lived that night I shared the Lord with her. Oh what a beautiful night; she was totally transformed and has lived a consistent christen life every since. She looks forward to that great ay she will be eternally in the presence of the Lord She is the second oldest daughter of Maude and Richard Lawton's.

7.2.8 *Charles Sheldon Sudduth*

My baby brother Charles Sheldon was born in Oklahoma in 1909. He was 3 1/2 older than me. They called him "Pretty boy".

He wasn't named Charles Sheldon until he was 3 years old. He was named Charles after my Papa and Sheldon after Charles Sheldon; who wrote the book "In His Steps". Charles Sheldon man was very prominent Christian Minister not far from where we lived who helped to make ways for the black people during the time of segregation. I guess Mama and Papa ran out of names after 7 kids *(Smiles)*.

Sheldon and I were close "Buddies". He and Poly called me "Pete". He taught me how to drive the first car our family bought, an old model "T" Ford.

By the way, Sheldon was converted at the Age of 12 and never knew what living a life of a worldly sinner was like.

Sheldon started dating Mildred Jones who lived in Oskaloosa Kansas, about 36 miles from Topeka Kansas our home town. When he was about 16 and I was 13 years old we would drive to see his girl friend Mildred. I often rode down there with him and played with Mildred's youngest sister Vadeth. We would teeter totter on a teeter totter. We don't hear of things for kids to play on today like that.

Sheldon married Mildred when he was 17 and she was 19 years old. They were married about 30 years when she died with breast cancer. They had 3 children (Names in order of their birth): Charles, Nadine and Edwyn Elon. Mildred was the love of his life a very sweet lady who died at the age of 50. They both were very devout Christians, and when she died he was afraid to be alone.

Women of course began to pursue this eligible bachelor. He needed to be protected and so he married a lady 9 years older than he was; her name was Ruth. Ruth was a lovely Christian; but never told him she had Cancer before they married. She died about 3 or 4 years after they married.

Margaret was available waiting for Ruth to pass, And about 7 weeks after Ruth's death she was the fortunate person to catch this handsome eligible bachelor. She had two young Daughters by a previous marriage; Sharon and Valorie. He adopted the two girls.

He was devoted to Mama. She never had to want for anything after Papa died. Sheldon was always there for her. He said one time; my wife comes first but Mama is next.

He went home to be with the Lord saying "Glory to God" when he was 86 years of age in 1995.

Sheldon wrote a book of poems; this was one of the gifts God Gave to him and of course he sang with the "Gospel four Quartette" for about 50 years. He was also a deacon in the Church Of God at 12th and Lane for many years. I remember my four brothers singing together many times with Buck directing. Buck Knew harmony like no one I've ever heard before. He sang tenor, Poly sang lead, Elsberry sang baritone, and Sheldon sang bass.

7.2.8.1 Children's memory of Sheldon

Figure 54 – Left – Sheldon and Mildred Jones Sudduth (1st wife) with Nadine and Charles. Right (2nd wife) Ruth and Sheldon Sudduth

I am sorry I don't have a picture of his 3rd wife Margaret. He was married to her 30 yeas before he passed. His 2nd wife Ruth died after only 4 years of marriage to him. He was married to his first wife Mildred for 30 years before she passed.

My brother Sheldon in the picture above wrote the following poems; I chose only two of the 100 book of poems he wrote to put in this book.

RIDING HOME ON A HEAVEN-BOUND TRAIN

Oh, my brother, the time is drawing nigh,
All our troubles will soon be o'er
We're traveling to our heavenly home on high:
Get your tickets now and get on board.

Chorus:
We are rolling on the that heaven-bound train,
Get your tickets today, don't wait;
We are striving with all our might and our main,
Just to pay fare through those pearly gates.

This train is now rolling right at hand;
God's agents are bidding you to board;
He will have mercy if you demand,
Save your soul from that hell-bound hoard.

You can't get the wrong train on this line,
There is only one traveling this way.
It has one track and on a heaven-bound time,
Going straight to where our God holds sway.

On this heaven-bound train there's room to spare,
God will take all who care to go;
Here on earth is where you pay your fare;
Do not pay it to that place of woe.

THE HEAVEN-SENT WIND

As I sit here at my writing desk
And hear the birds twittering in their nest;
The wind is rustling in the trees
And on my face come a fresh, cool breeze.

Who sent it, the God of love
He knows my trouble the way above;
Sent that cool breeze right in here
To let me know that He is near.

And as my trouble puts my brain to rack,
My poor heart is just about to crack;
A soothing breeze right to my soul
He send to push me to my goal.

Not just a mere cool earthly wind,
That is not the kind my Savior sends;
But one that pierces and soothes the heart
And causes sweet tears of joy to start.

It calms aching heart and troubled mind,
Oh! God is so merciful, just and kind;
He knows our cares, he knows our all,
He saved men from the Adamic fall.

Now brother, when you start to sink,

You feel that you are on the brink;
Pray for the wind God sent my way,
To blow you from sin and dismay.

That wind can stop all hell's wrath,
And blow even Satan from your path;
Just open your heart to God and pray,
He'll send that wind into your soul to stay.

GIVE UP YOUR ALL

Won't you come and give God your heart?
    Give up your heart today.
Will you please from sin depart?
    Leave it and from it stay.

O give up sin, my brother,
    Give up to God your all:
When you turn to Him, He will help you,
    If you give up to Him your all.

Will you give up your cards, my brother?
    Why do you so long delay?
Turn to God, there is no other,
    Throw all your trash away.

Now if you have given up your sins,
    Turn up the narrow way;
Praise God for his taking you in,
    And press on to the perfect day.

KNOW HIM

Christ, the mighty God of yore,
    Who in a manager was born;
He helped the rich as well as the poor,
    And from fearful death the sting has
drawn.

He who stilled the tempest wild,
    And calmed the raging sea;
The same who took a little child
    As and example for the older to be.

The God who delivered the Hebrew children,
    And Daniel from the lion's den;
One who many a shackle has broken,
    Stands ready to take you in.

He's wounded for all our transgressions,
    And by whose stripes we are healed;
Died and made our intercession,
    For our lives to God he appealed.

He to prove his Messiahship sign
    To his doubtful race the Jews;

Gave up life for three day's time,
    But has risen again, 'tis good new.

This same good, merciful Father,
    Who in all points was tempted as we;
Leaving for us an example to follow,
    And truly like him we'll be.

His head with radiant light is crowned,
    His lips with grace o'erflow;
With him Lord of beauty and renown,
    We shall live forevermore.

A WITSFUL PRAYER

Dear Christ, my comfort and my stay,

Please help me on life's rugged way;
Keep my feet ever in the path,
Till thy kingdom I shall reach at last.
May my will, Lord, be always thine,
Meek of heart and of a humble mind;
Help me dear Savior always to choose
The right words thou would have me to use.
Let my light shine as bright as day,
Thus to illuminate another's dark way;
Then, when at last my work here is done,
Evening has come at the set of sun.
Take my soul, Lord, to rest with thee,
We'll praise thy name through eternity.

I would like to say something that is so very special about my brother Sheldon right here; I feel that it bearers recognition. He was converted at the age of 12 and was consistent in living a beautiful Christian life all of his days. He sang with the gospel four quartet for forty years; was a deacon in the church of God in Topeka, Kansas; a man always in good standing. He worked in the Santa Fe Offices for years and had his own successful janitorial service for years. He married Margaret his third wife after both Mildred and Ruth were dead.

He lived a beautiful life with Margaret for 30 years before he went home to be with the Lord. Margaret had two lovely daughters before they were married by her first husband; who had passed away; Sharon and Valerie. Sheldon and hi first wife (his youth sweetheart Mildred Jones) had 3 wonderful children

Margaret was supposed to send me information about his life and ministry with Bay Ridge Christian College which I haven't received yet. I remember the ministry was second to none. But details I am not recalling at this time. I do remember he was an officer and one of the founders of that College. I put some of his 100 poems above. I do have his book of poems.

I must tell you he was a Mama boy. He loved my mother to the death. He was always there for her. Anything she wanted or needed he got it for her and he was there when ever she called.

7.2.9 Bettye Gyle Sudduth Guillory

Now for some stories about me.

I am, Bettye Gyle Sudduth, the youngest of the nine children born to Charles and Dora Sudduth in 1912 in Topeka Kansa.

I was a Change of Life baby. Mama had me at the age of 39. She never had hot flashes or had a period after I was born. At my birth she was very ill, near death, but the saints prayed for her. God healed her and me. So here I am writing this book today at 95 years of age; with a young heart and spirit.

I was born with out a name just like my brother Sheldon. Everybody called me "Deedlelump" until I was 3 years old. One day when I was 3 years old Mama took me to town shopping. She was shopping and I got lost. When Mama found me with two clerks, who had me sitting on the top of the counter in the jewelry department and who were talking to me. They asked me what my name was and I told them I didn't have a name. They told Mama if she would name me after them and would bring me back they would give me a diamond ring.

Their names were Bettye and Gyle. So my Mama named me Bettye Gyle after them. But Mama never took me back to pick up that ring. The church we went to in those days did not believe in wearing jewelry.

My Mama used to take me with her whenever she went to pray for the sick. I was like a little old lady, being a change of life baby. I grew up in Church. I took piano lessons and played the piano for the church as a teenager. I directed a youth choir and sang in a trio with my sister-in-law Mildred (my brother Sheldon's wife) and Edith Grizzel. Edith was my brother Sheldon's best friend Frank Grizzel's wife.

I graduated from Topeka High School in 1932 with a class of 425 Students. This was the first class to graduate from the newly built High school.

7.2.9.1 *Marriage and Children*

John Guillory was tall and handsome and very popular at Kansas Vocational School. He loved to play basketball. He graduated from Kansas Vocational School valedictorian of his class. I used to watch their games and met him there. Sometime after his graduation, I married John Louis Guillory May 30, 1937. He was 20 years old at the time and I was 24.

A year and one week after we married our first baby, Nesbia Greta was born on June 8 1938. She looked like a China doll. My 2nd born, John Basil, came the next year on July 19, 1939. He was a beautiful reddish brown color and looked like a little Indian papoose. Paquita Ylonne, my last born, came on September 16, 1941. She was gorgeous and prettiest of all *(Smiles)*. She looked like a little Italian baby.

People didn't want to believe the three children were mine because they didn't look like me. They all favored their Dad's side of the family. People thought I was the baby sitter. I had to take my children out of an all Black school and put then in Catholic School. When my children were young and were going to an all black school they were picked on by black children; because of their light skin and nice hair. By the way; their father was French Creole and I had the mixture of Irish, Indian and black. The melting pot or mixture of nationalities of course brought about the results of my children looking mulatto.

Figure 55 –Paquita Y Guillory Wheeler, Bettye Guillory, Johnny Guillory, and Nesbia Guillory Lopes

Nesbia was 7, Johnny was 6 and Paquita was 4 years old when I divorced their father in 1945. I was living in Topeka, Kansas at the time.

I met Richard Lavelle at a camp meeting in West Middlesex, Pennsylvania. We were married in 1946 and divorced 2 years later.

We moved in 1954 to Springfield, Massachusetts when Nesbia was 15, Johnny was 14, and Paquita was 12 years old. They spent their teenage years there.

Nesbia and Johnny both graduated from high school in Springfield, Massachusetts.

Paquita got sick in her senior year of high school. She never did to back to complete her schooling. She lacked 4 months of graduating from high school.

My youngest daughter Paquita was 4 months shy of completing her senior year in high School when she became ill. I took her to the doctor and I found out she had been using her lunch money to buy cigarettes. She was very anemic and to weak to deal with the stairs as school. Of course she promised me, she would go back the next year and finish school but didn't. When she did get better, she went to Beauty School and became a Beauty Operator. She never took the state board. She eventually did get her GED Certificate when she was in her fifties.

Johnny left home to join the Navy just before his 18th birthday. I had to sign for him to join. Nesbia left home when she married Ronny Lopes when she was 18. Paquita left home when she turned 18.

In 1959, I met Andrew Braxton, who was in the Air Force, while I was living in Springfield, Massachusetts. We married in 1959 and moved to Bangor, Maine in 1959 and then to Canada in 1962. In 1964, we moved to Spokane, Washington.

I sold my home in Spokane Washington and moved to Brooklyn New York in 1972 to live with my Daughter Paquita, her Husband Keith and 3 children for a year. At that time All three of her children were quite young. Angela was 12, Tony Was 9 and Deryck was 7 years old.

Although we divorced in 1972, I continued to make Spokane my home until 1981. Then I moved to Bellevue, Washington for 1 year. Since then Federal Way, Washington has been my home for the last 27 years.

Today my children are in their sixties they are very devoted to me and have spoiled me; I never have to want for a thing; they are exceptionally good to me.

The Lord has blessed me with my three children. All told, I have 3 children, 11 Grandchildren, 12 Great-Grandchildren and 1 little Great-Great-Grandson.

Figure 56 Bettye's 3 children and 9 of her 11 grand children

7.2.9.1.1   *Nesbia Greta Guillory Lopes*

Nesbia was a beautiful young girl, very industrious, and tall. Nesbia was self conscious of her height so I sent her to modeling school when she was 17. I told her that tall girls make the most beautiful models.

It must have worked because at 18 Nesbia met and married Ronald Anthony Lopes Senior in 1957. Ronnie Lopes who was of Portuguese decent and was in the Air Force as an Air Force Policeman. Ronnie was very handsome, an inch or so shorter than Nesbia.

Ronnie was transferred to Milldenhall, England for 2 years where their first child Gina Gyle was born in 1959. When they moved back to Springfield, Massachusetts, Rhonda Bridgette was born in 1961 and Ronald Anthony Junior in 1963. She later moved to Spokane, Washington in 1969 to be near me. She later moved to Seattle, Washington in 1975.

Figure 57 - Tony, Gina, Nesbia, and Rhonda Lopes

Nesbia was in Banking for almost 20 years; promoted from bank teller to customer service, to payroll, assistant bank manager, then became manager and up to a Bank officer. Nesbia has achieved many honors in banking through the years.

She started out as a bank teller for Sea First National Bank in Spokane Washington. She then was promoted to customer service. In 1975 she was transferred to Seattle, Washington to work in pay roll. She then went on to become Managers Assistant and then later became Manager of Madison Street Branch. Her last Promotion was to the head office as a Bank Officer. Sadly after 19 1/2 years of service with this bank she and 300 other Employees were laid off.

Nesbia's personality, ability and knowledge have earned her jobs with high positions that have made her popular and acquired many friends through the years. This severed her in good stead as she is currently an Assistant Manager at the American Pipleline Company.

Nesbia has also worked for many years in Crime Stoppers.

Nesbia G. Lopes, my first born daughter, is my computer helper. When I need help, and don't know about things on my new XP 2000 computer. She comes to my rescue. My youngest daughter Paquita and her two sons Anthony P Goss and Deryck K Goss blessed me with a new computer on my 91st birthday.

Nesbia is very kind to me, extremely generous to her Mother. She takes care of my immediate needs, and is my power of Attorney. She has been a great help to me in getting this book together.

Nesbia has been there for me through thick and thin. During the physical attacks I had from the year 2001 - 2006. She had a lot to deal with as I was rushed to the hospital emergency room 9 times through my 3 times in Rehab. She was a real jewel to me taking care of me. I depend on her a lot. I'm a blessed Mother to have her as my daughter. Thank God.

7.2.9.1.2   *John Basil Guillory*

John Basil (Johnny) my one and only son, after graduating from high school went into the Navy for three years. Johnny joined the Navy when he was 17 years old. I had to sign for him because he wasn't quite 18 years old.

When he came out of the Navy he decided he wanted to play a guitar, He worked hard to master the instrument. Music is his hobby. He is the only one in my immediate family that is following through on our family musical talent. He plays the lead and bass guitar and sings also. It thrills my heart to know that for years he played in worldly bands, and now he is singing and playing for the Lord and with worship teams.

After leaving the Navy, he also decided to become a master hair stylist. Over the next 35 years, he owned 4 different styling salons. He won first place in a National Hair styling contest in Philadelphia, Pennsylvania and was awarded a trophy. He became a famous hair stylist through out the Seattle area. He is a chip off of the old block *(Smiles)*. Yours truly was in the cosmetology profession for 53 years.

After he retired from the Beauty business he became a successful car sales man for about 10 years. He now works with his 2nd wife in the catering business.

Johnny married his first wife Patricia "Pattie" Saloy in 1967 and had two sons by her: John Basil Junior and Zarr Del. They divorced after 35 years of marriage.

John Basil Junior is a contractor in erecting buildings. He is a hard working gifted young man and is very successful in that business. He is married to Christie who is a lovely young lady who has a special gift of hair styling and owns her own home salon. They have a beautiful baby girl about 2 1/2 years old at this time named Lola Renee.

Johnny's youngest son Zarr Del Guillory, by Pattie, is working as successful hair stylist for the last 15 years and has his own cosmetic sales department. He gives services to the elite and is well liked with great hair styling unique techniques and skill. He is following in the family tradition like me (his grand Mother) and then his Dad.

Johnny has son, Mark Darnell Mc Fadden from Ruth Mc Fadden who is his oldest son. Mark is now 43. His mother, Ruth, was a singer of renown when Johnny met her some 40 years ago. Her story is told later in this section. She has been a good mother and has done an excellent job of raising Mark alone. She has been like a daughter to me through the years. Mark is a graduate of Howard University.

Johnny has a daughter, Suzette Lynn Georgia from Mamie Davis who is his oldest daughter. Mamie later married Joseph Davis. Joe died in his early fifties in the year 1991. He adopted Suzette Lynn when she was only 5 years old. Suzette graduated from Howard University also. Suzette was very popular through her school years and excelled in many activities. She was made queen of her high school prom. Suzzette has 3 brilliant daughters: Senta, Shalimar, and Serria. Senta, the oldest daughter, is now 28 years of age and is working on her Doctors Degree. Shalimar is married and has a son named Joseph Mathias (born September 29 2006). Shalimar's son Joseph has made me a Great-Great-Grandmother for the first time. Suzzette's youngest daughter, Serria, is in college.

Figure 58 Suzette Lynn Georgia (oldest daughter of Johnny Guillory), Bettye Guillory (Johnny's Mother), and Senta Georgia (Suzette's first daughter 2 more were born after Senta; Betty's great grand-daughter)

Johnny has a daughter, Leslie Diane Lattanzio by Delores Lattanzio who is his youngest daughter. Leslie's mother, Delores, is an Italian who was a very beautiful lady and also a Hair stylist. She was a good mother to Leslie and did a lovely job of raising her. Delores has never married through these 41 years since she gave birth to Leslie. Leslie after two years of College decided to train and sell Horses. I think she is a horse lover like her daddy was. The only difference is she has show horses that jumped fences etc. She trains them and sells them.

Figure 59 - Johnny Guillory and youngest daughter Leslie Lattanzio

I remember when Johnny lived in Chattaroy, Washington. He had three riding horses. One was named Dawn with a gray with blonde mane. Miss Chattaroy was brown with a black mane. Sonny was Brown and had a blonde mane. Johnny's boys rode Sonny in their younger years.

Johnny married again after being divorced about two years. His second wife is named Victoria Lopez a beautiful Mexican lady. She is and excellent cateress and has a top position with a Mexican Foods Company which services Mexican stores, restaurants, parties and weddings. Vickie has 3 grown up children by a previous marriage.

Victoria has a spiritual ministry and is connected with many evangelist and prophets, their services are phenomenal. She loves the Lord. I had prayed for Johnny's salvation for more than forty five year. Vickie led Johnny into a saving knowledge of Jesus Christ. He is now on fire for the Lord Jesus Christ growing by leaps and bounds.

Johnny has prophesied as well as Paquita over me and encouraged me to not give up the vision God gave me 21 years ago. That vision is now being fulfilled.

7.2.9.1.3   *Paquita Yvonne Guillory Goss Wheeler*

My daughter Paquita Wheeler, my youngest is my prayer partner and confident. We are very close spiritually. She has been and is faithful to pray with me and for me. At the beginning when I started working on this book she worked with me, by making contacts for me through calls and mailing to key people.

Paquita married her first husband Keith Bertrum Goss in 1960. He is half Chinese and half Jewish. Paquita was 18 years old at the time.

Keith in later life became President of a New York City Bank for some years. Paquita has 3 lovely wonderful children by him: "Angela Monique Goss," Anthony P. "Tony" Goss and Deryck Keith Goss. Keith and Paquita were married for 15 years before divorcing.

She later married James Wheeler Jr in 1976. They had no children together. Jim Wheeler who has been a good provided for his wife and he has been very gracious and kind and good to me. He is a very industrious person. He was in the Air Force for 20 years and worked at Grumman's for almost 20 years. He is still working at age 75 as a patrolman. Paquita lived in New York for more than 40 years; but she has now been living in Cornelius North Carolina for the last 4 years to be near her Granddaughter Angelina.

Figure 60 - Angela Goss

Her first child Angela Monique favors the Goss side of her family. She was born in 1960 in Bangor, Maine. I named her Angela and her Dad named her Monique, beautiful girl. Angela graduated from Mammoth University in New Jersey. She Graduated Magna Cum Laude. Her interests includes dance, theater, hiking and sky diving. She was sky diving even at the age of 40. She loves teaching special Education. Her heart is wrapped up in the welfare of these special children. She is deeply involved with social workers and with the parents of these children. This position must be quite a challenge; but extremely rewarding.

Her 2nd child is Anthony Patrick Goss. He grew to become one of The most brilliant, honorable young men I know. He is a young man that is blessed with great wisdom. He was a physical Ed. instructor for 14 years. He was then promoted to Vice Principal, and now is Principal of an elementary school with about 335 students. He is a stickler for eating and living a healthy life style.

He and I love to hold great conversations together. He is the one grand son that never fails to send me a beautiful card for every occasion, and most of the time there is a check with the card.

I must mention the fact that Tony also remembers his Mother; Father and Paternal Grandmother like he does me. He is the most thoughtful young man I have every known; of course very special to me. I do love all of my grand children. But honestly he is very close to me; we talk about deep Spiritual things. He is a young man whom God has given great Wisdom.

Figure 61 L-R Deryck and Estrelletta Goss, Daughter Angelina Niclole Goss

Deryck is Paquita's 3rd born child. He was born in May 30, 1965 in Maryland. He is a young man of great Integrity and wonderful family man finished college in two years. He is a very brilliant person who never had to study hard but had natural ability. He earned a high position as supervisor, earning 100 thousand dollars a year, over about 13 employees for a company that kept accounts for retired Teachers.

He married Estralletta "Starr" Goss who is a school teacher sometime around 2000. They have Paquita's first and only grand child, Angelina Nichol, a beautiful smart intelligent, active little 4 years old.

They were transferred to Charlotte North Carolina in the year 2000. He and his wife Estraletta Vega; who is from Puerto Rica; she was working for the same company he worked for.

Estraletta's nick name is "Star"; she and Deryck had a beautiful daughter born on November 26th 2003; Paquita's first and Only grand child. Paquita was 62 and just getting her first grand child. Paquita moved from New York after living there for more than 40 years to Charlotte North Carolina 2 years ago; where her youngest son Deryck and wife Star have lived for about 7 years.

I use calling cards and talk often with her.

She too is a woman of great faith and has many talents. God has endowed her with great wisdom. I would call her a Prophetess; because she has foretold so many things years ago that have come to pass, Like "Christian Theatre". She even organized a Christian Theater program named "The hallelujah Christian Theater". Together we organized other chapters. She set up a chapter in New York where she lived at that time, one in Spokane Washington and one in Seattle Washington. As you all may know Christian Theater has become prevalent in these last few years. The first Christian Theatre production I remember seeing is "China Cry", the life story of Nora Lamb.

Figure 62 - The Halleluiah Christian Theater Group of Seattle. Paquita is seated in bottom row center with the lavender blouse and boots on.

Another prophecy she gave years ago was that there would be "Christians taking communion together, through world wide Television". That happened years later, conducted by Kenneth Copeland Ministries over Christian Television.

She has multiple God given talents and has been a real servant of God by helping so many people; especially trouble young people.

One of her God given talents which she is presently doing is designing ethnic custom made Jewelry. She has sent me some very unique pieces, like ear rings and necklaces to match; only one of a kind.

She is my encourager. She knows me better than any one but the Lord. She knows both the natural and spiritual sides of me.

Paquita had a vision of starting Christian Theatre. She organized a chapter in New York called "The Hallelujah Christian Theatre". We were in close contact with Each other and so I started two chapters on the west coast, one in Spokane Washington and one in Seattle Washington. These never became full blown; however the vision has been fulfilled in recent years by many others writing plays that are now being shown in theatres all over the United States. She has had training as an interior decorator also.

7.2.9.1.4   *Naomi Ruth McFadden-Edwards*

Figure 63 - Naomi Ruth McFadden

I am a southern lady born in Charleston, S.C., raised and schooled in the city of New York. I'm compelled to mention Charleston because it's who I am in my sole. I dearly love being a native of this historic city and one must first know that in order to know who I am.

At the age of thirteen, while attending junior high school, I became a member of a gospel singing group, "The Dorothy Rivers Gospel Singers". Aside from performing for churches, we became a regular part of the Joe Bostic Gospel Hour heard Sunday Mornings on New York's radio station, WLIB. This was my entry into the world of entertainment. I was "bitten" by the bug and loved the attention. A few years later thanks to a neighbor, I was registered and called to perform on Harlem Apollo Theatre's Amateur hour. I won four weeks consequently, and was awarded a recording contract. Minimum success as a recording artist, but clearly put me on a road that would dictate the course of my life. At this time I was a high school student and the demands of the "business" was an unwelcome intrusion according to my Mom. This lead to a very short career. However, after graduation from high school, and one semester at Fordham University, the stage was calling and I began my career as an entertainer.

My travels as an entertainer took me all over the world; I worked with most of the famous names of that era, entertainers and political people of the day. It was exciting, rewarding and I had the time of my life, I felt blessed.

In 1961, a singing engagement took me to the lovely New England town of Springfield Massachusetts. While performing at a nightclub in

Springfield, I met John Basil Guillory, one of the most important relationships and lasting friendships of my life; hence, my connection to the Sudduth/Guillory family. A four year relationship produced a son for me, for John; and a grandson for Nana, Bettye Sudduth Guillory.

Having not met most of Nana's extended family, I'm certain many reading this book will ask, who the heck is Ruth McFadden, and why is she in this book. It's simple, aside from being the Mother of one of her grandsons; I became "a daughter" a very long time ago. She's an amazing lady, I love her, admire her; and she's my Nana, in the depths of my sole.

7.2.9.2 *My career in Cosmetology*

Being a single Mom after I divorced John was quite and experience. After two years of welfare, I determined to prepare my self to support my children. I hated being on welfare; John had migrated to California. The law in those days would not pursue men for child support if they left the state and went to another state.

I decided to go to the State supervisor "Frank Long" and ask him if they would support my children and send me to beauty school. I was determined to support my own children; if I had to work my fingers to the bone. It's for the birds to depend on welfare. He said he had never had anyone on welfare want to get off and go to school before. He admired me for having that desire.

He was able to get Welfare to send money to my sisters to support my children. But I had to borrow money to go to beauty school. I enrolled at the Madame CJ Walker Beauty School in Kansas City Missouri in January 1946 and finished in July 1946. I received 1000 hours training; which in those days was all I needed to get my state license. It was in an all black school; those were the days when every thing was segregated. However, 8 years later I had moved to Springfield Massachusetts and went to Trade Beauty School. I received 500 more hours of training in learning how to do the white techniques; thus I was able to work on both white and blacks hair. When desegregation laws were passed I then worked in salons that were mixed and taught in white schools both techniques; after I received my teacher's certificate.

I worked with Ava and Albelle Atkinson in their salon until my mother gave me space to build my own salon on the east side of my family home.

After five years I moved to California, worked in a beauty salon there. I stayed in California about 9 months at that time.

Through the years I owned my own salons for more than 25 years. While teaching at Spokane Community College in Washington state, I was called to become a State Board examiner. Governor Dixie Lee Ray had appointed me as the only person of color to work with 4 Caucasian examiners. It was exciting and rewarding for 6 years when the state took practical exams out of the schools for 8 years. I and several other examiners worked hard to get regulation again.

Cosmetology exams were finally voted in again within Washington. But it was not the same; because working on mannequins is not like having live models to work on.

I became a Cosmetologist; Beauty School Instructor; then joined the Alpha Chi Pi Omega international Greek letter Organization for cosmetologist. Marjory Stewart Joyner the President of that organization who lived in Chicago Illinois

Appointed me Basilus of the Springfield Massachusetts chapter. I was promoted then to an international organizer for the sorority and held that position for 17 years; I received a Plaque of honor for my years of service.

I taught about 35 instructors how to give state board exams. Seven schools joined me as I started and examining service of my own in 1993. I directed "Cosmetology Practical Evaluation Service" for about 9 years. Praise God for the talents he has given me and the blessings; I was able to extend toward many others through the years. If I have accomplished any thing through the years; I owe all the credit honor and Praise to my Lord and Savior Jesus Christ.

7.2.9.3 *Becoming a Book Author*

In October 23' 2000, I moved to Patchogue, New York from Federal Way, Washington. There I spent eleven and a half months with my daughter Paquita and Her husband "Jim" Wheeler.

The presidential election was occurring that year. Shortly after arriving there The Lord began to give me prophetic words for George W. Bush, then Governor of Texas, who was running for office of The President of the United States. I got 3 different prophecies, one right after another came to me. I sent copies of these prophecies to many Executives and Pastors.

While I was in New York, my adopted spiritual Granddaughter Donna Olson from Federal Way, Washington, sent me a Book titled "The Final Quest" written by Rick Joyner, Pastor of the "Morning of Star Church" in Charlotte, North Carolina. When I read this book I thought it was one of the greatest books I had ever read. Of course, I've read a lot of Books through the Years. "The Final Quest" was about Heaven. God had shown Rick visions and dreams. There were so many things it revealed that were new to me, and were in keeping with the Word of God. I became so excited; right away my desire was to be under Rick's ministry in Charlotte, North Carolina.

My grand son Deryck Goss (Paquita's youngest son) and his wife Estraletta both worked for the same company which in 2001 moved their Business headquarters to Charlotte North Carolina. They had a home built for them before moving to Charlotte. It was a big beautiful 5 bed room home.

I moved from Patchogue, New York to Charlotte, North Caroling on October 3, 2001. I believed the Lord had given me the desire to move to Charlotte and my Grandchildren welcomed me into their home where I spent the next 3 months in their home with them.

I then moved into a senior citizen's apartment in Charlotte. Shortly after moving there and getting settled, I read an announcement in a paper that Margaret Bigger, a popular writer and Instructor, was starting a class on "How to write Memoirs" on January 20th 2002.

I was inspired just thinking about what it would mean to me to attended this class. I would get ideas about how to write my book which I had started writing on in 1989. Through the years, I only taken time out occasionally from my busy schedule to sit down and write on this manuscript.

So, I had great anticipation about my enrolling in her class. It was designed especially for senior citizens; who were either writers or interested in learning how to write. There were 13 of us who attended this class, both men and women ranging in ages from 55 on Up. I finished the class with flying colors. I have benefited tremendously from the book provided in the class and the things I learned in class. As a matter of fact, I am still using the ideas I've have taken away from her class for this book.

During the class, I told Margaret Bigger about the book I was writing on my Family Tree. She wanted to make sure the title of my book would grab the interest of people, and motivate them to read it. Margaret and the class thought the title, "How the Sudduth Melting Pot Began", would be good. I believe when people see the title they will be curious to know what the melting pot means and what the story is all about.

7.3 Mama and Papa: Their later Years

Figure 64 - Mama and Papa Charles (2 years before his passing in 1945)

I will proceed with my story about my Papa Charles after telling you a little bit about his and Mama Dora's offspring.

My Papa, besides having all those Gifts I related to you at the beginning of this chapter, was a Minister of the Gospel, and pastor for the "Church of God" at 11th And Freeman in Kansas City Kansas at one time. He loved the Lord; He was a very meek and humble man who loved his colored Children. For in those days, we were called colored because we were of mixed blood. I was surprised when in the fifties people started calling themselves black; all dark skins or African Americans began to be black and beautiful. I don't know who started that one; but I've had a hard time getting use being called black because of the segregation in the south.

For instance the bus driver ordered my mom to sit in the back of the bus with the Blacks and Papa to sit in the front with the white people. Of Course, no way Papa was going to sit in the front with the whites and Mama sits in the back with the Blacks. My brother Buck was 14 years old at that time and was endowed with a high temper that could have caused a lot of trouble. So in order to avoid problems my parents thought it best to move our family up north to Kansas from Oklahoma.

Segregation was the norm in the south especially, riots were happening of which my uncle Elsberry (Ebb) got involved. There have been different stories told about the riots at that time; but this was before I was born and so I will tell the story as I remember Mama telling it to me. This black 14 year old kid was walking down the side walk and of course black people had to get off the side walk when they passed white folks in those days. This kid didn't and a white guy and his girl friend were coming down the street and the white guy deliberately kicks the kid off the side walk. Seemingly it happened in front of my Uncle Ebbs barber shop.

Mama said Uncle Ebb was not married; he was a handsome young red headed man, very nice, never drank or ever harmed any one before. But this day, he went to a bar and got drunk. He was really angry and killed 7 white men. Uncle Ebb was strung up, by some whites but wasn't able to be killed that way. He was put in the back seat of a car. They were carrying him to jail, when some one shot him through the back of the Ford car and killed him. My parents took their family and headed north after that. They landed in Independence Missouri; stayed there only a short time, then moved to Topeka Kansas; the Capital of Kansas; where I was born.

My parents joined the Church of God; at that time it was located on Lincoln Street and Brother John Clark was the pastor. We had one white family that attended out church at that time. They were the Beechums. They had one son. It was a very strict church that had a lot dos and don'ts; no jewelry, no short skirts of pants and no make up for women. The church finally built a bigger church on 12th and Lane Street. Our family was very active in the church.

I played the piano, directed a youth choir, and sang in a trio with my sister-in-law Mildred and a friend Edith Grizzell. We wore dresses made alike.

Here's more about Papa's life, he loved cats, and we always owned one. Funny I never really liked cats; but we had rats. Mister Frank Ford, a neighbor across the alley from us had horses, I think they draw rats. I remember standing on a stool with a cup of water on a little table combing Papa's hair. I was a natural born hair dresser, even as a kid I loved to do hair. Papa was faithful in bringing his check home to Mama, she would give him a couple of dollars and he would go buy tobacco. Papa loved coffee and of course Mama didn't approve of him chewing tobacco or drinking coffee. But Papa's only pleasures I think were, the tobacco chewing, drinking coffee and eating sweets. I don't think drinking coffee or chewing tobacco and eating sweets would keep him out of heaven; but perhaps it could have sent him to heaven quicker.

Papa was a good father and a very good provider; it's for sure he loved Mama. On their 50th wedding anniversary he said he loved her better than he did the day he married her. I remember him saying the blacker the berry the sweeter the juice; referring to my Mama color.

She definitely was the boss. She handled those 4 boys like she was as big as they were, she was only 5 feet "tall.

Even though Papa was white he loved his colored children. I remember people whispering; I could tell what they were saying when we were with Papa "look at that white man with those black kids". Segregation was prevalent in those days; we had to sit up in peanut heaven if we went to a white theater (up in the third balcony). When we went up town shopping and got hungry we would have to stand at a counter in the dime store to eat a hamburger or a hot dog; we couldn't sit at a counter with white folks to have a meal.

I am remembering incidents that happen during my childhood; Mama planted a garden every year; and raised chickens, we had our own eggs. I remember when our hens hatched baby chicks and we kept them in the house until they had grown a little; especially when it was so cold in the winter time. We had a cherry tree in our back yard; I can almost taste the pie now Mama made from the pie cherries we picked from the old cherry tree. I visualize seeing the ole white horse Papa owned that was blind in one eye; and the green wagon Papa put chairs in, for us to sit on as we were driven to church out in pierce addition; it was about a five mile ride, bumping along in the ole wagon on Sunday morning.

We had a state camp meeting in Kansas in July each year for one week and international camp meeting in Sharon Pennsylvania in August each year. Mama always wore white dresses and white shoes, every body called her Mother Sudduth, she was noted for her leaping and shouting and praising the Lord. She and Papa would sing duets together. The Charles Sudduth family was a very musical family.

I was married and had moved to Kansas City Missouri; my children were; like Nesbia 7, Johnny 6 and Paquita 4 years old in 1945. John and I were have marital problems, and so Papa came to visit us and as he left he said; Bettye if I were like I use to be I would take a gun and shoot John; for mistreating you and the children; but the Lord had changed him. He was on the way to the train station and he turned around and came back to tell us good by again and left. I watched him as far as I could see him for some reason.

Shortly after he returned to Topeka he called me and said; Bettye you had better come home; the doctor says I have cancer of the stomach. I prepared to leave and went home; two months later Papa went home to be with the Lord. He was so sweet and as very patient as he suffered with that horrible disease. We made him a bed in the living room where we wouldn't have to go up stairs and down to the stairs to take care of him. I trimmed his toe nails one day and he said; I believe the Lord has allowed me to have this disease to take me home, and I said don't say that Papa it might happen; he said but it is true. I ask him if he was ready and he said yes; I said are you afraid and he said no I am not afraid. He saw words written over the top of the piano that said; why should I care? The answer; I shouldn't care, because Jesus cares. He would cry Take it out! But in those days doctors didn't have a cure for cancer.

One night it was pouring down rain and we all came down stairs and Paquita said "It's raining on my grandpa". She was only 4 years old at that time. The Camp meeting was convening that summer when Papa went home to be with the Lord. He passed on my sister Ella Mae's birth day the 14th day of July 1945.

As I was trimming Papa's toe nails one day; he said he believed God had allowed him to have cancer to take him home and I said don't say that Papa, it might come true. He said; but it is true. I said Papa are you ready to go, are you afraid? He said he was ready to go; no I'm not afraid. My father was so sweet, never wanted to be any trouble.

I remember my sister Maude sitting by his bed, and I was standing between the living room and dinning room when he turned and looked at my sister Maude then turned his eyes up toward heaven and breathed his life out sweetly. Pastor Ray S. Jackson was at the camp meeting; from Detroit Michigan. It was perfect timing since Papa had previously requested him to preach his funeral. He was buried in a white suit.

Mama passed four years later and camp meeting was convening around that time also. She went home to receive her reward on July 13th 1949. Her death was very sweet. She had lost weight and was very frail although she was only sick 11 hours with just nausea, she really didn't do a lot of suffering. Mama quoted scriptures all night long saints came and prayed for her.

About 9 O'clock in the morning Mama called Trudy and I to her bed side; as she ask for her written will to sign; while Mildred My sister-in-law and Charlotte Queenery were witnesses to her signing of her will. Mama didn't believe in vitamins and had every thing she wanted to eat, supplied by her children; especially my brother Sheldon who was exceptionally kind to Mama. Next to his wife he made it known Mama was next in his heart and life. The Sunday before Mama passed Sheldon carried her up the steep steps at church; she was so weak, and the following Tuesday she passed. Mama was preparing two years before she passed to go home; she really didn't want to live after Papa died. Sister Edna Burnett loved Mama and made her a beautiful white satin dress.

Mama boldly and proudly announced to all that this dress was going to be her shroud. Mama was preparing to go home two years before she passed. She and Papa were married 52 years when he passed.

Mama did not want any one to mourn when she graduated to Glory; but wanted every one to rejoice. Her request was that all the girls wore white dresses and the boys rented white suits to wear at her celebration. Both Papa and Mama wanted their bible laid on their chest with the 23rd Psalms open as they were laid to rest.

I am still learning and receiving new revelations I have never known before; even though I have read the Holy Bible and receive a lot of knowledge of the word through the years. But I know now it was mostly book knowledge; not revelation knowledge. There is a difference I've found out. I'm so glad God has no respecter of persons, he loves us all the same and believe it or not, age makes no difference. He told me to-day; that I am the apple of His eye, Deuteronomy 32:10. You know what; His timing is not the same as our timing; He is the same yesterday, to-day and for ever Hebrews 13:8.

There will be written manuscripts and Writings about Papa's off-springs and descendents; many of them have Written about their lives and their own families. From the 9 of us who are his birth children; there are many grandchildren and greats; you will find some very interesting stories about their lives. We came from a very talented, and I might say brilliant heritage of accomplishments; you will find that the prayers and examples of our fore parents have been past on to their descendents. Mama and Papa we are truly prayer warriors, they loved the Lord and raised us kids in the admonition and fear of God. I remember as we sat around the old pot belly stove; burning up in front and freezing on our backs, we would have to kneel in prayer at night before we went to bed. Some nights my brother Buck would be their and play the guitar as we would march up to bed, or Mama would play the accordion. We would sing "Little David play on your harp", Hallelujah!

Even today I often dream about the old home place and dream especially about my mom. We would be in church or visiting or something like that.

May you enjoy and may God Bless these stories to your hearts as you read about our loved ones

Chapter 8 -Joseph Sudduth, "Remnants of Grace"

Written by:
Ramel McClelland Eubanks who is great great Granddaughters of Joseph "Joe" Sudduth

Figure 65 – Left - Joseph Sudduth 1870-1917 Right - Daughters of Joseph Sudduth: Naomi, Rose, and Ruby Sudduth

Figure 66 - Leonard Joseph Parker and Rose Sudduth Parker

Figure 67 - Ophelia (daughter), Gywn (granddaughter), and Rose Sudduth Parker

Joseph Sudduth was born to William and Lucy Sudduth around 1878. Ophelia Stone was born to Isabelle Stone, Father's name unknown around 1877. Joseph and Ophelia were united in matrimony in 1893.In Tallapoosa county Alabama as recorded in vital statistics data from rootsweb.com. To this union bore 6 children two deceased in childhood.

Ruby Sudduth	1897-1985
Rafel Sudduth	1898-1919
Naomi Sudduth	1899-1991
Rose Sudduth Parker	1905-2000

Naomi married Johnnie Kaufman and had no children.

Ruby married David Shaw, and had one son Demonthaus (Milton) Shaw, who had one son Herbert Shaw, who had 3 children. Anthony, Trina, and Troy.

Rose married Eddie Boyer and had two girls Laverne, who died from pneumonia while still a baby and Ophelia Isabelle. She had 3 children, one son who was still born and 2 daughters Gwynetta Rose Nevils, and Ramelle Naomi McClelland. Gwynetta had one son, Vincent Timothy Jarrett. Vincent has to date 2 children, Michael and Mikayla.

My Grandmother Rose held us all together; above all she held the hand of God. Some of the stories she shared would have you sitting on the edge of your seat waiting to hear more. Grandmother wanted to be a nurse, and was enrolled in the Kellogg School of Nursing in Michigan. Her brother Rafel was paying her tuition, when he died from black lung disease working in the coal mines. She had to leave school. I remember her saying she wondered why her older sister's wouldn't help. They were too busy with their lives, but she managed to let go of those hurt feelings.

Rose was off to Chicago where she went to beauty school in Waukegan Illinois. She became the first black woman to open a school of cosmetology for women of color.

My Grandmother Rose later in life married Leonard Joseph Parker in the late 1940's whom I knew and loved as a wonderful Grandfather. I remember Grandma saying "he's the only husband I've ever had. "In other words she'd been married before, but this was her husband!

Now when Grandmother was a little girl growing up in Alabama her Mother Ophelia had a dear friend by the name of Leanna Parker Montgomery who was the Mother of Leonard Parker.

Leanna left Alabama and moved to Kansas City, Ophelia moved to Ohio. Now over the years they stayed in touch through letters. I read one of these letters when going through some of Grandmothers things. They talked one to another about how good God had been. They looked forward to seeing each other again one day. This letter was dated 1918. The next year Grandmothers Mother (Ophelia) died. Shortly after that her brother (Rafel) died. My dear Grandmother kept in touch with her Mother's friend over many years.

Bringing you up to speed, as Grandmother told me the story, around the late 40's she received a letter from Leanna telling her that her son Leonard was stationed up her way in Wisconsin. She asked if she could give him information on how to contact her. Needless to say Grandmother agreed. With a smile on her face when telling me this story she said, "I remembered him, but I never imagined he'd be my husband! I was a little girl and he was my brother's age.

My Grandmother and Aunt Naomi (Tuttie) as we called her growing up were 2 praying women and active in church. My Aunt Naomi liked the city life and lived in Chicago as far back as I can remember. We lived in suburb about 45 miles north of Waukegan, which today is a small city itself.

As the 2 sister's were getting older, my Grandmother would try to talk her sister into moving to Waukegan. My Grandfather had built a little studio apartment for Grandmother so that when guests came, they would have a private place of their own. I know my Grandmother had thoughts of her sister.

Naomi and Uncle Johnnie split up. Funny they never divorced. Uncle Johnnie liked his liquor and Naomi loved God. Naomi wouldn't hear of it, however she'd come to visit us on a regular basis. She'd say "Rose, I'm happy where I'm at. "I've got my own place and I've got my church and all. So we were one happy family. Back and forth, and of course visiting one another's churches.

Now Aunt Ruby went for the gold. She moved to California in 1929, and later took up residence in Alaska. She was one of the first black women to work as a welder on the pipe lines. I called Cousin Milton (her son) "Uncle Milton" because she was so much older. My Mother and he were the only 2 children born in that generation. We lived far apart, Uncle Milton in California and us in Illinois. Mom and Uncle Milton were like brother and sister, so Uncle Milton it was, and it rested well with him.

As I look back over the years, Grandmother has been gone 6 years now, it seems like yesterday. Precious memories we hold in our hearts of those gone before us, the heritage we inherited. It's time to pass it on for the generations to come. There are no words to express the joy in knowing the grace of God through the prayers of the generations before us. Many death angels have passed me by. God said "No", I send an angel before you to keep you in the way, and to bring you into the place which I have prepared. Your latter shall be greater than your former.

James 5:16b The effective, fervent prayer of the righteous man avails much.

Psalms 37:25-26 The writer says: I have been young and now I am old: yet I have not seen the righteous forsaken, nor his descendants begging bread. He (God the Father) is ever merciful, and lends; and his descendants are blessed. Family we are blessed!

My sister Gwyn is happily married with 1 son and 2 grandchildren of her own.

My life has taken many twists and turns. I have returned to the land of the living from a 20 plus years of addiction to drugs and alcohol. It's been 4 years now, and I am still free of addictions. But by the grace of God, do I live! Today I'm married to a wonderful man, Mr. Eubanks.

Figure 68 - Joseph and Ramel McCleland Eubanks

God redeems the time not as lost years, but as an experience and an opportunity to share the goodness of God with His people. God's will is that none perish, but all come into the knowledge and acceptance of Him through grace (Christ).

God has restored my life!

God has restored my relationship with my sister whom I love dearly!

God is restoring the Sudduth family, His family!

The grace of God, by Lord and Savior is upon this day!

For I know the plans I have for you, plans for a hope and future hold oh so true, from my heart to your heart. From the heart of God. We are remnants of His Grace!

Chapter 9 - "John Sudduth's Genealogy"

Written by: Robert Blakesleay Senior and Bettye Guillory; Robert was a grand son of Uncle John; Uncle John was the youngest child of the 12 children of William and Lucy Sudduth Senior

Figure 69 – L-R John A. Sudduth,   His wife Holly Mae (Mattox) Sudduth

    1. Hollie Mae ………………………Robert J.

       Mae G. Blakesleay

       Michael G. Latimer …………..Viveanne

       Patricia F. ………………………Brent

       Kathleen Echol

       Brittany"

       Blair "

       Boston"

Christina "

Douglas"

Corey"

Justin "

Ashley"

Brent Elazier

Earl"

Robert R. Blakesleay ....Evelyn-Rosanne

Robert Blaklesleay ....Deidre

Terrance" Urlesse

Robert T. Blakesleay

Steven T. " Snowber

Essence ....Blakesleay

Brittany"

Richard R. Blakesleaay Kimbley

Rhonda "

Bria "

Shelley"

Kenndy"

Robert R. Blakesleay

Ruby"

Joey"

Jamie J. Rainone ....Blakesleay

    2. Anderson Wn. Sudduth

    3. John A. SuduthHazel

    Dwayn Sudduth

    4. Sarah M. Sudduth Barnard

    Barnard J. Snowden

    Anita "

    William A."Yvonne

    Jennifer Snowden

    Marilyn J."

    Sarah Gilmore

    Carol Ann Snowden

    Amanda"

    Suzanne "

    Dondi "

    William "

    4. Anderson J. Sudduth Louise

The names above are all the information I have received on Uncle John's chapter. Robert Blakesleay Sr., Uncle John's grandson promised to write the chapter. The last he told me his computer was out of order.

Figure 70 - John A. Sudduth's children

My Uncle John was married to Hollie Mattox, they lived in Detroit Michigan and had 5 children. I went to visited Aunt Hollie in Detroit many years ago; Uncle John had been died for years at that time. Their oldest son called "Buster" was living with her and was the one to look after his Mother; because I think she was in her 80's at that time.

I remember Aunt Hollie was very heavy and had mingled gray hair; she had on a dirty apron at that time. I caught her as a surprise. Surprisingly enough I seldom ever saw people wearing aprons, only if they were cooks.

Robert Blakesleay Sr. was married to Evelyn Rosanne and they live in Essex Ontario; Robert came to Patchogue Long Island New York in the year 2001 to visit my daughter Paquita, her husband "Jim" Wheeler and me. He only stayed a few hours. At that time he was traveling across country to California where he has a couple of sons; whom he told me were professional and very busy. He did not want to give me their names because of their being so busy, and he didn't want to bother them. I thought he was extremely interested in finding out about his relatives; because he was going to different parts of the country to find them and seemingly was gathering a lot of information I thought. I was very surprised when he didn't send me the information he promised through the years. I had called him and we exchanged e-mail for almost 6 years. I thought he had compiled a lot of information; especially about his grand Father John Sudduth and their family.

Figure 71 - Robert Blakesley

I have heard my Uncle John was a very handsome man and died at a young age. I remember before I came to know Robert I met his Mother by telephone; she was named after her Mother Hollie Mae. I remember talking several times to her over the phone; but I didn't think to get a lot of information from her about the family. I was surprise to know she had passed; she at that time I found out she was in her eighties when she passed. Through the years I have been able to hold conversations with so many of my cousins and relatives by phone, especially as I retired from working so hard as a cosmetologist and had more time on my hands. They didn't call me so much; but I was and even now am the one who believes in making calls to family and friends; especially on special occasions; like Christmas, Thanksgiving and Birthdays.

The youngest of the twelve children in my Father's family was my "Uncle John". I understand he like my Papa was very handsome. But as a matter of fact, I think my Papa's whole family was attractive. I have seen pictures of most all of them. Half of the family was white like Grandma and the other half of them were red skinned like Grandpa.

I received a surprise from Robert Blakesleay last Friday. I received a picture of Uncle John and Aunt Holly. Uncle John looks like Papa he is white with a mustache. I have added a few things recently. However I must cut it off promptly as I wish to have this book finished by August 8th for the Family Reunion date.

Uncle John was the youngest in Papa's family. Uncle John's grandson, Robert Blakesleay, lives in Ontario Canada. He has been working on a chapter about that side of the family tree titled, "John Sudduth's Genealogy". I never saw Uncle John. I think he died when he was fairly young.

Just before the book was completed and ready to send to the publisher I received a picture of Uncle John and Aunt Holly. I also received a picture of their five children and believe it or not A picture of himself. Thanks Robert for telling me you'd send all these things and the information you were gathering. This is all I received and I'm very happy to have it.

Chapter 10- Dora (Culpepper) Sudduth, "Experiences with the Father and Miracles of Today"

Written by:
Sister Beecham; dictated by my Mom in 1935. This is a Phenomenal Story of my Mothers life and ministry that will bring tears to your eyes, and joy to your souls; it is an extra ordinary story that will also warm your heart and make you realize the power of Almighty God and how he works through his children; if they make Him Lord of their lives!

9.1 Introduction

As the number of milestones of our life have been reached, and have passed out of sight forever, and we now stand on the sunset side of time while great eternity draws nearer and nearer, we have become increasingly burdened for the souls of men.

While we see with one glance the appalling traffic of immortal souls to the certain destruction of eternal darkness, the cares and burdens that confront us here, as well as the distress common to men, and with another glorious reward that awaits the faithful servant of God, we cannot but say with Paul of old, (Phil 1:23,24) : *I am in a strait betwixt the two, having a desire to depart, and to be with Christ; which is far better, never the less to abide in the flesh is more needful for you."*

Knowing that sometime (we know neither the day nor the hour), we must bid farewell to all we love and answer to the call of the Father above. We wish to leave a footprint, if but a tiny one upon the sands of time, in the hope that it may encourage some precious soul, and make a little brighter the pathway to heaven.

We have not wished to make it an exhibition of eloquence for the benefit of those who love 'the king's English' neither a sensational story to excite the emotional or superstitious, but rather we have wanted simply to tell all

"The old, old story of unseen things above, of Jesus and His glory, of Jesus and His love."

Humbly, lovingly, therefore we submit to whosoever will read these few words with a prayer that God may bless it to the purpose whereto it has been sent.

The Author;
Dora (Culpepper) Sudduth,
Mother of Bettye (Sudduth) Guillory

9.2 Truths Revealed in Visions

I was converted more than thirty-five years ago, and my soul created anew by the Spirit of God, but from the many things I had heard others relate about their conversions, I felt I had to see a vision of something as a witness of my salvation. For thirteen months, I prayed that I might have a like witness, when a meeting opened at

Mount Zion Baptist Church in Rupesville, Georgia, where we lived at the time. I had been attending for a week when God rewarded my prayers with a vision I shall here endeavor to tell.

It was Sunday morning service, and the power of the Spirit was strongly felt. I was standing on a bench at the rear of the church looking on with others, when suddenly a weak feeling came over me, and I fell backward. The young woman who stood near me caught me as I fell and laid me on one of the benches. I saw them, heard all they said, but I could make no reply. My tongue clove to the roof of my mouth. They felt that death was upon me, and indeed so it seemed to me. Seemingly the breath left my body, and in some strange unexplainable way, my own soul stood before me. The people about me faded from my sight and as I stood in the spiritual world I discovered that wings had been given to me. Then an angel appeared before me saying, *"Follow me."*

Happy to be released from the body which now appeared to be only an old and forsaken shell in which I once lived, I joyously went with my guide, who led me through a narrow path which was enclosed on both sides by lakes. Finally we stepped into a cloud which carried us far, far up in the heavens, past the kingdoms of the sun, the moon and the stars, all of which my angelic guide called to my attention as we went. Then, as we still continued, he said, *"Behold the Holy City!"*

The glory and beauty of this I cannot fitly describe to you; but as the writer of Revelations described the New Jerusalem, (Rev. 21:12-27) just so I saw it foursquare. Twelve angels stood, one at each of the twelve gates. With my guide I entered the east side, which was called Sapphire, the Chief cornerstone, where stood Jesus, with twelve angels, who bowed to welcome me therein.

Once inside the gates, I beheld three arch angels coming to meet me. They carried me away to a stream of clear pure water in which I was immersed. As I went down into the stream, a heavenly host with gold-edged wings and harps of gold were singing. "Jesus will be with you, with you always." As they brought me again out of the water, the archangels said, *"Now you are quickened,"* then turned again, saying *"Behold the Father of all!"* I looked and saw the great God sitting on His throne. He had one eye in the center of His forehead, an all seeing one which pierced to the ends of all His creations. The apostle Paul tells us (1Cor. 13:12) *"Now we see through a glass darkly, but then face to face; now I know in part, but then I shall know even as I also am known."* In this vision I saw face to face, I knew as God the Father had known me, and as He has ever known you. I saw heaven, its hosts, the earth and all its peoples, saw the great fishes of the sea, and all the creatures of the deep, and looking into space could see the other worlds, the sun, the moon and the stars. I saw the angels flying hither and yon to do the bidding of their Lord and King, saw the grim reapers of death on their fatal mission, and saw the guiding spirits that keep from harm and danger helpless humanity. I was in the spirit for three days. On the third day I saw a light coming form the east which came nearer and nearer, which proved to be God himself. Three times, He called me by name. The first and second times I did not answer, but the third time I said, *"Yes Lord!."* He said, *"This is not your salvation. I forgave you your sins thirteen months ago, and gave you a new heart, but I have given you this vision because of your unbelief. Go now, lest I be angry and be baptized in my name."* There were three wrinkles in His forehead as He spoke, and as He finished I awoke from my vision, my soul once more in its house of clay. The doctors had told my people to wait three days before they buried me as there seemed a little warmth about my heart, and they could not be sure that I was dead. And now as I opened my eyes and spoke to the hundreds who had waited to see the outcome of this strange happening, you can only imagine the scene that ensued when I told them of the wonderful things that I had seen.

9.2.1 *Truths Revealed in Visions, My Work*

One morning while sitting at home a vision appeared before me of a large temple filled with people. All these people were the same stature and size. As I went down from the pulpit where I seemed to be sitting, to make the alter call, I saw a table before me filled with books. One of the books lay open on the page which contained the following song:

> *O glorious hope of perfect love,*
> *That lifts me up to things above.*
> *It bears on eagle wings,*
> *It bears on eagle wings.*
> *Gives my rapture soul a taste,*
> *And makes me for some moments feast*
> *With Jesus, the Priest and King.*
> *Rejoicing now in earnest hope,*
> *Standing on the mountain top*
> *Seeing all the land below,*
> *Seeing all the land below.*
> *Rivers of milk and honey rise And all the fruits of paradise*
> *With every blessing blest.*
> *In a land of corn, of oil and wine,*
> *Flavored with God's peculiar smile*
> *And ever blessed bliss,*
> *And ever blessed bliss.*
> *Shall I live out my three-score years*
> *Now dwells the Lord, our righteousness.*
> *He keeps His own in perfect peace.*

While this song was being sung, a number came to the altar. I asked them if they were saved. They replied that they were. Then I asked *"Have you received the Holy Ghost?"* They answered, *"No, that is what we came for."* I laid hands on them and they received the Holy Ghost. When I had finished I heard a voice saying, *"This is your work."*

There were others who came forward for healing, and for salvation and the people appeared in multitudes as I still stayed in the temple. I realized then what God has more forcibly made me to know in later years, that truly it has been the work He put upon me to do, to lay hands on the afflicted that they might be healed, the sinner, that He might be saved and the converted that they might be sanctified through His power.

9.2.2 *God's Children Are One*

At one time I was much burdened for the people of God because not much healing was done, neither were many miracles performed. While earnestly praying, God gave me this vision. An angel appeared and said to me *"You will have to meet the Trinity."* I answered that I was not ready. I did not understand the meaning of it and thought it meant that I was to die, while at the same time I thought there was still more work for me to do on earth.

However, after much persuasion I consented and the triune God appeared, Father, Son and Holy Ghost, side by side. *They came together till they merged into one, and He spoke to me saying, "When the saints are become one as We are one, then you will see signs and wonders as there were in the morning time."* I could hear the angels singing, *"The comforter has come,"* and I ran to tell the saints. When I reached them we went together to a place where there stood a temple. Three of the gospel workers in our congregation were in the lead and many others of the saints were there whom I recognized. I asked someone what they were there for and they replied that they were waiting for the funeral procession of Brother Waters, one of the brethren who, they informed me, had just died.

The saints became thirsty and came to me saying, *"We want water."* Once inside the temple, I went to the body of Brother Waters and laying my hands on his head, asked him to arise in the name of Jesus and give us water. Whereupon the soul returned to the body and he immediately arose and took us to a beautiful stream of water, where we drank until we were satisfied. Truly it is a reality that it is the water of Life only which can satisfy the soul of man and make one the children of God.

9.2.3 *"Ask In My Name"*

I therefore continued in this work a good many years but finally as my little ones came one by one till they were nine, I found the cares so heavy and work so constant that it seemed I could not leave my family so I felt I could no longer continue. But one evening about six o'clock a woman in the neighborhood, Sister Hammond by name, came to my door and said to me, *"Is this Sister Sudduth?"* I replied that I was. She said, *"I was seated this morning reading my Bible, and while doing so, you appeared before me, and God told me to come to you and tell you to go with me to pray for a woman who is afflicted with paralysis."* I said, *"Won't you come in?"* But she replied, *"No, I just came to deliver the message, and I must go now."*

After she left, while in meditation over this strange occurrence, I decided, *"If God really wants me to go with this woman, He will surely have to reveal it to me some way!"*

Then again the things of earth faded from my sight and the angel of the Lord appeared saying to me, *"Look!"* Before me I saw a lady afflicted with paralysis sitting in a chair. He said to me, *"Tell Sister Hammond that healing for this affliction comes only by fasting and prayer."*

Then I saw three barrels: The center one had a key in it and by this I was made to understand that there were to be three of us to pray for the afflicted woman. Then the angel spoke again saying *"Go and I will be with you. Ask for anything in my name, not only for small things but ask for anything from the lease to the greatest, and it shall be done."*

The angel faded from the vision in a cloud and I found myself still in my home. I decided I could do no other thing than what God had shown me, and I accordingly sent word late that evening that I would go with her. The next morning I went to the house of Sister Hammond to accompany her and as the two of us reached the home where the sick woman lay, Sister Parr, the third one whom I had been told of in the vision, met us at the gate to join us in prayer. We went in. Sister Hammond anointed her, and we laid hands on her in the name Jesus and when we prayed for her, God instantly healed her. Later, Sister Hammond and I were sent to pray for another sister who the doctors had said could not live, as she had a broken blood vessel that formed a blood clot on the brain, and she also had been paralyzed. We laid hands on her after anointing and praying for her in Jesus' name. God rebuked the disease, and she was able to sit upright in her bed. The second day, when we went back, she was able to walk about the house. The third morning, we went to her home and found her returning there after going herself to pray for a young man who had the typhoid fever, who was healed by her prayer. She had walked nine blocks to his home and back again. All of this experience, together with the vision God had shown me beforehand convinced me that I owed my life to Him in an active way, despite the family cares and burdens which fall to the lot of every wife and Mother. I could not again refuse to use what ever time required of me for His service.

9.2.4 *The Temple Of God Is Holy*

Though I had lived a Christian life for years, I had not yet received light on the use of tobacco, and I had acquired the use of snuff. My husband often objected to my using tobacco; as he said it was wrong for Christians to use it. I insisted that it was God who had made everything, and certainly everything he made was good…yes very good indeed. As time passed however he still continued to speak of it. I told him one day that I would ask the Lord to show me in some way if it was really wrong.

This was the way the Lord used to show me it was wrong. I was standing at the door of my home at the noon tide, when all at once it seemed I stood inside a beautiful glass house. I took a dip of my snuff while there, and soon the saliva filed my mouth so full I was forced to rid myself of it. But it occurred to me this was such a beautiful house it was such a pity to mar it with that filth, I looked this way, then that from the ceiling to the floor of the pearly white structure, but nowhere could I find a place that seemed suitable for the filthy snuff to fall. Finally, in desperation I spat on the side wall. It looked so very bad, I decided it must be wiped away. Finding nothing at hand convenient, I at last raised the hem of my dress skirt and tried to absorb it. But the more I attempted to wipe it away, the more it spread, until at last it covered the house from floor to ceiling.

I still stood surveying the situation, completely dismayed at the result of my deed when that scene disappeared and an angel appeared on a ladder out of heaven. Stepping to the end of the ladder he said to me, *"The beautiful house you admired so much was your own...The house of clay in which you live and like it, you were pure and clean until you dipped the snuff, but as the filth spread all over the beautiful house, so the poison and Uncleanness of the snuff has spread all over your body. Now I, the Lord will not dwell in an Unclean temple."* So saying, he fled on the heavenly ladder, and I was still standing in the door of my little home. Falling on my knees, I said, *"Now Lord, I know that this is indeed a sin. Take away the desire for it. Forgive me and I will never use it again."* And from that day until now, even the odor of tobacco in any form makes me feel ill.

9.3 *When Jesus Healed My Life Extended*

Though, as I have formerly said, I was converted more than thirty-five years ago, I did not have the full light of the gospel, and therefore did many things I should not, and that I would never have done, had I realized it was not according to the will of God. How tenderly He cares for His children! How forgiving and compassionate and with how few stripes does He punish the children of His kingdom who do not understand His will concerning them! Such have I been who had not suffered in the manner that I hear shall give an account of, if I had known the things I later learned. But bless His name, He knew I did not understand, and I give all honor and glory to Him today, for had it not been for His mercy I would not have been living at this date.

It is, I believe nearly twenty-five years since the incident happened. I lay in bed with a tiny three day old child at my side. My husband was at work, and my Mother had been caring for me but was called away to my sister's home, as she had been taken suddenly ill. My second oldest child, a little boy of school age, failed to come home when school turned out. Childlike, he had gone to a neighbor's home to play with other boys and did not come back till late in the evening. I was very much out of patience with him for having failed to come when I needed him so much. When I heard him whistling as he came, I got out of bed, not stopping to dress myself properly. I ran out in the cold snowy air, down to the honeysuckle vine, in my bare feet and pulled some switches. Then I returned to the house where I wore them away on his little back. I went again to bed but the exposure I had put myself through brought on a congestive chill which curdled the blood in my veins and clotted the blood vessels near my heart so that it almost stopped the heart action. Five doctors were called into consultation, and they all agreed that there was no hope for my life. It was then 10 p.m. and they said that in two hours (at midnight) I should die. I at first suffered violent pains so great that I was held down by two bed sheets across my body, but gradually I grew weaker and weaker until at last I could not speak, though I still was conscious. Indeed I was so near death that they laid a veil over my face that they might see if any dampness gathered and thereby know I was yet alive. At that time I did not believe in Holiness, though we had heard of it, for some of the people who lived in the neighborhood near us then had taught it, but we paid no heed to it, as we were not interested.

However, one of the men in the faith was acquainted with one of the doctors. He talked with the doctor after they had left our home, and the doctor informed him of my condition. The man got another brother to join him, and they came to our house late that night. God had not lost His power they said. The read Mark 11:23-24, then, after anointing me, laid hand on me and prayed, *"Lord God in the name of Jesus we ask thee to rebuke death and extend this woman's life and cause her heart to function normally."*

It was a short simple prayer; much different to the lengthy ones that today are considered by many so essential. When they took their hands off me, I realized that a radical change was effected. A cooling, soothing refreshing feeling coursed through my body, and I realized then that the healing virtue with which Jesus of Galilee made whole the leper, opened the eyes of the blind, and made the lame to walk was not only for the people of His day, but also for all those that *"believe on His name"* even unto this day.

I wanted to get up even then, but my husband would not consent, as he did not believe it possible for me to be healed in this manner. The next morning (Friday), I was still more anxious than ever to get up and my husband still was fearful of the result. As my Mother told him that I could not live just to let me do as I wished, I crept out and knelt by my bedside and earnestly prayed. *"Lord now let my will be lost in Thine, and Thine in mine. Whatever you want me to, I will do it if you will only raise me up in health and strength."* I arose perfectly well, only a little weak. My family still expected me to die and could not understand why I lingered. I stayed in bed until Saturday evening. I could not contain myself longer for joy because I knew I was healed. I arose and walked the floor shouting for joy! There was to be a business meeting at the Baptist church where we attended. My husband went to the chapel telling them that God had stricken me with death and that I was walking the floor. They closed the meeting and a number of the women came to watch throughout the night. Expecting me to die, they didn't want me to know they were there. They stayed in another room, peering into the bedroom to see if I was dead. When Sunday morning came, I awoke feeling much rested and stronger than ever. I arose a five o'clock telling my Mother that I would cook breakfast for her. The women slipped out quietly when they heard this and went to their respective homes. From that day on, I continued doing my own work.

9.3.1 A Ruptured Appendix Healed

The second time God came to my rescue in healing my body was fourteen years ago. I had a ruptured appendix and suffered intensely.

When the doctor came he held no hope for my life. As a last resort, he offered an emergency operation. He said there was slight hope of ever awakening for the anesthetic. One of my sons fell to the floor and lay face down weeping. He implored me, *"Mother please go and have the operation and perhaps you will live a little longer anyway."* After the doctor offered no hope with or without the operation, I had given up completely. I was so weak and ill that I too felt I should not survive.

As I lay for the second time so near death, I looked up to God saying, *"Lord not my will but Thy will be done."* I called my husband to me and said to him, *"See that you teach our children the way they should go. Keep them in Sunday school as we have started to do. And when the girls go out in the evening, either have their brother go with them or accompany them yourself."* I had no further desire for the affairs of the earth and now fixed all my attention on eternity. I prayed again, *"Lord now let my will be Thine and Thy will mine. If you can get more glory from my life by taking me unto Thyself in heaven than by permitting me to remain, amen."* When I submitted fully all things into His hands, to my surprise and joy, God raised me immediately in health and strength. I have not been troubled since with my appendix.

9.3.2 *Healed of Hemorrhages*

About thirteen years ago I was seized with an attack of bloody flux and for thirteen days had hemorrhages. I was lying down resting one day during my illness and dreamed that I felt normal and as well as I ever had. I later went to one of the saints' homes where they all agreed in prayer for me that I might be healed, and be as normal as I was in my dream. I returned home where I discovered that I was indeed completely healed. From that hour, I had no hemorrhages.

9.3.3 *A Deadly Poison*

About ten years ago, I was picking potatoes in a field that bordered a lake at Silver Lake, Kansas. Our two youngest daughters and our youngest son were with us. I was out in the center of the field when I felt something bite and sting the back of my shoulder. In an instant, my whole body was filled with intense pain and burning till I felt near death. I grasped my dress and held it tightly over the place where I was stung and screamed out.

The little girls came running to see what caused the trouble. What they saw frightened them, so they ran away and left me. A man plowing near by saw my plight and came to me. He told me to let loose of my dress, which I did. He knocked a centipede off me to the ground and killed it. *"Lady,"* he said, *"This is a centipede, very poisonous."* He called my husband immediately from the end of the field and told him to hitch the horses quickly and take me to the doctor. My husband had long since become acquainted with the power of God to heal. He calmly replied that I would be alright.

The man was only a sinner, but he did believe in God's healing virtue. He said to me, *"I have a sister who believes in divine healing. Do you remember how Paul felt no harm when at Melita the serpent came out of the fire and attached itself to his arm?"*

(Acts 28:3) I had only a moment to look up to my God saying, *"Lord save me, else I perish."* And now by his words of faith I was strengthened tenfold. I answered, *"Yes and neither shall I feel any harm."*

That was about ten o'clock in the morning. The pain left me and I had such a soothing feeling of relief that I was able to continue working, so that by evening I had picked sixty bushels of potatoes. It was so.

9.3.4 Dye Poisoning

Five years ago while living in Kansas City, Kansas, my oldest daughter gave me a pair of brown three strap slippers with which I was very much pleased, except for the color. That, I felt was too noticeable. Therefore, I purchased a bottle of dye to change the color to black. This resulted in a bad case of poisoning which caused my feet to swell so greatly that they burst open in great cracks. Underneath, they were covered with sores that seemed to eat into the flesh.

For three weeks I was unable to walk. During this time many were brought to me for prayer. When I laid hands on them they were instantly healed, but I myself could receive no relief. Among those who were healed, was a man who had been suddenly stricken with paralysis. He was speechless. His eyes were bloodshot and the doctors had given him up to die. They sent for me. Being unable to walk, three women came to our home and took me to him. They carried me into the house and set me down on a chair by his bedside. I sat there praying for him, while I suffered intensely with swollen feet. God healed him. The next morning he arose and ate breakfast as usual. The second morning he walked downtown to attend to his business affairs. He is alive and well at this writing.

Many will consider it strange that while through my prayers many were healed, but I remained afflicted. This is the explanation. Many of the sectarian sisters used all their persuasion to get me to employ a doctor's assistance. They even advised me to go to the hospital and have my feet removed, as they said it would be better for me to loose a limb than loose my life. One woman came with some sort of liquid which she said would keep my feet from swelling. In spite of my objections, she insisted on painting my toes with it. In five minutes or less, I was suffering almost beyond endurance. Instead of the swelling reducing, the toes now also became so swollen that they burst open. When I poured olive oil on my feet, the poisoning was so rank that it turned green.

Unbelievers talking to me so much had the affect of discouraging me. While not to the extent that it caused me to yield to the use of all those remedies, it was enough to hinder me in grasping faith to obtain my blessing. I am convinced that often this is all that hinders the child of God from being healed. If we can only burst the bands of unbelief asunder, the blessing will be ours.

But the affliction gradually grew worse and daily brought me nearer to a decision. I knew that a change must come soon in some way. Would I submit to remedies or an operation? If I did, would my life be spared? All these and many other thoughts crossed my mind. But I settled on the Wednesday night before Thanksgiving, that whether He healed me or not, I would not use any of the things suggested to me. I would trust Him whether I lived or died.

The next morning, the swelling was gone from my feet. I got out of bed and walked to the city and came on a bus to Topeka. I went to my daughter-in-law's home where we anointed my feet with oil and agreed in prayer that God would restore them to normal condition. I wrapped them in gauze. All the old skin came off with it as the reptile's skin is shed. My feet were really clothed with anew with healthy skin. My daughter-in-law and I shouted aloud fro joy! Oh wondrous, wondrous love of our Redeemer, that He cares for even the least of His children answers without fail their pleading petition. Praise God! I have tried Him and proved Him and found that His promises are as true as He that made them. Oh doubting, fearing, tempest-tossed suffering one. Fear not to trust Him for *"He careth for you"* and is able to do for you even abundantly above all that you can think to ask.

When I returned to Kansas City, a blind woman (Mrs. Minter by name) was brought to me. I anointed and prayed for her that her sight might be restored. She washed her face and dried it. As she opened her eyes she said, *"Why I see as well as I ever did in my life."* And she remained with sight as long as she lived.

9.4 *Miracles of Today*

I know that the world today is full of the scoffing and unbelieving. It has ever been thus, and now in these last days there is less faith than ever before. I know there are many that say there are no miracles; that healing is not for the church of today. That is a lie as God Himself lives. His Word is true and He promised that signs shall follow them that believe.

As I begin the writing of this chapter, I hesitate somewhat for I feel entirely inadequate to portray in a manner that fitly expresses the beauty, majesty and the faithfulness of the great God, before the tremendous manifestation of His power availed to me. I am lost in wonder, love and praise. I cannot tell it all, but in my faltering way, I shall endeavor to place before your vision a few of the marvelous things that God hath done.

9.4.1 *The return of The Spirit*

Something like nine years ago, we were called to a home where a man who was a rank sinner was dying. Mrs. K..., his wife, had heard of our congregation and of the healings God had done. She sent for me. His was a case of pneumonia. They had been seen by three doctors, all of whom had given up. When I first saw him, his face around his eyes, down his nose and over his mouth was as red and inflamed as if it were raw flesh.

The window was open and he lay covered with a thin spread. Nothing but the whites of his eyes could be seen. He was cursing and saying that God had told him that at eleven o'clock that morning, he must take a train that was bound for hell. A little later, he became very still. He no longer was able to speak. He lay in that state of coma which frequently precedes death. Everyone about the place was awaiting his death and expecting that he would soon be gone. Many of his friends were gathered there.

Outside, my husband and I were holding a controversy. My husband said, *"Mother, you know this man is a rank sinner. The doctors have agreed that nothing can be done to save his life. I do not want you going in there to pray for him and put holiness to the wall. He is talking of dying and going to hell and you can't stop him. You will only bring reproach on the church of God. Come home with me now, and leave this thing alone."*

Ah, my dear Christian friend. This is the fatal cry of opposition that so often comes between us, to keep us from victory that comes through obedience to the vision God gives us. So often those who are nearest and dearest to us unwittingly hinder the good that God wills to do. And as we listen to them, we forget that we ought to obey God rather than man. (Acts 5:29)

There are many times when we must turn a deaf ear to all remonstration, even from those we love more dearly than life itself. We must courageously and steadfastly keep our eyes on the vision God has given us, if ever we are to accomplish what He has given us to do. At the same time, we should look with compassion and patience at their attitude. We must understand that they have not been given the vision God has given us. Therefore, they cannot see with our eyes. They look with fearful hearts on circumstances, realizing that man is nothing and can do nothing on his own power. Before it, they are helpless.

It takes a vision to accomplish the work of God. Let us keep that vision though our dearest sometimes cannot understand. If we keep it, wondrous joy shall be theirs as well as ours. They will rejoice with us that we were heedless of their fears when they witness the wonderful things that God shall do.

Did Jesus falter before the unbelieving in the house of Jairus? (Luke 8:41-56) Nay, rather He put the unbelievers out of the room and restored the maiden to her sorrowing loved ones. Did He hesitate an instant when the timid Martha informed him that her brother had been dead for four days? Ah, no. He had the vision! He insisted that the stone be removed from the door of the tomb and commanded fearlessly that Lazarus come forth. Lazarus came forth, and it was said in John 11:45, that *"many of the Jews who had come to Mary, and had seen the things Jesus did, believed in Him."* Aye, let us follow Jesus and do the will of our Father that many may believe in this day.

Three times, my husband drew me off the porch to get me to return home with him. The third time I firmly withdrew from him and answered,

"Husband, you may go home if you wish, but I am going to pray for this man. He may be dying now, but he'll not be when I finish praying for him."

He left me and returned home. My daughter-in-law and I stepped into the sick-room. I anointed his head and face with oil, and we knelt to pray. I do not know how long I prayed. But I do know that before I ceased I had the witness that this man would be restored to health. I prayed that he might be made whole and that if he were dead, the spirit might return to his body.

Then followed such a manifestation of His power as I had heard told in olden times, but had never before seen. The house was shaken so mightily that his wife fell to the floor. When I opened my eyes there was only she, a young woman who stayed with them and the man who was his partner in business. He stood with his face to the wall, weeping. The others had become frightened at the extraordinary occurrence and fled the house. My daughter-in-law and I stood with our backs against the wall amazed. The manifestation had been so great as to almost frighten even me.

Mr. K... sat up in his bed. As he came to consciousness he was saying, *"Yes Lord, just give me one more chance and I will serve you."* Then he told us that a short time before, he had stood at the lake that burns with fire and brimstone, and that God had said to him, *"There are two women praying for your life. Now go back to earth and sin no more lest a worse thing come upon you."* The Lord raised him up to normal health and converted both his companion and himself. Such is the power of God in this day. He is mighty to save, mighty to keep and mighty to heal if we will but believe.

9.4.2 *Operation of the Heavenly Physician*

Five years ago, in the springtime, I received a telephone call from Paola, Kansas. I was asked to pray for the sister of one of our saint ministers. I immediately set about preparations for leaving and arrive in Paola after nightfall. They had told me somewhat of her condition over the phone. It seemed the dire extremity of the case nearly discouraged me, till I willingly would have returned to my home without seeing her. I feared it might mean a reproach to the cause. But the voice from the skies said to me, *"Have I not told you, if you abide in me and my words abide in you, ye shall ask what ye will and it shall be done for you?"* (John 15:7) This encouraged me somewhat and as I got a little nearer, again the words came. *"Whatsoever things ye desire, when ye pray, believe that ye receive them, and ye shall have them."* (Mark 11:24)

I entered the home where the woman lay. Like many of the others of whom I have given account, she was given up by the doctors as being beyond their help. She had a large tumor which had four smaller growths attached to it. By taking an x-ray, the doctors had learned that the largest tumor had been eaten away in the center by cancer. The cancer had eaten into her back. She also had cancer in her stomach and dropsy. They had been keeping under the influence of hypodermics to lessen the suffering until they dared do so no longer. She was so weak the doctors said she would die from it. She had wasted away till the bones were plainly seen and had scarcely any vitality left. She tried to speak to me when I first came into the room, but could not be understood.

I anointed her with oil over the abdomen, and then prayed that God would let her sleep the night. The agony of pain ceased and slumber came to her. She had before been held down by bed sheet at times when suffering was unendurable. I sat keeping watch bedside till one o'clock in the morning. Her sister and minister suggested that I go home and rest till day. I did accordingly.

After I went to sleep, I dreamed I saw her arise from the bed and connect the floor lamp to current, light it and sit down beneath it to comb her hair. I awoke laughing for joy. I could no longer sleep and spent the time until dawn in prayer. I asked God to let it be with her just as I had seen in my dream. In the morning when I entered her room, she was still in no pain. I stood over her bed, anointing her with oil as God had commanded, for nearly an hour. I was looking for her to be completely healed as I had asked when she began vomiting. Her bowels began to move. The roots of cancer and unhealthy flesh were expelled. Some pieces were so large as to nearly strangle her. When this all had been expelled, she lay very quiet at rest.

Soon, she said, *"I am hungry. I wasn't something to eat."* They got some steak, ground it, cooked it and gave her the broth from it. She did not vomit this, but was not satisfied and wanted meat itself. We would not let her have it as we felt her stomach was too weak. We gave her some toast with butter on it and that did not hurt her. Then she said, *"I want to get up."* We tried to keep her in bed as we felt she was too weak for such exertion. She continued, *"I want to get up and comb my hair. It has not been combed as it should be for six months."* In spite of all we could say, she arose and attached the lamp as I had seen her doing in my dream. At this, my joy knew no bounds. I left the house to rejoice to my heart's content in praise to the God who once again had answered the pleading of his children.

Later, she said to me, *"Woman, may I go home with you?"* *"Oh,"* I said, *"I do not think you are strong enough yet. You might take a cold on the way or get too weary."* But she answered, *"If I were depending on you I should not be strong enough. But I am depending on God."* I could no longer refuse. The following day we started. She did not even try to sleep till we arrived in Kansas City and changed trains at Union Station.

She stayed at my home for three weeks and gained in flesh and strength. When I was away from home, she would cook anything she wished. On one occasion, she ate a full meal of beef and cabbage with no injury. When I scolded, she merely said she was hungry and had to have something to eat. She is at this writing, in Detroit, Michigan working as a pastry cook in a large restaurant. Last summer, she sent me word that she was perfectly well and weighed 140 pounds.

9.4.3 When the Doctors Were Cheated

Mrs. T..., of Kinsley, Kansas came to Topeka to Christ's Hospital five years ago, for treatment of diabetes. A specialist here gave her treatment that she might be in better condition for the operation of removing a cancerous breast. It was considered her only hope for life. Before he released her to the surgeon, he told her, *"If you have a will to make you had better make it now. If you have not already made your peace with God, you had better to that."*

Her daughters learned of his statement and sent for me, that I might pray for her. It was on Tuesday that I first saw her and anointed her breasts and prayed for her healing. The next morning when I arrived again at the hospital, the lumps on her breast had disappeared with the exception of one small one. I anointed her the second time and prayed. She said to me, *"I am going to be operated on tomorrow morning. My husband is coming from Kinsley tonight to be here during the operation. I want you to give him the address of the place where your prayer meeting will be held. I am going to ask the doctors if I can go."*

The doctors gave her permission to go, but did not expect she would be able to do so. She walked six blocks to the chapel with her husband that night. She had been completely healed before she ever came. After she arrived, she also received salvation and was shouting praises in the building till eleven o'clock, before she could be persuaded to return to the hospital. The next morning, the surgeons examined her and took her temperature, which was normal. They said, *"We cannot understand."* God has healed her, she told them. They answered her somewhat sarcastically, *"He had done a pretty poor job."* But she left the hospital a well woman, without having to pay the one hundred fifty dollars for the operation. God had freely made her whole!

9.4.4 A Broken Back

Charles E...Jr., a child about seven years of age, was in the hospital in Chicago, Illinois, for eleven months and three weeks with a broken back. He developed tuberculosis and had a weak heart. His Grandmother brought him to Topeka and sent for me. On being anointed and prayed for, he was instantly healed.

9.4.5 Hemorrhage of the Brain

Mrs. D...lay at St. Francis hospital with a hemorrhage of the brain. The doctors could not stop the flow of blood which issued from her mouth and nose. Her daughter-in-law sent for me. With another of the saints, I went on a Thursday to pray for her. She was instantly healed and the following day returned to her home.

9.4.6 Tuberculosis

Mrs. ...was taken from Hillcrest Sanatorium to die. Two of the saints sent for me and we prayed over her anointing her with oil in the name of the Lord. That hour, she began to mend. She was completely healed and has since given birth to a child. Not long ago, I saw her and she was robust and healthy.

9.4.7 Other Healings

Among the many others whom I have witnessed the healing of are a few instances which I submit as the more remarkable:

Mrs. E.J. - healed of tuberculosis

Mrs. J.B. - healed of a cancer

Mrs. C - pneumonia Mary Fisher - healed before an operation

Lillian Harris - rheumatism

Mrs. H - life restored (Miracle)

Mrs. Anna Haywood - tuberculosis

Mrs. Evelyn Slaughter - healed of a goiter

Mrs. M.J. - shingles

Rebecca Boland - muscular rheumatism

Frank Payne - strychnine poisoning

Mrs. S… was healed of gall stones and an abscess on her liver. The doctors had said there was no hope of her recovery. After I prayed for her, God removed the gall stones and abscess without an operation. I saw the gall stones and they looked much like cancer.

How merciful our God is, both to the just and the unjust. Though one of the vilest women, she was completely healed four years ago. Like the nine lepers of long ago, she did not turn to give God her life and praise. She still continues on her ungodly way. As far as I know, she is still well.

Mrs. L.E….was healed of complications after being bedfast for seven years. I further testify to two healings of the insane, as otherwise expressed, the devil possessed. This is in reality the condition of most of those who are called insane.

At the state hospital seven years ago, a woman who had lived near me as a neighbor was confined. I felt impressed to pray for her. When I reached the hospital, the nurse brought me to her and locked us together in a room. *"Do you know me Mrs. Cooper?"* I began. At this she laughed and ran to the window acting in an unseemly way. Fear took hold of me. I was not accustomed to being with people in such a condition.

I looked furtively at the fastened door, speculating the chance I might have to escape in case she attacked me. A second time I asked, *"Do you know me?"* This time she acted more foolishly than before. She came and sat down on a chair near me. I quickly turned over in my mind what would be best or possible for me to do. I had come to help her if possible and did not intend to be frightened away without at least making the effort.

Gently, quietly, I laid my hand on her knee. Lifting my face to heaven, I asked God in the name of Jesus our Savior to rebuke the devils and cast them out, and clothe her once more in her right mind.

I moved my chair some distance away from her and said for a third time, *"Mrs. Cooper, do you know me?"* This time the light of recognition appeared in her eyes and she spoke normally answering, *"Why isn't this Mrs. Sudduth?"* *"Yes"* I replied joyfully. *"Oh, I'm so glad to see you"* she said.

Later during the conversation we had, she asked me of her people and if they still lived on College Avenue. She told me to tell them to write to her and come to see her. From that day, her mind was normal and at this date she lives at her home not a block away. She often comes to see me.

9.4.8 *Personal Guidance through Revelation*

Time and memory fail me to tell of the many times I have been shown things to come in my personal life, which have been invaluable assistance and joy to me. But I have selected a few out of them all, which have seemed most wonderful.

9.4.9 *Death*

I was sitting in my home one day sewing when I glanced out the window. In the vision I saw there appeared a large automobile. It approached my home and stopped. Out of it, the occupants produced a long black casket and placed it at my door. *"There is no one either ill or dead here,"* I told them. *"Do not bring that casket in my house."*

But Death, the grim reaper, sat beneath a tree in the yard and answered, *"Let it alone. It will not touch you or your immediate family. But it is coming to your house."*

The scene vanished and left me still sitting in my chair, my sewing on my lap. Soon after this, my grandson who was at my house was taken ill with whooping cough and pneumonia and died. Five years ago while visiting Akron, Ohio, I was called with some other saints to pray for a young man who had been kicked by a horse. It caused a concussion which left him without speech or hearing and rendered him insane. He had been in this pitiful condition for thirteen years. Hearing of divine healing, his Mother sent for us that we might pray for him. They brought him home from the asylum for the occasion. We gathered around him to ask God to rebuke the Unclean spirits and restore him to normal condition. He was instantly healed. The first word he spoke was *"Hallelujah!"* He also became a devout Christian and a constant student of the God's Word.

9.4.10 *The Reward of Faith*

In the fall of 1928, I had a vision in which I saw my son who lived in Pueblo, Colorado, carried form the mine in which he worked. He was hurt, mangled and bleeding. I told my husband and some of the other children of it and sent my son a telegram warning him to leave the mine. He paid no attention to the warning as it meant nothing more than a dream to him. I later sent a special delivery letter to him, begging hi to go to Akron, Ohio where I had been for two weeks. There was splendid opportunity at that time to obtain work there. Still, he and his family were content to stay in Pueblo.

He vision however, I could not forget. It continued to trouble me. One morning in the winter several months after I saw the vision, I became much burdened. *"Oh."* I said once more to my family. *"I do wish Elsbury would leave the mine. I am so afraid something will happen to him."* At four o'clock that afternoon, came a telegram saying that if I wished to see him alive, to come at once as his body had been crushed in the mine. One of his kidneys would have to be removed. I did not have a cent of money with which to pay for my fare. How I could get it, I did not know. But I did believe that my Father had it within His power to give and I asked Him for a way to go.

I received a witness clearly and plainly that my railroad fee would be provided. While my son, his wife and daughter along with one of my daughters, (who traveling with passes) packed their grips, I confidently made my own ready. I fully believed that my ticket would be forthcoming before train time.

I told one of my sons-in-law to come by my home and take me to the station before train time. One of the saints who live near me gave me the last three dollars she had to help me. But nothing more was in sight and the fare to Pueblo was $21.00.

Train time drew near. My son-in-law came and took me to the depot. The train whistled and the children picked up their grips and started for the door. Nothing more had been given me as yet. I followed them to the train that my Father had promised was to take me to my dying son. Confident, though I saw not the way, it was provided none the less. Just as I was ready to step on the train, the son-in-law who had taken me to the station came to me and put the ticket in my hand. He said, *"Mother, here is your fare."* He had tried all evening to get the money. When at last he took me to the depot, he went away as he could not bear to see me grieve at being left behind while the children went. He went to the drug store close to where we lived and mentioned the matter to the druggist who became very much concerned when he found out I had no way to go. He gave him the price of the fare, telling him to rush it to me.

When we arrived at the hospital the following evening, we found my son in the room where the dying are laid. We were told at first that we could not see him. When we explained to the head nurse that we had come such a great distance, she told us we might go in for just a few minutes, but to be very quiet. We found him so weak he could not talk. He was still having hemorrhages from the kidneys. I anointed his head with oil and laid my face against his praying earnestly that he might be healed.

The following day when I went to the hospital, I found he had been removed from the room and was instead in a room upstairs. This time, he was able to smile and talk a little. The nurse told me that from the time I had left the night before, the action of one kidney had been normal and there was hope for his life. The next day, they showed me how his body had been cut half way around. They placed him in a cast. In three weeks he was able to sit up. The week after I came home, they wrote and told me he was able to be up and out of the house.

While visiting the same son who was now living in Lester, Colorado, my daughter-in-law and me were asked to pray for a woman who had been stricken with paralysis. We did so and she was healed. In turn, another woman who had heard of us asked us to come pray for her. She had a gunshot wound in her ankle and her foot and leg half way to the knee had been poisoned. As a result, it was black and puffed with swelling. We anointed her with oil and prayed for her. The swelling went instantly out of her leg and left it normal. She was then able to walk. She said there was no sin in her life and that she wanted the Holy Ghost. We laid hands on her and prayed and she was sanctified. The following morning as we were praying for another woman, this woman's husband came out of their home and told us that he was waiting for us that we might pray for him also to receive the Holy Spirit. "If you can live like that, I can too" he told us. We stopped again at their house and prayed with him and he also received the gift of the Holy Ghost.

At this time I decided to start homeward. My son took me to Trinidad, (which is about thirty miles from his home) so that I might board the train there. I was to change trains at another station after which I was told, my ticket would be invalid after midnight. I was to be put off at the next station which was sixty miles beyond. I did not know what to do and did not even have money to send a telegram to my people. I sat in the station till morning, and then inquired of where I might get help. I was told of a home of a home about 2 ½ blocks away, where I might go. A widow and her two daughters lived there. She kept me for the day and gave me a ticket for part of the way. She told me when I got to Dodge City to go to the Methodist church and give them her name. They would give me fare to get the rest of the way home. While on the train, I met a little woman who was in the gospel work. As we talked, I told her how I had overstayed my time unknowingly and of the work we had been doing. She took a tin cup and arose saying, *"I'm going to make myself a missionary right here."* She went through all the car and when she came back to me she had received ten dollars. Some of the people on the car bought the ticket and made up the five dollars beside and gave it to me. This is the way God has provided for me many times, when there seemed no way. *"According to your faith, so be it unto you. If ye abide in me, and my words abide in you, ye shall ask what ye will, and it shall be done."*

9.4.11 *"Whosoever Cometh Unto Me, I Will in No Wise Cast Out"*

A ninety year old man lay dying in his home. Mostly from old age. He was ill though he had a minor ailment. His time was near to go. The doctors told his daughter that there was nothing more they could do, and he was not likely to last through the night. When he was first taken sick he had said he did not want to die until he was saved and forgiven by God. But he grew weaker and had not had the chance to make his peace with the Lord. His daughter sent for me that I might pray for his life to be extended till he had the opportunity to count the cost and the price. When I prayed for him, his life was extended three weeks. During that time he was saved and sanctified. Shortly before he died he sent for a rich man of the city for whom he had worked for thirty years. When the man came he said, *"I am here Joe. What is it you wanted?"* He said, *"I've a message for you from heaven. I saw your Mother and she told me to tell you that unless you repented you would be cast into the lake that burns with fire and brimstone."*

The man put his hands over his face and went away weeping. Then he said to me, *"Wash my feet."* His daughter went to town and bought a pan and a long towel with which I girded myself. I washed and wiped his feet. After this was done he said, *"Now I want you to preach my funeral and I want to have them sing, 'Beautiful Robes' and 'I'm Redeemed'"*. When he had done giving directions, he looked up saying, *"Now finally farewell."* He turned his face to the wall and his spirit quietly ascended back to God the Father who gave it.

9.5 Miracles of Today

While living in Coweta, Oklahoma, I was standing out in the yard of my home one day when a vision appeared before me of a great herd of cows. One of them had a rope around its neck and was struggling to get it off. Soon they stampeded. As I stood wondering at the sight, a man appeared and asked, *"Do you see the cow with the rope about her neck?"* *"Yes"* I answered. *"Well,"* said he, *"That represents a riot."*

Then the scene changed and I saw a man approaching dressed in brown with a tan hat and shoes. He was carrying a suitcase. By the time he came even with me, he was dressed instead in a suit of overalls. I asked him what had become of his new clothes and suitcase. He replied that he did not have any. This same man whom I had seen in the vision was killed the following Sunday in a riot.

9.5.1 The Plot of a Deceiver

At one time a young man was keeping company with my eldest daughter who wished to marry him. I had always told my daughters that they should marry men who were honest and industrious and would make a good living for them. My daughter knew little of this young man, so I was anxious to know whether he could care for a wife or not.

Then God gave me another vision in which I saw the young man seated in his home writing a letter to my daughter. In it he told her that he had a home which was completely paid for, containing eight rooms, all waiting for her, and that he was buying a piano and having everything put in order so that she might be happy when she came.

But as he sat there writing, a woman stood beside him telling him, *"These things do not belong to you. They are mine."* She seemed to be his step-Mother. Still he paid no heed and sealed the letter and mailed it. I told my daughter of the vision and that she would receive a letter. The letter soon came. When my daughter read it, she found it contained just what I saw in the vision.

9.5.2 The Prince of Peace

In early autumn of 1918, two nights before the 92nd division boarded the train at Camp Funston for New York. They were to sail from there for the battle fields of France. I saw them in a vision board a ship which was to carry them over. As they put out to sea the Christ appeared out of the heavens and alighted on the ship.

After they got some distance out, they experienced some difficulty with the ship and returned to New York for repair. During this time, the Savior disappeared. When for the second time they left the harbor, He came again to them to attend their journey.

I saw them again as they stood in the hills of France, ready to charge in battle. They stood with guns in their hands held straight, ready for firing. But out of the heavens came the Christ again, down to the valley beyond which lay the enemy they were to meet. As He set His feet in the valley, He stretched wide his arms to the ends of the earth. I heard Him declare peace. The legion of guns dropped and all was quiet.

The following evening was just the night before they were to leave for New York. We lived in the Army city at the time. It adjoined Camp Funston. None might pass the camp to the city that night and none might enter the camp. I stood on the border by the ditch which lay between and told the 92nd division that they need not fear, for the peace would be declared. I told them that I had seen the Prince of Peace spread wide His arms to command the war to cease and that none of them would have to face battle.

How fervently they believed my words. Many came the following day just before they left and bade me goodbye. It was something like two months later that the Armistice was signed. Oh how many letters I received from those boys as the later returned to American soil, in memory of my farewell words to them. *"We did not see the Christ,"* they said *"but He did declare peace."*

9.6 Miracles and Visions

9.6.1 The Power of Darkness

How the devil and all his angels oppose the servants of God in their efforts to accomplish His works. To those who serve Satan, he may seem but a figurehead and a myth. But those who serve the true and living God must wage constantly and openly face to face war with him as an evil spirit.

Several years ago I was called to pray for an elderly sister who had been blind for a long period of time. Ah, how the devil hates to see the deaf made to hear, the dumb to speak, the lame to walk, the blind to see and the dead raised. Each time it is done, it scores a victory for Jesus of Nazareth who nearly 2000 years ago walked the shores of Galilee to kindle a fire which burns in the hearts of His own unto this day.

Let us take courage, go forward, facing all things, fearing nothing. *"He that is within us is greater than he that is in the world."* The powers of darkness may sometimes almost overwhelm us. But God is sufficient to lay them low and conquer for us of we do not leave the scene ourselves at the crucial moment.

Had this not been the case with me, the incident I shall here relate might have been a different story. I believe that many times the only reason the wondrous miracles of the morning time are not more frequently seen is because of those who pray the prayer of faith, giving way to the awful powers of darkness at the moment when just beyond is certain victory.

I give this chapter with a prayerful heart, trusting in God that it may work for the ultimate and lasting benefit of all who read it. Especially to encourage those whose work may be to pray for the afflicted.

I anointed this woman's eyes and stepped behind her chair, placing both hands clasped over her eyes. I had not the thought of time. I was completely lost in my labor. So earnestly did I pray that she might see. I do not know how long it had been. Suddenly it seemed a stream of water coursed through my body. As it went, terrific pain centered in my eyes. It blinded me for a time so that I myself could not see. I felt ill unto death. But when I tried to unclasp my hands and remove them from her eyes, I could not. It was as if they fastened by an unseen power. The more I struggled to loosen my hands, the tighter they seemed to stay. Even the chair in which the woman sat swayed in the air.

Finally my hands were released and I leaned against the wall in misery for a moment. As my sight came to me, I fled from the house in terror of the awful experience. The woman saw for a time better than for years. But gradually she became blind as before. I am persuaded that had I had enough strength to avail myself to God and have another to agree with me, we would have been gloriously rewarded by our sister's sight being fully restored.

9.6.2 Kidney Stones Pass

I had been ill often with a complaint which was of unknown origin to me. All I knew was, oft-times my pain would become so intense that a doctor had to be called in to give me shots to relieve the pain. This condition continued for several years. It grew worse each year until finally I was sent to another doctor for an x-ray to determine the cause of my trouble. The x-ray revealed the fact that I had kidney stones lodged in my right tube and would not move.

The doctor gave me a prescription for medicine, stating that if the medicine did not remove the stones, an operation would be the only alternative. I took the medicine for two or three months with no results. At last, I went to bed very ill. One night after staying in bed for a week or two, my pains became so great that a shot in the arm did not give relief at all. I suffered in terrible agony, tumbling and groaning with my bladder completely obstructed. It was impossible to pass water. I felt that this must be the end and could not live through the night without relief of some kind. Giving up all hope of being helped by anyone but God, I called Mother and my sister Betty in the room to pray for me. Both bowed in earnest prayer for God to ease and remove the pain. For an hour after prayer I continued to toss and groan. Then all of a sudden something started pulling in my side, as if the very life was being pulled from me. A slop jar was given me and a stone hit the bottom, sounding as tough a rock had fallen. After that, ten smaller ones passed. I truly thank God for sending those stones from my body and trust others who may be afflicted will have faith enough to believe that God is the same today and can still heal the body He made.

St. Luke, chapter 16:17-18

"And these signs shall follow them that believe; In my name they shall cast out devils; They shall speak with new tongues; They shall take up serpents, and if they drink any deadly thing, it shall not hurt them; They shall lay hands on the sick and they shall recover."

9.6.3 Caterpillars

During the national camp meeting, in Middlessex, Pa., I was called to the linen room to pray for a sister who had been seriously ill and brought from Sharon, Pa. hospital. The extent of her illness was not known at the time. I anointed and prayed for her. She returned to her home in Sharon and reported later that her trouble was caused from eating vegetables that had not been washed clean. The vegetables had caterpillar eggs on them that were taken into her body. When the sister returned home, five caterpillars passed and were opened by her husband and some neighbors, disclosing five beautiful butterflies. Again, showing God in His infinite power.

9.6.4 Tumor

Mrs. E of Buffalo, N.Y. happened to run across one of my books on Miracles and Visions of Today. She wrote me asking for a prayer for a tumor. The doctors could not remove it as it had grown to her intestines.

She had just one child and wanted so much to be with her as long as possible. She was asked to compare the time there with the time here in order that she might be able to pray with us for her healing. On this night we were holding our weekly Bible classes. At the appointed hour, I had the class close their Bibles. We sang, 'He is Just the Same Today' and read the fifth chapter of James, the thirteenth verse.

I had told Mrs. E to do the same thing at this time and requested her to apply an anointed handkerchief to the affected part of her body. She later sent word that while we were praying the house quaked. Never before had she seen such power. Each person present was blessed and her tumor vanished.

Having been healed and so wonderfully blessed by our Father, she wanted to see me and wished me to see and know that the tumor was truly gone. My fare was sent and I made the trip to Buffalo. While there, it was requested that I run a healing service. During these ten days of services, each person prayed for was instantly healed. In one of the apartments above where I was staying, a lady had been ill for about a year. She was unable to do anything. They brought her downstairs on a cot. When she saw me, she said, *"You are the little woman I saw in a vision coming to pray for me that I may be healed, and to show me the real church."*

We started reading Mark, chapter 11:24 and before we could finish praying for her, she started leaping and jumping, giving thanks to God for healing her body. She had not been in the services for a year due to her illness. This miraculous healing of her body caused her and her husband to unite with the church of God.

To each church of God wherever they may be, if they will live right, tarry as Jesus commanded, they will be endowed with the Holy Ghost. Then power will come into their lives. God can use them to His glory. Reading the 19th chapter of Acts, the 11th and 12th verses, we can see why anointed kerchiefs are used. *"And God wrought special miracles by the hands of Paul that from his body were brought unto the sick, handkerchiefs or aprons and the diseases departed from them and the evil spirits went out from them."*

9.6.5 Snake Experience

Mrs. A… of Leavenworth, Kansas was confronted with the following experience which sounds impossible but is true. Mrs. A became very sick, losing weight and growing smaller all the time. She would eat the normal mount of food required for nourishment of her body as usual, but to no avail. She continued to get worse. The doctors thought perhaps she had a tape worm. They tried various medicines to kill it without killing Mrs. A. Failing in this it was decided to x-ray her stomach. To their amazement the x-ray showed a snake inside her stomach. Mr. and Mrs. A then recalled having drawn a snake from the well in a bucket one time. They had been drinking water from the well located in the yard. All this added up and it was determined that she must have unknowingly swallowed a snake egg in the water. The warmth of her body hatched the snake causing her illness.

I was called to her home to pray for her and God wonderfully healed her and sent the snake in pieces through her intestines and out of her body. Each experience such as this should bring the fact home to each and every one that, God is the same today, yesterday and at all times. He just wants us to consecrate our lives and have faith in Him.

9.6.6 Tuberculosis

Mr. D of Twinsburg, Ohio was in the last stage of tuberculosis. No one but those who administered to him was allowed to enter the room. His condition was truly deplorable. I went to his home, anointed his body and prayed to God earnestly to heal him. God sent His supernatural power and instantly healed Mr. D. He had been in bed for six months, but after being healed, went back to his work the following week. When our heavenly Father does something for us, He does it well and makes no mistakes.

9.6.7 Gall Stones

In the same town, a sister had gall stones. For some reason the doctors could not operate and the stones were too large to pass through her bladder. She too was told that there was no hop for her. In the healing services that I was running at the time, I prayed. The Lord looked down upon her pain racked body and so mercifully sent seven stones from her and she was healed.

9.6.8 Baby's Life Extended

A party of us returning from the national camp meeting in Middlessex, Pa. had a very sad experience shortly after starting for home. Unexpectedly, Rev and Sister Thomas' baby was stricken with pneumonia. It so happened that we were near my daughter's home in Akron, Ohio. The baby was taken there and all of us postponed our trip home on account of the sick child. She was put to bed upstairs and grew worse each passing hour. She became so ill until we expected her to pass any moment. The child was struggling and panting for breath of life so fast that the people in the home were afraid because she was dying. The doctor was called and told that the baby was dying. Knowing it was too late to do any good, the doctor did not visit the home.

We bowed in prayer for the healing of her body. It seemed our prayers were not doing any good. Rev. Thomas' wife became discouraged and upset. She started crying and went downstairs. Brother Thomas, feeling that there was nothing to be done fro his baby, started downstairs to comfort his wife. I then told him that I would pray once again.

Returning to the room, I anointed her and prayed asking the Lord to send the soul back into the body. While anointing the baby and praying, she suddenly said, *"Stop! Stop! Stop that"*, I said! She wanted me to stop rubbing her little chest. The Lord instantly healed the child and she jumped out of bed, ran downstairs asked her Daddy to pick her up. We as God's children should lift Him up so that He may be glorified with our lives and work that we do for Him.

9.6.9 Pneumonia

While visiting in Los Angeles in 1944, Brother Wellington and I were called to pray for Mrs. L. She was given up by the doctors. We anointed and prayed asking God to restore her soul. He wonderfully did so and healed her body.

While visiting and praying for Mrs. L we were called next door to pray door to pray for a neighbor's baby who had lost its hearing. The Lord touched the baby's ear and restored her hearing. God is so very good to all of us that it behooves us to live for Him in this present world. If we do this there is nothing that we ask Him for that He will not grant to us.

9.6.10 *Healed of Infantile Paralysis*

This incident also happened while I was visiting in California and running a healing meeting. A little girl was brought up for prayer for infantile paralysis. Her little body and feet were drawn and so badly affected that she was unable to walk without aid. I anointed and prayed for her. She was instantly healed. Her limbs straightened and next week she was able to walk to school. All of us need that child-like faith.

9.6.11 *Tumor*

I want to tell my experience to the world with the hope that in doing so, it will be the means of some sick soul to be healed in body and soul. I had many afflictions and wish to tell of one of the most outstanding of all. I had a tumor that was sapping the very life out of me. The doctor stated that an operation was the only possible course for me. I had to make up my mind to have the operation or trust God for the healing of my body. I called on the Christian people of the church to pray for me. Then, Mother Sudduth came to my home and prayed. God wonderfully delivered me causing the tumor to pass in pieces. Today I too can with the rest of those who were miraculously healed report victory and truly know that if we meet the conditions, having faith in God at the same time, He will heal us. ---Signed, Mrs. Laura Thurston, 855 Lovers Lane, Akron, Ohio.

Sister M... of Los Angles, California sent for me to come to the Union Hospital to pray for her. The doctors had done all they could for her. I sent up petition to the Lord for the healing of her body which He did. I told her that if she would obey God's word, the affliction would not return. Mrs. M went home from the hospital. The Lord blessed her giving her strength to work.

However, she failed to obey. He tells us to serve Him when He heals our body or worse things will come upon us. He wants us to lift Him up that all men may come unto him. But not obeying His word, she suffered the affliction worse than the first time. Mrs. M was given up again and her people sent for me to return and pray for her. She was in a coma for two days when I arrived. I told her Mother that God would let Mrs. M speak to her. She did so after I prayed for God to rebuke the death and let her speak. She became better for a while, but later on my way home, I received a telegram that she was worse and asking for prayer. She died. It pays to obey, for obedience is better than sacrifice.

I accompanied Rev. and Mrs. Ray Jackson to the national camp meeting in Middlessex, Pa. one summer. On our return trip, we stopped in Three Rivers, Michigan to visit the Jackson's friends and relatives. One of Rev. Jackson's deacons from his former church had been in the hospital for nine months without cure. They carried me to his home where he had been taken when nothing more could be done in the hospital. I anointed him and prayed for his healing. He became so overjoyed that he ran out into the yard, praising and thanking God for touching his body. This brother's wife and daughter were united to the church through the miracle that happened to their husband and Father.

At this time, Rev. Jackson's nephew was stricken with tuberculosis. He also was healed through prayer. The family traveled to Kalamazoo, Michigan, leaving me in a meeting at his former church. During the services there, the Lord marvelously restored the eyesight of one of the members.

End

Chapter 10 - A Glimpse of the Culpeppers

Some information given by Rosalie Davis, Uncle Dokes grand daughter
and great-great grand son Charles Davis 3rd
Written by:
Bettye G Guillory

I feel very strongly to mention my Mother's side of my family to honor them by telling what little I know about them in this Book. My Maternal Grandparents; Mama's Mother and Father were Named Benjamin and Mollie Culpepper. They both had passed before I was born. But Mama shared some things about her family with me during my teenage years. I am the youngest of the 9 children in our family and was at home longer than any of my brothers and sisters. I didn't get married until I was 24 years of age. I was always younger than my years; my parent's kept me a baby as long as they could. My "Papa" went home to be with the Lord when I was 32 years of age; Mama passed 4 years after Papa's home going, and I was 36 when Mama passed.

Grandpa "Ben" my Mama's Father was jet black with straight Black hair, a Black hawk Indian. Grandma Molly his wife was Brown skin with kinky hair. They had 7 children; I only have the names and information about five of the seven. The other two, the only information to speak of I have about them is; I believe Mama told me they died as infants, if I remember correctly.

Mama's oldest brother was named Doke, Uncle Doke had six or seven children. His oldest daughter was named Melissa. I remember meeting his son named Robert in California many years ago. Robert was very dark like Grandpa with cold black straight Hair and was a very handsome man. I also met Uncle Doke's daughter Julia, who lived in Los Angeles California also. Uncle Doke had a daughter named Roxie, one named Pinkie and another son named Zagzee. I haven't been able to get any information about them: Roxie, Pinkie and Zagzee.

About 15 years ago someone told me about Melissa's Daughter Kathryn Bell who lived in Chicago Illinois. Melissa was Uncle Doke's oldest daughter. I called Kathryn and we kept in touch with each other by phone through the years. Then I called one day and her granddaughter told me she had passed. The granddaughter gave me the phone number of Kathryn's sister Rosalie Davis who lives in Chicago also. I called Rosalie; she referred me to her daughter for information about their side of the family tree (the Culpepper's).

I was introduced to Rosalie's daughter Daphne over the phone. Daphne is a very prestigious lady. She teaches and is very busy. I tried to get her to write about her side of the family; believe it or not she tells me to call her Mother back because of her extremely busy schedule; of course her time was limited.

Rosalie told me a few things; her grandson Charles Davis III was married here in my area about 3 year ago and now Lives in De Moines Washington; which is the next city to my place Federal Way Washington. Charles the 3rd is a commercial Pilot Working for the Alaska Air Lines;

his wife is a stewardess who works for the same airline company. They have a new little Daughter.

Mama's oldest sister was named Ella May, she married my Father's oldest brother William Sudduth the 2nd. This meant two sisters were married to two brothers. Uncle "Will" and Aunt Ella had 9 children and my Papa and Mama had 9 children; Of course their children were our Double cousins. Mama named my sister Ella May after Aunt Ella and also named my sister Emma Lou after her other sister named Aunt Emma. In those day's people named their children after Aunts and Uncles and other family members. You will find in this book much Repetition of names.

Robert Culpepper, Mama's youngest brother was a fine young Man with red hair and was loved by many people Mama said. Everybody loved him. He had favor with several prominent white people. But he had enemies who were jealous of him and of course at that time segregation was prevalent. Some one killed Uncle Robert.

A couple of people were fishing in a boat one day and it started to rain, it thundered and a bolt of lightening struck him and brought up Uncle Roberts body out of the water. He had chains and some iron wrapped around his body that held him down under the water. He fell in the boat which startled the two people fishing. They laid his body on the shore. How they recognized him was because of his sandy red hair. The murderer was never found.

The story of my Aunt Ella and her family is told in Chapter 2, written by her off springs and my Mother Dora's is told in the Chapter 6 about my Father and our family. Aunt Emma the little I know about her has been written in another chapter.

Mama had a great Uncle she called Uncle "Ben". I feel compelled to tell the great Story she told me about him. He was Phenomenal. My great Uncle Ben lived very close to God. When he walked in a room where some one was sick, if he groaned in the Spirit you would know they would not get well, but if he smiled they would know that person would be healed. He was loved by most every body because of his love for God and people and the wonderful gifts God had blessed him with. He had prophesied about the day he would be translated; which meant he would not have a normal death; but like Enoch and Elijah in the Bible did not see Death but God just took them. That day he walked out of the door and some one remembered that was the day he was going to be translated; they went out to check and to see where he went. People drug the creeks and logs were turned over they looked everywhere and his body were never found.

I remember Aunt Emma and one of her daughters named Lillie coming to visit us when I was a girl and we were living in Topeka Kansas. Strange thing happened Papa and Uncle George were the last two in their family living and Uncle George died in January 1945 and Papa passed July 1945; 6 months later. Aunt Emma passed In January 1949; she and Mama were the last two living in their Family and Mama died 6 months later on the 13 of July 1949.

I have tried to contact Charles III several times and only received a reply to my phone call one time. I gave up trying. It is unfortunate that my Mother's side of the family seems to come to a halt with Charles's generation; even though he is the fourth generation I had hoped my children would meet him and carry on as it is doing on my Father's side of our family. I am in touch with the fourth generation on my Father's side who are extremely interested in knowing about their Ancestors; and are working with me to carry on.

Figure 72 - Indigo Davis the little daughter of Charles Davis the 3rd and his wife Lena

Ironically enough I did received a Christmas letter from Charles Davis III and His wife Lena just this past Christmas with this picture above of their 2 year daughter above. The letter was quite informative of their accomplishments of the past year. He was just promoted to Captain and is pilot of a special plane for the Alaskan Air Lines Company. His wife Lena also works for the same company. They have purchased a home in De Moines Washington. They travel extensively. They are very active and are accomplishing great successes.

Chapter 11 - My Spiritual Quest

Written by:
Bettye G. Guillory

I remember when I was 76 years of age, I read Ethel water's Book telling the story of her life; she was 76 years of Age when She wrote her book. I thought since I was the same age as she was when I read her book; why not write my autobiography? It's not too late; and so that is when I started to write.

I've had quite an eventful life; my life has been very interesting. I feel strongly I have a lot to share with the world even. There is a lot that many can learn if they are seeking answers to life and their purpose for living. Many will be able to profit by my mistakes as well as my successes. God has given me a lot of Wisdom through my experiences as well as my observations through The years.

At this time I would like to reveal to you the greatest Testimonies of my life. So I have also started writing a second book. The title of my Second Book is "She Was Born Without A Name." When people see this title, I am sure it will raise questions in people's minds. Who is she? Why didn't she have a Name? Yes you guessed it. I will be writing my autobiography.

I am writing my Autobiography as a Testimony to pass on to those who choose to read these Books. My life's story will be a story of how God has brought a member of the Sudduth off springs through an awesome and unbelievable Journey over the period of my 95 years of life. I do hope many people will be able to profit by my mistakes and be motivated and inspired by my successes. I have been made very much aware that life is a challenge from the day of birth until the end of life. God has given me great favor in answers to my prayers. When I ask Him for wisdom, He has given it to me as he has promised in His word. The things He has taught me, what I have learned by reading, seeing and by experience; and most of all by receiving revelation from God (through the power of His Word; and the Holy Spirit), I want to share with you. It almost boggles my mind.

The Greatest of all has been my relationship with my Lord and Savior Jesus Christ. God has sustained me and brought me through many trails and test in life; which has really been a blessing. I was so busy doing good things that I missed the God things. Being quieted by pain and misery I began to seek God in a special way. As I began to see and feel the pain others have felt. God in a new way has been giving me revelation knowledge rather than just Book knowledge. I don't know how many times I have read the Bible and through other books galore, ever learning, but never coming into the knowledge of Spiritual truths.

It seems hard to believe after attending seminars, traveling going to classes, getting the book knowledge, earning certificates, etc., I am now receiving the revelation knowledge I never knew before. It is very exciting because I am learning so many things about the

Lord and His word which I didn't know or understand before. I have grown spiritually through being taught So many things by the Holy Spirit.

I am indeed thankful that God has so graciously given me longevity. The fact that I am still on this planet earth is amazing. I still have a sharp mind and a very young spirit. Although I have had many reverses, I can say I am in good health for my age today. If people don't know me, they cannot believe my age when they meet me.

I praise Almighty God for His Love, Mercy and Great Favor He gives to me daily. I do believe with all my heart that Jeremiah 29:11-13 is the Answer. God has a plan for me yet, and His plan for me is good. My goal is to fulfill his purpose for me. I do want Him to say *"Well done thou Good and faithful Servant, inter in to the joys of heaven"*, when he calls me home on my final graduation day. In seeking His will and the knowledge of his word; I have read the Holy Bible over and over again through the years; attended Seminars, watched Christian television programs, and read Hundreds of books.

In 1971 I went to Gerald Derstines Christian retreat in Bradenton Florida. I was seeking the Baptism of the Holy Spirit and His Holy Anointing. I wanted a deeper experience with The Lord. I made many new friends while I was in Florida. I had an hour conference With David Duplesse to receive prayer and Direction, David was the Father of Glosselalia, Speaking in Tongues. From the retreat I was invited to the Home of Glenda Miller, a prophetess. She had a teenage son and daughter. I stayed a few days at her home. From There I was invited to the home of Norma and Norman Fore, in Indian Harbor Beach, Florida. There is where I fasted, prayed and received the Baptism of the Holy Spirit. I had a chance to Visit Jamie Buckingham's Spirit filled church while I was there. Today I still keep in Contact with Brooks and Laura Watson who live in Palm Bay Florida. I spent a week at The Bethune Cookman College. Altogether I spent the whole month of February 1971 in Florida.

I was an International organizer for the Alpha Chi Pi Omega Sorority and Fraternity then; consequently that earned my stay free at Bethune Cookman College. I traveled to the Holy Land with Kash Amburgy's tour a Christian group of 210 people on a 747, and was baptized in the River of Jordan on November 9/1972.

While I was in NY in 1972, I joined a Spirit filled Church there and Sang in the choir. I made several friends in the church; who went on the Holy land Trip with the group from all over the USA. It was my first trip over seas. This tour to Israel in 1972 was one of the greatest Highlights of my life. I remember a storm came up as we were flying over the sea; I began to pray, the Lord directed me to just open a book I had been reading; without even turning the Page it read and the Lord said; *"you know I have the wind in my fist don't you"*, I laid back and went to sleep, as I said *"Peace be still"*; it reminded me of the Bible story how Jesus Spoke to the wind and said *"Peace be still"* the wind obeyed His Command. Mark 11:24 tell us to speak to the mountain and it shall Obey us.

I have learned the importance of speaking Gods word. God has given us authority to speak the word in His Name. I received the revelation of who I am in Christ by meditating the Word. Saint Paul wrote in Ephesians chapter 1:3-23. Most Christians do not realize who they are in Christ. I want to add Here John 6:53 to impress upon your minds the importance of the also partaking of the Blood of Jesus (Holy Communion) which gives us life; Jesus shed his precious Blood that we may have eternal Life. I feel led to take communion daily as I confess my sins To Him, read and speak his word aloud. Romans 10:17 says faith Comes by hearing and hearing the message that comes from our lips.

We went to so many memorable places on our tour like to Jacobs well, the shepherds cave, Golgotha, the Wailing Wall, the Tomb, the Dead Sea, etc. I will never forget the river Jordon. I was baptized in the River of Jordon on November 9th 1972. What a blessing to have had the privilege of being Baptized in the same River our Lord was baptized in.

In 1977 I went with Francis and Charles Hunter to Hawaii on a Nine day retreat. We went to a couple of different Islands. I met new friends there. We went to Alueowe, the beach and sight seeing. The meetings were very inspiring; especially the teaching On the Holy Spirit and healing meetings.

I toured the Country attending conventions; also Retreats Throughout the years, I was so hungry to be close to the Lord and to know him better. I think most people ask themselves the Question; what on earth am I here for? By the way I have a little Booklet that has that title written by: Rick Warren. This little Booklet inspires me.

It is amazing how God has revealed things to me I never understood I know now that with all my learning through the years there is always a new and fresh revelation we learn from time to time; really some time daily. I was just getting book knowledge. Some people thought I was a Bible scholar; because I could quote so many scriptures. Yet, I was so thirsty for more of Jesus. There is a difference in Book knowledge and Revelation knowledge. God says in His word He will never leave us or for sake us. It is amazing the difference in our lives once the Holy Spirit Quickens His word to our spirit. I am an impetuous person like Peter; who loved the Lord with All his heart; yet Peter was quick to speak before he thought sometimes and had to repent. But on the day of Pentecost, He was totally transformed like 180 degrees. He preached to 3000 Souls that day and even when people passed his Shadow they were healed.

I would love to be able to heal others through the Power of the Holy Spirit; who lives in my spirit. I am reminded of the words of St Paul who was one of the greatest disciples of Christ in the New Testament. He wrote about 2 thirds of the New Testament. Romans 7:18, relating to the Battles he had in the flesh when he was tempted. He said in the Flesh he would do the things he shouldn't do and also not do the Things he should; yet Romans 8: 1,2 Tells us; but God and the Holy Spirit only is able to keep us from sin and temptation.

The experiences I have come through all my life; but especially since the year 2000 have been phenomenal. God has been so good to me. No one could have stood the pain emotionally and physically, that I have experienced with out Gods sustaining, Amazing Grace. To come through the high blood pressure and emotional anxiety attacks and on top of being given medication that caused side affects and not have a stroke or heart attack is impossible at my age. It had to be God Almighty Who has done the impossible with man kind and worked miracles in my life. I believe He has a plan and a purpose for me to fulfill yet. Each of the 9 times I was rushed to the Hospital in emergency over a Period of 6 years I would quote Gods Word. Psalms 118: 17 & 18 *"I shall not die, but live, and declare The works and recount the Illustrious acts of the Lord". "The Lord has chastened me sorely, but He has not given me over to Death."*

The Holy Spirit has taught me so much during this period. I am amazed at the revelations that the Holy Spirit has given to me. Even though I have read the same scriptures so many times through the years, I want to say here (regardless of my Age and the slowing down of my body) my spirit and my mind are like a 47 year old. I feel in a way like Caleb in Joshua 14: 10-15 when he was 85 he said, he was as strong as he was at 45 and was ready to take that mountain. So I'm ready to do what ever it takes to fulfill my purpose in this life.

I strongly believe that the vision God gave me 20 years ago; which is to walk in the manifestation of healing in every atom of my being, is yet to come and will come quickly as Habakkuk 2:2,3 says. Even in old age I believe the gifts I have walked in; in the past are being restored by the Holy Spirit. The desire of my heart is to be used as Peter to heal the sick and raise the dead. People were healed even as they walked by Peter's shadow. That has to be the anointing of the Holy Spirit. God has shown me older people don't have to die sick; should walk in health even though they are aging. Amazingly, I still love life and feel like this is the greatest age to live in. I believe life is a challenge from the time one is born until they die.

I believe the key to all of Gods promises is speaking the Word of God, standing on the word praising God without ceasing, believing it and receiving His word without wavering. We must visualize ourselves walking in and living an abundant life. To confirm this vision God gave me scriptures like Psalms 71: 18, *"O God yes, even when I am old and gray for sake me not, but Keep me alive until I have declared your mighty strength to this Generation, and your might and power to all that are to come"*; Also Psalms 92:12-15 *"the uncompromisingly righteous shall Flourish like the palm tree {be long lived, stately, upright, Useful Fruitful}; he shall grow like a cedar in Lebanon {Majestic, Stable durable and incorruptible}. Planted in the House of the Lord, they shall flourish in the courts of our God. {Growing in Grace} they shall still bring forth fruit in old age; They shall be full of sap {of spiritual vitality} and rich in the Verdure {of trust, love and contentment}; {they are living Memorials} to show that the Lord is upright and faithful to His Promises; He is my rock and there is no unrighteous in Him"*..

During this period of testing; God has revealed so many new Things to me; especially at times I was diligently seeking Him. I Heard Andrew Wommack at 5:30 AM one morning on Christian TV; his Message was so powerful, I was compelled to send for 20 of His tapes and meditate on the word God had given him. The names of his tapes were; "A better way to pray", six tapes on Spirit, soul and body. "The Baptism of the Holy spirit" "Growing In the Spirit". I thank God because now that I have retired from working out in the world as I've done for so many years, I now am learning so many things I didn't know. The Holy Spirit Being is my teacher as I review the word, watch Christian Television, listen to Christian radio, meditate the word and Pray, and observing what's is going on in the world. I find life very interesting; really exciting.

As I close this chapter I want to share a couple of short poems by my brother Sheldon's from his book of poems:

"It Might Have Been"

God had need of you and me
In this sin cursed world below;
To cast out all evil that we spy,
Save souls from that place of woe.
Don't be slow to start out,
To put old Satan's host to route;
Friend don't wait to late to begin,
And at last to say it might have been.
While the blood runs yet in your veins,
Put forth new effort with might and main;
To save lost souls yet out in sin,
Then it surely is not might have been.

"What a Friend"

Dear brother if you lose your soul,
Miss Heaven, fail to reach your goal;
What pleasure then would you gain,
With your riches, pride and worldly fame?
Though the whole wide world lay at your feet,
Everyone is your friend that you meet;
But your riches and fame you lose You have no friends from which to choose.
Then brother why not God's friendship obtain,
He'll share His glory and immortal fame;
Give you a home, a mansion rare, In the heavenly city so fair.

Sheldon's poems are so beautiful it was hard for me to choose; However, I believe they have blessed many souls and still will be instrumental in winning souls to Christ.

May this chapter give all who read it a hunger and desire to seek the Lord for a deeper experience with Christ at any age; and make you know that at any age God is your only hope for living the Abundant life with him only meeting your every need Spiritual, Physically, mentally, emotionally; I might add financially too.

May God bless you and give you a joyful, happy and healthy long life is my prayer for you! Ephesians Chapter 1 will tell you who you are in Christ Jesus. Read it over and over again and ask the Holy Spirit to help you receive it in your Spirit: may it Become life to you.

Chapter 12 - " The Summary"

Written by:
Bettye G. Guillory

As I come to the end of the first book I have written; "How The Sudduth Melting Pot Began" I wish to express my gratitude to my relatives who are much younger than I; that have so graciously taken time out of their busy schedules to write chapters, and other contributors who met with those writing Chapters to talk about their side of Our Family Tree -- their Great Grandparents, Grandparents and other members of their families. The truth of the matter is I must say WE HAVE COME TO THE END OF WRITING THIS BOOK TOGETHER, even though I have initiated the writing of it. It has been a journey for all who participated in so many different ways.

I must give God Honor first and then all the family members that have worked to put this book together.

Figure 73 – Elizabeth holding her baby Makayla; Bruce the proud grandfather, and father of Elizabeth

I wish to especially honorably mention Bruce Petersen; my brother Elsberry's grand son. His mother Elizabeth "Beth", my brother's youngest daughter passed at the age of 43. She was a beautiful and gifted young lady. Bruce who so graciously offered to print and bind this book for distribution is very special to me and is a man of great faith. His daughter Elizabeth (named for his mother) was in a terrible accident October 27, 2007. She was hit by an 18-wheeler truck and injured badly, hospitalized and went through rehab for sometime. She is doing wonderfully and planning to go back to school. I was impressed by his great faith in God and his devotion to his daughter and the baby. God miraculously continues to heal her. Praise God! I can't praise God enough for Bruce.

Bruce is the Manager of FedEx Kinko's in Raleigh North Carolina, holding a prestigious position. I am so proud of him. Although this book was delayed, it is going great now and will soon be in the hands of all those God has ordained to be blessed by reading it. Thanks be to God Almighty and thank you Bruce, may God restore to you 1000 fold Deuteronomy 1:11.

I will also mention the following names because they have helped make this book a success:

Rasheeda Garner, my Uncle "Will's" Great-Great-Grand daughter, contacted several relative from Uncle "Will's' side of the Family; namely -- Roy Roberson, Eugene Logan, Calvin Spann, Megan Spann and Juarezetta Bass. They have put together a beautiful memoir in Chapter 2. It really warmed my heart inspired me. The chapter gave me information that was new to me even though I had met and seen a number of the older members of their family before they passed way.

Under Chapter 2, Calvin Spann was able to pass on his memories about the Sudduth Clan. Unfortunately, Calvin suddenly passed away not too long ago. He will not have the enjoyment of seeing his writings in print. The book also contains the writings of Jodette Spann who is a daughter of Calvin Spann.

NaDel Justice a granddaughter of Larry B. Sudduth has writings about her Grandfather Larry who was my double cousin (his Father was my Father's oldest brother who married my Mother's oldest sister). This also makes NaDel my Uncle "Will's" Great Granddaughter.

Billie Ruth Parker is my Uncle "Jim's" Great Granddaughter. She has written Chapter 3. She is to be commended for having contacted so many relatives in Tulsa Oklahoma and elsewhere whose names are mentioned in Chapter 3.

I especially want to mention Juanita Wilson because she and I talked often now on the phone. Juanita is just 2 months younger than I am. Her writing is very good, and I admire her sharpness and ability at such a young age *(Smiles)*.

The Chapter 5 title, "Mudda the Tie That Binds", was chosen by Patricia Buckner the Great Granddaughter of my Aunt Lucy (Sudduth) Marcus and also by Anita Culp a Grand daughter of Aunt Lucy. The two of them worked together to create this chapter.

I wrote what I knew about that side of our family tree in Chapter 6 "George Sudduth a Journey of Faith". His mother Lucille Johnson told me recently he had a stroke and had to give up his pastor position in Cleveland, Ohio. He has also some what of a memory loss. Barbara Jones, granddaughter of Uncle George, daughter of George, Jr. gave me the title for Chapter 6. I took what I could draw from her and completed Uncle George's chapter. My desire has been that there would be someone from each one's off springs who would elaborate on their side of the family tree. They know so much more about their family than I do and especially know more about the younger Generation. I have written some things that I know about each of my Father's brothers and sisters also my Father's parents in Chapter 1, Chapter 7, and Chapter 9 just in case all the requested information does not come in.

Chapter 7 was written by yours truly about my parents, brothers, sisters, and my children. I have been so blessed by so many of my Father and Mother's descendants responding to my request to send in writings. These testimonies and writings have their names recognized with their writings. I am sure you were blessed by their messages.

Chapter 8 was written by Ramel McClelland Eubanks I commend her for her dedication.

"Experiences with the Father" was a booklet written by Sister Beecham about my Mama's healing ministry. The words were actually dictated to her by my Mother in 1935. Sister Beecham was a member of the "Church of God" in Topeka, Kansas. I was born and raised in Topeka and was raised up in the Church of God there. My Mama's testimony, I believe, is one of the most outstanding in the book. Mama was a saint and ministered to many people in her day. She was a woman of great faith, with multiple talents. She was moved by the Holy Spirit and was a Blessing to many people. I believe her chapter will even touch many lives today and will live on through the years; for the generations to come. This is one reason alone this book must be published and her Message live on.

An exciting story about my spiritual adopted grand daughter Christina Portillo; on Sunday the 4th of may this year 2008 Christina invited me and Aukash the care giver where I live here at "Tuscany Adult Family Home". Well - she invited us to go to church with her and then out to a Chinese restaurant for lunch after church. We were just talking about different things and my book came up. Christina asked me how the book was going. I told her it was finished all except the editing and checking the format. She then said she could finish the book in a day. Wow, I got excited. I then called my nephew Bruce Petersen in Raleigh North Carolina; who had offered to put the book together. He sent the book by CD to my daughter Nesbia. Christina immediately started editing the book. She and I found out it would take days instead of a day to finish editing the book. Christina has worked diligently giving me so far about 6 days of her time on Saturday's and Sundays from 7 to 9 hours a day. May God return to Christina a 1000 (thousand fold) "Deuteronomy 11:1. I can not thank and praise God enough for Christina. May every body that reads this book know that Christina Portillo, Bruce Petersen, and Elizabeth Jean Rattray are heading this project and should be accredited under God for the success of this book!

Deuteronomy 1:11 is my prayer for all who read this book, "*May the Good Lord, the God of our Fathers make you 1000 times as Many as you are, and bless you as He has promised to do so.*" I'm believing you all love Him and serve Him.

To those who don't know him, if you will repeat the following simple prayer and mean it sincerely from your heart; he will save you and come in to your heart and will give you Eternal Life.

"*I believe Jesus Christ is the only begotten son of God, and that He was crucified; died, shed his life's blood for me. He arose after 3 days and now forever lives to intercede to the Father for my sins. I ask you*

Father in Jesus name for give me of all my Sin. Come into my Heart; take over my life; be my Lord and Savior. I accept you as my Lord and Savior and will Love you and serve you for the rest of my days. Thank you Lord for saving my soul; fill me with your Holy Spirit. Thank You, Amen!"

It is now important to find a Bible believing Church to attend for fellowship. Then ask God to reveal Himself to you in His word as you read the Bible. God's word and the Holy Spirit will be your teacher. You will grow daily as you feast on His word. There will be no end to your success in life if you live by Gods word. Follow it's instructions and teachings.

Do not let this Book of the Law depart from your mouth; meditate on it day and night, so that you may be careful to do everything written in it. Then you will be prosperous and successful. Have I not commanded you? Be strong and courageous. Do not be terrified; do not be discouraged, for the LORD your God will be with you wherever you go." Joshua 1: 8- 9

This is NOT the end

Addendum & Acknowledgements

Figure 74 -Northwest Church, Federal Way, Washington Ref. page 20

Figure 75 - Coy & Judy Mc Elderry Are my
Spiritual adopted Children see - page 22

Uncle Will's Descendents
Chapter 2 - Memoirs - page 54

**Figure 76-Sadie R. (Hill) 1st - wife of Larry B. Sudduth
And Mother of Nadine & Geraldine**

Figure 77-Nadine "Dean" (Sudduth) Thompson

Figure 78-Geraldine "Chick" (Sudduth) Monroe

Figure 79- Nillus NaDel Justice Daughter of Nadine
And Delmar Thompson

Uncle Jim's Descendants

Chapter 3 - Ref. -pages 62

Figure 80-

FRONT ROW: IDA;EMMA;ELIZABETH; FRANK
BACK ROW: CARL;LEROY;FRED;HERMAN

Figure 81

EDDIE;BILLY;FRED;JAMES

FRANK JR

Figure 82

Charles J. Sudduth Legacy

Figure 83- Sheldon & Margaret Sudduth chapter 7 - pages 150

Figure 84 - Twelve of the 32 grandchildren Of Charles J. Sudduth
When they were kids / grandpa Charles standing on right in back

Figure 85 -Elizabeth Jean & Kirk Rattray & their
Children Morgan and Carson
Chapter 7 page 109

Bettye Guillory's Children

Figure 86-Johnny & Vickie Guillory Ref. - Chapter 7 - page 157

Figure 87 – L-R Four generations

Nesbia is Bettye's daughter, Gina & Rhonda are Nesbia daughters, and Dionna in front of Bettye is Gina's daughter

Figure 88 - There were about 90 members of the
Sudduth descendants in this picture approximately 6 or 7 who were at
the reunion missed the picture setting

By: Bettye Guillory

I was delighted to know that most every one at the reunion was a born again Christians. Several nephews, 2nd and 3rd cousins were either ministers of the Gospel or evangelists. Some of them were professionals; and many had degrees of some kind, others had their own businesses. God has blessed our family tree supper abundantly. We give God all the glory and Honor! My nephew Howard Sudduth who is a minister and my nieces Judy Dyer and Lynette Kidd were the ones who Hosted the family reunion, I want to give sincere Thanks again for a beautiful exciting time; they did an excellent job preparing for the occasion.

Early in the morning on Monday July 27th I was preparing for the day, thinking about the family reunion and listening to Breakthrough on Christian TV. Rod Parsley was preparing millions of people through out the world for a special Service to be held 8/8/2008 for 3 days at World Harvest church; People sent in their seed of $88.08 and prayer requests believing for a New Beginning in their lives. Biblically the number 8 means a New Beginning. It clicked in my spirit; I knew I was to be at the family Reunion, because we were getting together on the same identical days and all of the Sudduth Descendants needed to be blessed with a New Beginning.

God miraculously provided the way for me to go to the family reunion on Friday 8/8/2008. I stayed 3 days from Friday to Sunday. I planted a seed of $38.08 into Rod Parsley's ministry and sent in my prayer request; we flew to Kansas City Missouri where my Nephew Marvin Lawton and his sister Gloria (Lawton) Williams from Rome, New York picked us up and drove us Topeka, Kansas. This was one of the greatest high lights of my life. I was treated like a queen being the Matriarch of the family. It was like Heaven on earth.

I called my oldest granddaughter Gina she readily consented to go with me; bought me new clothes and treated me royal. The flight going there was smooth and beautiful; returning home there was turbulence; Speaking Gods word aloud works, I had no fear I Quoted the scriptures of Jesus "Peace be Still".

God gave me prophetic words for several people at the reunion which I related to them privately. I had asked Rod's ministry to pray for all of us who were at our reunion.

In the Sunday morning service those who attended and heard me speak, for you and your families who believe, your New Beginning began on the eighth month, eighth day, and 2008th year. By the faith of God who dwells within you and me we shall walk in health, prosperity, and grow spiritually. Our needs will be met, even our God given desires as we delight ourselves in Him and seek His face diligently. Psalms 37 : 4

We shall meet in two years, 2010, in Tennessee at our next Family reunion with good reports! Amen

Legacy of Life - Bios of Donna Kidd's Children
Figure 42- Chapter 7 page 137

Rudy L. Dyer, III, the eldest child born to Donna Jean Lorraine Sudduth and Rudy L. Dyer, II on January 6, 1946 in Topeka, Kansas.

Attended Buchanan Middle School, Lowman Hill Middle School, and Boswell Junior High and graduated from Topeka High School, June of 1964. I joined the U.S. Naval Reserves while in high school. After high school, I attended Ark City Junior College. My second year of junior college, I received a football scholarship. I then received a walk-on scholarship to Langston University but was unable to accept it due to being called into U.S. Naval Military in December of 1965.

I had an honorable discharge from the Navy in 1967. I spent six years in the Naval Military. After leaving the Navy, I moved to Inglewood, California where I married my childhood sweetheart, Diedra Kay Akers. I enrolled into Cal State Los Angeles University majoring in Business Administration Marketing. I graduated from Cal State Los Angeles University in 1973 with a B. S. Degree in Business Administration Marketing.

I was employed with Exxon Mobil from 1968 until retirement in 2001. After my retirement, I moved to Madison, Wisconsin where I am currently a Transitional Foster Parent working with the Dane County Human Services.

"I have a daughter, Mikel Dyer, (step) son Cory who is 26 years old and two grandchildren, Taylor who is 15 years old and Brandon who is 5 years old.

Michael Armound Dyer, the second son and child of Donna Jean Lorraine Sudduth and Rudy LaValle Dyer II. I was born on November 11, 1946 in Topeka, Kansas. My first name comes from the Archangel Michael and my middle name comes from Armistice the day in which the treaty was signed to end WWII.

I graduated from Loman Hill Elementary School, Boswell Junior High School, Topeka High School, Butler County Community Junior College AA Degree, Washburn University B-Ed Degree, University of Wisconsin-Milwaukee Master's Degree in Educational Psychology.

I attended Butler County Junior College on a basketball scholarship, Highland University in New Mexico on a basketball scholarship. I played Semi-Professional Basketball for 3 years. I later became the Head Women's Basketball Coach, Head Men's Tennis Coach and Head Men's Basketball Coach at Madison Area Technical College.

I graduated from Washburn University and was certified in elementary education. I began my teaching career in Milwaukee, Wisconsin in 1968 at the age of 21. I taught elementary education for 4 years and later became a guidance counselor. I received my Master's Degree in Educational Psychology in 1972. In 1974 I moved to Madison, Wisconsin and began a teaching career at Madison Area Technical College as a Psychology Instructor. I retired from teaching in 2001.

I am currently semi-retired and am working in an innovative program of foster care in Madison. I developed the concept of Therapeutic Transition Foster Care in which I am an independent contractor with Dane County. I provide services to disturbed adolescent boys who are labeled SED's (Serious Emotionally Disturbed- they are adolescent boys).

I was married to Ellen Blackwell and am currently married, for the past 22 years, to Janet Lee Huff. I have 5 children, Christopher 38, Stephany 36, Muhibb 33, Angelene 25 and Makailah 14. I have 6 grandchildren.

Julia Marie Dyer, the eldest daughter of Donna Jean Lorraine Sudduth and Rudy L. Dyer, Sr. Judy was born on Mother's Day May 9, 1948 in Topeka, Kansas. My family and friends call me "Judy". I am the third child of Donna Sudduth.

I was raised in Topeka, Kansas and graduated from Topeka High School May 30, 1966. I was very fortunate to receive a 4-year athletic scholarship in 1966 to Texas Southern University in Houston, Texas. I was one of the original six women chosen to start the women's track and field team at Texas Southern University in Houston, Texas in 1966. I receive my B.S. Degree in Psychology in 1971 and a Master's Degree in Counseling and Guidance in 1974.

In 1968, I was a member of the United States Track and Field Olympic Team in Mexico City, Mexico where I participated in the 80 meter hurdlers. I tied the American Record in the 80 meter hurdles in 1968 before the Olympic Games in Mexico City. During my athletic career (which began at the age of nine years old) I participated in track and field events for over 13 years achieving many AAU records and national records in various events. My best events were the long jump (18ft.6") and the 80 meter hurdles.

I was the first Topeka Olympian and the first Texas Southern University female Olympian. In 1986, I was the first female athlete inducted into the Texas Southern University Hall of Fame. In 1987 I was inducted in the Who's Who in Professional and Executive Women that was dedicated to the 200th anniversary of the Constitution of the United States.

Judy was also inducted into the Southwest Athletic Conference (SWAC) Hall of Fame in 2001 in Birmingham, Alabama. On March 22, 2008, Texas Southern University honored Judy as the first athlete to have their jersey (track and field) hung in the new Southwest Athletic Conference (SWAC) Lounge at the Student Union Center on the campus of Texas Southern University.

Since my retirement from athletics, I was a Vocational Rehabilitation Counselor in Houston, Texas for five years. After leaving my counseling position, I adventured into sales and marketing for various companies throughout the United States for 20 years. I have owned and operated three businesses. The first business was a limousine company (Los Angeles, CA), a fitness center (Topeka, Kansas) and now a medical case management company in Houston, Texas for the past 14 years.

I was a USA track and field official and a board member with the Gulf Association Track and Field organization for over twelve years working with young boys and girls in Houston, Texas. I retired from this position in 2002.

Currently, I am the Chair Person for the Texas Southern University Track and Field Relays which is the 4th largest track and field relays in the nation and the largest minority relays in the nation at Texas Southern University, Houston, Texas.

I am now single and I do not have any children. I do have many, many, nieces and nephews, along with many great nieces and nephews. I was a member of the Topeka and Houston Chapter of the Link's Inc. for over 12 years. I am a current member of the Brentwood Baptist Church in Houston, Texas and I truly" Love The Lord"

Karla B. McClelland-Jackson, I'm the daughter of Donna J. Kidd and Paul R. McClelland both of Topeka, KS. I'm 56 year old, single mother of three children: Ameesah A. Jackson, Jamison R. McQuiller and Kellen C.R. McQuiller. Out of Donna's seven children I'm the middle child and the middle daughter.

I lived most of my life in Topeka Kansas; and graduated from Topeka High School in 1970. Later on I went to College and graduated from Friends University with a Degree in Human Resource. I currently work at the Michael E. DeBakey VA Medical Center in Houston, TX. I have worked with the Federal Government for ten years. After mother passed away, Jamison, Kellen and I moved to Houston in 2004. My daughter Ameesah soon followed by moving to Houston about two years ago with her two children, Zacchias; seven, Ezavyar; six , and had her third son, Lazarus who is about to be two; later after she made the move to Texas.

Ameesah is 25 years old. After she moved from Kansas she completed courses from the Texas School of Business last year. She is currently employed at Sprint, as a customer service rep. Both of her older children are both in elementary school where the are doing quite will adjusting to their new life in the big city of Houston, as we all have. My daughter Jamison is 19. She graduated from Lamar High School in Houston, Texas in 2007. She is currently enrolled in the Art Intuition of Houston working toward a degree in Baking and Pastry/ Culinary Arts. She also has two part-time jobs; one at Delia's clothing store and the other at Hollister's Clothing Store.

Kellen is 17, this coming year will be his last year of high school he will graduate in 2009, also from Lamar High School, in Houston, TX. He also works a part- time job at Sweetwater Country Club and plays football at Lamar as a wide receiver. In addition to his hard and dedication playing football last year, he also ran track with the Houston Track team.

Chalmus Ray Kidd was the fifth child and third son born to Donna Jean Lorraine Sudduth and Wilbur L. Kidd on April 3, 1956. He was raised in Topeka, Kansas and graduated from Topeka High School. Chalmus as one of the first minority males to become a member of the Topeka High School Debate Team. He was an excellent debater and won many awards. He also participated in sports. Chalmus played basketball and was an awesome 400 meter runner in high school. He also played the saxophone. He attended Fisk University and Washburn University before he passed away on October 4, 1998. Chalmus has two sons, Jordan and Gabriel Kidd. Jordan Kidd lives in Denver, Colorado and Gabriel Kidd lives in Topeka, Kansas. Chalmus was a member of the Mt. Asbury Methodist Church in Topeka, Kansas.

Lynnette Kay Kidd born August 8, 1958 - daughter of Donnajean Lorraine Sudduth-Kidd and Wilbur Linton Kidd I am the sixth of seven. I have two children, Tiffany Nicole Kidd in Houston, Texas 29 born September 17, 1978 and James Lee Johnson 27, born June 30, 1980. Four grand-children, DeAundre Sivon Kidd born April 1, Jashawn Ronnell Kidd born October 15, 1998, Trayton Lewis born March 26, 2001 and Samaris Johnson 6 born December   , 2001. Lynnette Graduated from Robert E. Lee High School in Houston, TX, attended Texas Southern University. Presently employed with Memorial Hermann HealthCare Systems as a Patient Business Service Coordinator in Houston, Texas for the past five and half years. I also serve on the Board for Texas Southern University Track and Field and the USA Gulf Association Track and Field.

Linton Stewart Kidd born August 8, 1958 - son of Donna jean Lorraine Sudduth-Kidd and Wilbur Linton Kidd the seventh of seven children. Linton has 4 children, Marcus Kidd of Madison, WI, Tanisha Kidd of Denver, CO., Brionna Kidd of Topeka, KS and Cozette Kidd of Madison, WI with seven grandchildren of the eight a set of twins. There are five grandsons and two granddaughters.

Linton graduated from Highland Park High School in 1976 from there Linton moved to Madison, WI where he obtained his apprentice License in Iron working.

Proof

Made in the USA